The Goddess Myth
in Contemporary Literature
and Popular Culture

The Goddess Myth
in Contemporary Literature and Popular Culture

A Feminist Critique

Mary J. Magoulick

University Press of Mississippi / Jackson

The University Press of Mississippi is the scholarly publishing agency of the Mississippi Institutions of Higher Learning: Alcorn State University, Delta State University, Jackson State University, Mississippi State University, Mississippi University for Women, Mississippi Valley State University, University of Mississippi, and University of Southern Mississippi.

www.upress.state.ms.us
The University Press of Mississippi is a member of the Association of University Presses.

First printing 2022
∞

Library of Congress Cataloging-in-Publication Data

Names: Magoulick, Mary J., author.
Title: The goddess myth in contemporary literature and popular culture: a feminist critique / Mary J. Magoulick.
Description: Jackson: University Press of Mississippi, 2022. | Includes bibliographical references and index.
Identifiers: LCCN 2021046127 (print) | LCCN 2021046128 (ebook) | ISBN 978-1-4968-3706-6 (hardback) | ISBN 978-1-4968-3705-9 (paperback) | ISBN 978-1-4968-3708-0 (epub) | ISBN 978-1-4968-3707-3 (epub) | ISBN 978-1-4968-3710-3 (pdf) | ISBN 978-1-4968-3709-7 (pdf)
Subjects: LCSH: Goddesses—Mythology. | Goddesses in literature. | Goddess religion. | Goddess religion in literature. | Goddesses in art. | Goddesses—Miscellanea. | Goddesses—Folklore.
Classification: LCC BL325.F4 .M34 2022 (print) | LCC BL325.F4 (ebook) | DDC 809/.9338202114—dc23/eng/20211128
LC record available at https://lccn.loc.gov/2021046127
LC ebook record available at https://lccn.loc.gov/2021046128

British Library Cataloging-in-Publication Data available

Contents

The Goddess Myth
in Contemporary Literature
and Popular Culture

Appropriative Roots and (Un?)Feminist Resonances of the Goddess Myth

Myth appeals to us deeply enough that we use the word liberally in modern English, applying it to many kinds of narratives and simply ideas.[1] The word has a soft and pleasant sound in English, but most people know enough about myths to respect the genre as carrying some gravitas. Though many people use the term *myth* dismissively—"it's just a myth"—most know that actual myths stretch back at least to Homer and ancient Greece, a culture we respect as inspiring democracy and fostering rich philosophy, literature, and art. Humans love any good story, which also likely accounts for myth's appeal. During my doctoral studies in folklore, I focused particularly on myth, but I had been drawn to the genre earlier, immersing myself in mythology, the study of myth, at least since college. This fundamental, ancient form of story can be powerful, making it worthy of profound attention. I've been interested in popular culture for most of my life as well, especially films, television shows, and speculative fiction (science fiction and fantasy), many versions of which are textually rich art forms, sometimes newly conceived and emergent, other times recycled (though possibly exciting) ways of telling stories.[2] All forms of good story merit critical analysis.

I use the term *goddess myth* to mean creative stories where characters are nominally or descriptively identifiable as having godly powers or lineage, or where the imagined world significantly involves goddesses or goddess mythology. Applying theoretical insights from mythology, literary studies, and feminism to contemporary literary and popular culture versions of goddess myths allows us to investigate overt or hidden messages in these works that help us to gain insights into our culture today. To better understand how ancient goddess figures, mythological women, and superheroic women generally have become popular for contemporary audiences, I also consider how we understand, or misunderstand, appropriate, and reimagine prehistory—the time when goddesses are thought to have been more revered and prevalent. Since representations and imaginings of prehistoric women are often evoked by proponents of goddess culture (i.e., as evidence of some goddess myths), we attend to expert insight about prehistoric cultures, women therein, and some context of ancient art. We also use a feminist lens to examine goddesses in literature and popular culture (films, television shows, and popular novels), asking whether the stories serve as empowering new myths that fulfill a promised feminist potential to liberate women and point the way to a brighter future, or whether they tend to be less feminist and promising than many perceive or hope. Analyses herein reveal the deep entrenchment of patriarchy throughout our culture, including in goddess myths, except for occasional examples with hopeful potential.

The ancient Greek word for myth meant "word," especially spoken words, and came to mean "story," as words that are artful and not verifiable, in contrast to *logos* (also Greek for "word"), verifiable words and speaking (as in science or history). If we consider myth as artful language, as in Aristotle's use of it as "plot" or "fabula," then any stories woven of words, including most literature and popular culture today, could be called myths (Doty 1986, 3). But the stem Proto-Indo-European word for myth (*mu-*) also connotes mystery, allowing for possible metaphorical "truth" even if not fully understood (4). In other words, members of the culture who tell and believe myths perceive necessary, fundamental, "crucial" truths in them, meaning myths are "special" stories, connected to truths (Doty 1986, 8; Geertz 1973, 129). Myth scholar William G. Doty (1986, 8) explains: "They are not little but big stories, touching not just the everyday but sacred or specially marked topics that concern much more than the immediate situation . . . common themes that humans face" repeatedly, or a story "so vital or 'alive' that it shapes and 'in-forms' the culture." Myth scholars thus reserve *myth* for powerful, possibly sacred stories that move us deeply, that contain messages and metaphoric truths for how to live, that involve culture heroes and tricksters, and that shape and reflect our lives fundamentally. Even considering this scholarly definitional framework, we could call some of the stories of popular culture myths.[3] *Star Wars*, for instance, is as much a part of many people's consciousness and worldview, shaping values and providing memes, morals, and some truth, as are traditional myths. Like origin myths, *Star Wars* is also set in a different world in the distant past, but a world enough like ours to constitute a relatable primordial structure. Contemporary genres and media do convey mythic stories, though not all such stories would fit definitions of myth. Popular culture can convey any variety of messages through diverse frameworks. I focus particularly on recent works that overtly evoke goddesses or a goddess framework within the narrative, to see what messages they convey to audiences today.

Myth and popular culture may seem opposite topics, since myth evokes ancient, sacred wisdom, perhaps performed in liminal spaces like stone churches or caves, with ritualized singing or chanting of poetic verses telling worldview-shaping stories of our origins. Popular culture, recognized since the mid-nineteenth century by scholars, was originally perceived as lower-class, less-educated expressions—stories and other art forms—paralleling the rise of a mass middle-class consumer culture and often compared to official, "higher" culture (canonical writers, museum art, etc.).[4] Ray Browne (2006, 21), American pioneer in academic study of popular culture, says popular culture "embraces all levels of our society and culture other than the Elite—the 'popular,' 'mass' and 'folk.' It includes most of the bewildering aspects of life which hammer us daily."[5] Often thus broadly defined, popular culture is most commonly understood, in terms of word-oriented art, to encompass popular fiction, such as pulp fiction, sci-fi, romance, mystery, and comic books. Popular culture also includes expressive media produced for mass consumption—music, comics, sports, games, objects, films, books—all phenomena of post-industrial society that reflect interests, practices, trends, and beliefs of a mass of people within a society. Originally, pop culture was, like folklore, considered less worthy of academic and critical attention than the definitionally contrasted "high culture" (Browne's "elite"). But definitions and perceptions of pop culture, and our reactions to and considerations of it have evolved over time, and many now consider it worthy of critical attention.

Popular culture may, as Browne asserts, "hammer us daily," but it also reflects and sometimes delights us, featuring any and all manner and mode of expression, including vibrant, gaudy, violent, lush, intense, sappy, silly, sophomoric, cheesy, mundane, subtle, or profound *stories* on screens, from speakers, in print sources, and through live interactions. Myths in the distant past were probably recited or performed only at special, possibly sacred times and were eventually carved in stone or scratched on paper using symbols most could not understand. But now we need never be without story, and virtually any kind of story with all manner of messages and images can be found or created through many diverse media, available often or always. Some stories classified as popular culture because of their media—genre fiction, television, film, comic books—are highly regarded by critics, studied seriously, and can be as stylistically, symbolically artful and rich as any more established, traditional expressive forms.

The goddess myths I analyze herein include nine novels (at least half of which are written by writers that most critics regard as highly cultivated, though some also write genre fiction), four television series, and five films (one discussed very briefly). These vary in quality, but all feature worlds in which exist goddesses, or characters identifiable or arguable as goddesses: female beings with godly power and characteristics, or named as godly. The works vary in terms of setting, tone, style, and other elements. Some are novels written by literarily acclaimed writers (Margaret Atwood, Leslie Marmon Silko, Alice Walker); others are typically categorized as genre fiction, particularly science fiction and fantasy, which has, like all popular culture, gone through cycles of being dismissed, ignored, mocked, belittled, and, sometimes, taken seriously or highly regarded. All of the writers of novels analyzed deeply herein are women, four of them women of color, and their main characters are all women, including women connected to goddess culture and sometimes goddesses themselves. Perspectives of gender and intersectionality inform analyses of these most promisingly feminist works. These women writers published between the 1980s and 2020. The television series and films I analyze emerge from production teams dominated by men, ranging similarly from the 1970s up to 2020, though some women are involved, as most films and television shows generally have very large crews. The films and television series feature characters clearly identifiable as goddesses or as goddess-related, sometimes named as such within their worlds. All the works could be categorized as popular culture, though in terms of chapter organization and generalizations, I mainly use that phrase to refer to films, television shows, and genre fiction (sci-fi/fantasy), though all the novels have also been termed literature or fiction.[6]

Minimally and somewhat superficially, all these stories can be called *myths* because they include goddesses or goddess culture. Myths are generally considered sacred narratives, and a goddess is technically definitionally connected to sacredness. More importantly, myths have metaphoric power to shape our lives and influence or reflect worldview. I delve much more deeply into generic definitions of myth at the end of chapter 2, right before we begin actually analyzing some myths (and thus applying those definitions). The way myths function can also reveal deeper structures of our society—like the continued dominance of the patriarchy—explaining why I call the works examined herein "myths." Since they are newly created and reflective of Western culture over the last fifty-plus years, they are new goddess myths. These new myths might seem empowering for women simply in that they recognize goddesses as a previous reality (however imagined) and include goddess characters (as very powerful women) or cultures with goddesses (and sometimes with women in power, i.e., matriarchies). But the way women are presented in most of these myths can be perceived to reduce them thematically and structurally to patterns that are often not actually feminist or empowering. The goddesses we mythologize today often lack agency, are caricatures drawn in extremes, or rest in patterns very familiar in our sexist, patriarchal world. The presence of mythic, powerful women is not always indicative of feminist messages.

Many of our stories today are still traditionally patriarchal and feature male heroes using their strength, cunning, or other skills to overcome obstacles and fulfill quests, or fail at them, spurring reflection. We also find psychopathic heroes (or anti-heroes) compelling, even while we cringe at their narcissism and sociopathic natures (Tony Soprano, Walter White, Dexter Morgan, etc., from popular television series). Female heroes also get center stage regularly these days, including powerfully gifted and sometimes complicated heroines such as Daenerys Targaryen (from HBO's *Game of Thrones*), Hermione Granger (from *Harry Potter*), and Rey from *Star Wars*. Superheroic women such as Buffy (from *Buffy the Vampire Slayer*), Xena (from *Xena: Warrior Princess*), and Captain Marvel (a Marvel Cinematic Universe or MCU film of the same name from 2019) are thrilling. There are dark, tortured, but also capable heroes such as Michonne (from AMC's *The Walking Dead*), Carrie Mathison (from Showtime's *Homeland*), and Jessica Jones (from Netflix's *Jessica Jones*). We find as well goodhearted, strong women fighting evil forces, like Katniss Everdeen (from *The Hunger Games*) and several women in the MCU film *Black Panther*. We generally admire these women, though none are technically goddesses, and I too celebrate such heroically powerful female characters as admirable, clever, strong, funny, enduring, kind, and/or loyal, high points of recent popular culture. But these stories tend to reflect and shape today's world in patterns familiar to our culture rather than shaping revolutionary or new patterns, as myths have historically worked. As promising and exciting as some characters appear, they often do not advance a feminist narrative very convincingly, partly because they emerge from a still unequal, problematically patriarchal (written, directed, and produced mostly by men), and discriminatory (racist and sexist) culture.

Many feminists hail stories of powerful women as having mythic potential to usher in a new age of feminist dreams—more woman-centered or egalitarian if not outright matriarchal. Some feminists' faith in these stories to effect change reflects our overall faith in stories as a species. We all love stories and perceive ways they provoke thought and make our lives better. We look to stories to inspire, entertain, soothe, anger, provoke, and provide cathartic release. Our whole lives revolve around stories that evoke emotional and intellectual responses of every variety in myriad ways. Stories, along with other forms of artistic expression, may represent what most differentiates our species from any other on the planet. While other animals might communicate in sophisticated ways, and might even dance (bees and cranes), decorate (birds in nests), or express themselves playfully or purposefully (dolphins, chimps, and dogs), members of no other species *live* inside stories and art, resonate with such expressiveness, shape their existence through and around narratives, and have them so much at the center of *being* as we humans. We are *Homo narrans*, beings with stories as our special gift and defining nature, many have pointed out.[7] Some scholars of prehistory believe that our oldest art, Paleolithic art, likely gave humans an evolutionary advantage when competing for resources with rival hominid species.[8] The general assumption is that most of the ancient Stone Age art and human symbolism—of which there was an "explosion" in Europe during the Upper Paleolithic (40,000–10,000 years ago)—reflects stories, probably myths, rituals, and shared belief systems that tied humans together (White 2003). We cannot know exactly what those specific stories or beliefs were. But humans likely used shared culture, including stories reflecting beliefs (myths), to survive and thrive as a species, meaning narrative may literally be what makes us human, a successful species with stories as the most powerful force shaping our lives.

Powerful and pervasive narratives that dominate human existence are artistic creations, meaning they are layered with levels of deeper meaning and complexities, including symbolism, irony, and all manner of nuance and context, rendering them *interpretable*—and the better the story, the more there is to interpret. Hermeneutics—the art of interpretation—is itself complex and multilayered enough to be theorized into schools. Rarely is any one interpretation for any story agreed upon. Fairy tales, for instance, seem simple or childish to casual audiences, but when we look deeper, we find gruesome, disturbing, or alien messages that many readers may not see. In fairy tales, Bluebeard is a serial killer; parents abandon or even cook and eat their children; other children face hostile, adult situations; and sexual symbolism is common.[9] Seventeenth-century author Charles Perrault narrates Bluebeard in such a way as to scold women about being obedient and to quell their curiosity. Modern feminist folklore scholars perceive it instead as a story told among women—likely from older women to younger ones—as a coded warning about marriage and the potential of metaphorically monstrous or beastly husbands.[10] People spend careers writing interpretations of fairy tales and other forms of narrative, from literature to film, television, comic books, and more. Methods and schools of interpretation explore and sometimes debate meanings, moods, tones, and all conceivable implications or forms of artistic expression, speculating on mixed messages, interpretive ideologies, and other aspects of form and content.

Films like *Wonder Woman* (2017) and *Captain Marvel* (2019) that feature powerful, good women characters seem like a happy development of our time. But female heroes have long demonstrated agency, strength, and cunning. For example,

1) The heroine from "East of the Sun, West of the Moon" follows the same basic plot as the at-least-two-thousand-year-old myth of Cupid and Psyche. The heroine boldly accepts various quests, such as saving her family's lives and finances by marrying a large white bear and then undertaking a dangerous journey to refind or claim him as a good husband. She even travels to outer space—the place described in the title—all *without fear*, emphasized in the text: "Are you afraid? No she wasn't" (Asbjørnsen and Moe 1859).

2) Scheherazade, the wise, well-educated, lovely heroine of what is often called *The Arabian Nights*, who saves women in her culture by telling stories—implied in the frame story as a process that lasts 1,001 nights—to teach her vengeful, murderous husband (who was killing a new wife every day, out of distrust) wisdom, compassion, and good governance, first recorded more than a thousand years ago in Persia.

3) American culture's own beloved Dorothy from *The Wizard of Oz*, who many consider an inspiration for Luke in *Star Wars*, appears many years before him, a young woman swept into a sort of "outer space"— over the rainbow—on a similar adventure with similar companions, comparable to Luke, but predating him by seventy-seven years.[11]

Our culture has enjoyed many female heroines as popular, appealing, even iconic and influential characters.[12] In the phenomenal Harry Potter series, many consider Hermione Granger to be a favorite character who resonates most as heroic.[13] Is Hermione, even named after a character from Greek myth, a mythic-level heroine, a kind of modern goddess, as some have argued?[14] In the third *Star Wars* trilogy, consisting of *The Force Awakens* (2015), *The Last Jedi* (2017) and *The Rise of Skywalker* (2019), we also find women heroes foregrounded—more so than before in the Star Wars franchise. Some of these women are refreshingly humble and less classically beautiful than is typical of Hollywood. While many fans and critics heralded characters like Rey (played by Daisy Ridley) and Rose Tico (played by Kelly Marie Tran), these films and those characters and actors have also received notable backlash, especially in reaction to *The Last Jedi*, with the anger coming from "traditional male viewers" who, some speculate, are angry at the prominence of stronger women characters and lack of concomitant, more traditionally white male heroes.[15]

Dan Brown's *The Da Vinci Code* incorporates the goddess myth overtly and became one of the best-selling novels of all time soon after its publication, mainly telling the story of the sacred feminine, lost female goddesses, and symbols thereof, including a Christian goddess.[16] The hidden truths of the significance of and need for a goddess to "balance" earth—and all life thereon—resound throughout Brown's influential novel. Many other writers, including literary superstars such as James Joyce, T. S. Eliot, and Ezra Pound, also incorporate goddess worship and lost matriarchy themes in some of their work. Early twentieth-century men theorists such as James G. Frazer, Sigmund Freud, Carl Jung, Erich Neumann, and others supported the narrative of prehistoric matriarchy and goddess worship but also of heroes vanquishing those inferior cultural patterns. Many literary works, as well as popular culture films, television shows, and genre fiction, accept and project that goddess-centered, probably matriarchal prehistory is a given. Since early archaeologists first speculated that the distant past was matriarchal, and especially since the publication of work in the sixties and seventies by women promoting such theories (like Marija Gimbutas and her followers, explained more in part I), positive portrayals of goddesses and matriarchy have become more prevalent in the imaginative writings of women (chapter 5). Men writers promote this perspective popularly as well, including Dan Brown and Joseph Campbell.

Many within our culture accept or at least enjoy strong female characters, even goddesses, and our perceived need for them, to the extent that we have been creating and receiving enthusiastically many newly imagined goddesses and super-strong female characters in popular culture for well over 150 years.[17] Classics scholars such as Mary Lefkowitz (1993, 268) demonstrate skeptical appraisal of today's goddess "cults," as she terms them, though her study does not scrutinize many popular culture versions of goddesses. There were so many Amazonian heroines in the early twentieth century, for instance, that historian Jill Lepore, in researching the origins of Wonder Woman, finds the main frame plot of the original comics to have been largely borrowed from popular novels, poetry, and other comics that preceded creator William Marston's work.[18] Cynthia Eller (2011) traces a continual fascination and appropriation of

Amazon-like characters (like Wonder Woman) throughout European history, starting early in medieval times. How remarkable that characters inspired by goddesses or super-strong women from largely forgotten or little-understood ancient cultures, *completely reimagined* for contemporary audiences, capture our attention and reflect and influence contemporary culture.

Goddess Culture's Influence

Much of the popularity of goddesses in popular culture today derives from the influence of "goddess culture," a catchall term I use to refer to neo-pagan and New Age types of groups or beliefs that posit or assume a prehistory where goddesses, or a goddess, dominated or were at least prevalent and powerful.[19] Let me be clear that my main purpose herein is not to offer ethnological or comprehensive research or information on any specific contemporary community of goddess culture or goddess worshippers but mainly to analyze literary and popular culture "myths"—powerful stories with a sacred tinge— that incorporate goddesses and cultures related to them as they are more generally perceived in our culture at large. In order to understand patterns and influences of such beliefs and practices and how they manifest in our myths, I present and analyze some of the most commonly understood and often-stated ideas and aspects of goddess culture as explained and evinced today.

Recent goddess-related cultural practices and beliefs represent contemporary worldviews, often reflective of how we appropriate or misappropriate ideas and assumptions about the past but nonetheless deeply informative about our own culture—especially in terms of the goddess myths that many who are not members of these communities tell and enjoy. Beliefs and practices associated with goddesses and "the Great Goddess," while variable and complex, are often conflated and praised, by those inside and outside goddess-believing communities, as offering exciting, new, feminist, empowering, and ethically superior inspirations or examples. But when deeper mythological structures are analyzed in these modern myths, their patterns and messages often appear less exciting, new, or feminist. Why do we cheer, revile, and generally love—even when we love hating them—goddesses and super-strong women? We don't in fact always love them, one could argue, as seen with recent *Star Wars* films, whose strong women characters many fans hated.[20] Strong women are often figures in pop culture to be hated or feared, forces of destruction and chaos. Consider Cersei Lannister and ultimately Daenerys Targaryen from *Game of Thrones* (HBO, 2011–2019); Hela from *Thor:*

Ragnarok (2017); Lilith from the television series *True Blood* (2012); and many wicked witches, including Bellatrix Lestrange from Harry Potter, the Wicked Witch of the West from *The Wizard of Oz* (film 1939), and Maleficent (2014), to name but a few.[21] But however we portray and respond to powerful and magical women characters, new goddesses and powerful women hold our attention and often succeed commercially in popular culture.

As much as we need, want, enjoy, mock, glorify, or despise goddesses and powerful women in current popular culture and literature, many of them serve less as beacons of a hopeful, more feminist future than simply as reflections of our still-patriarchal society, with occasional feminist incursions or promises that are often fantastically unlikely. Consider that most powerful women exist in *speculative fictional* worlds, not realistic ones. New myths, or at least mythically tinged narratives, of imagined goddesses and related worlds, however fantastical, reveal much about our culture, including values and fundamental life patterns. Myths function often to comfort and offer distant hope, confirming our world and lives are *good* and livable now, however confusing or troubling the times may seem—as in the era of #MeToo, #TimesUp, groundbreaking anti-sexual assault and women's empowerment movements especially popular in 2017–18. There are some recent, more promising goddesses too, but virtually all suffer (see table 4), and all are comprehensible and familiar to us, because ultimately they are about us and our world.

The Pull of Prehistory

My interest in this project was partly sparked during a trip to France in 2001, where I visited ancient sites of early human art, seeing and considering many figurines and images, including many of women, some named as goddesses. This trip inspired reading, research, fieldwork, and consideration of both prehistory and contemporary goddess culture, including goddess incarnations and uses in our popular culture. There is an epistemological continuum between the discovery and recognition of this ancient art and our contemporary ideas of goddesses. In order to fully understand goddess culture today, we thus examine some specific goddess artifacts from prehistory to delve more deeply into their contexts and complexity (chapter 1). Experts situate ancient artifacts in very different contexts (leading to different understandings of the past) many assume or imagine today. Since ideas of prehistory spur so much of goddess culture, consideration of some source inspirations helps us see how most aspects of goddess culture are actually contemporary, imagined, or imposed.

We modern humans have been reimagining and appropriating goddesses—even calling them "goddesses" is an assumption—creating *our myth* of ancient times, only loosely inspired by archaeological evidence, which remains emergent and negotiated: "images from the European Upper Palaeolithic and Neolithic periods (c. 40,000 to 5,000 years ago) are claimed to represent fertility and other positively-valued attributes and thus are often taken as material and symbolic evidence for the existence of a world in which females, as a generic category, were valued positively" (Tringham and Conkey 1998, 22). Goddess culture proponents' invocation and definitive interpretations of art from this region as evidence of a superior past where women ruled or were worshiped explains how my interest in this project was ignited by a visit to the southwestern region of France, where one can "bathe in prehistory," as some locals say.[22]

France's well-developed tourism industry surrounding all these sites of patrimony makes them easy to visit and relatively easy to comprehend, at least at a basic level, with the help of well-trained guides and thoughtful displays.[23] Many visitors like me enjoy learning what they can of this ancient, distant, totally foreign culture from the Paleolithic era, absorbing what's left and visitable of this ancient art.[24] Prehistoric artifacts (figs. 1–11), handprints (fig. 2), tools, living sites, and so on seem to come to life at the spot where they were created, making these ancestors feel remarkably close to visitors and residents.[25] One guide told tourists (including me) at Lascaux II in 2018 to think of Jesus Christ, from "only about two thousand years ago," one whom many find relatable and not too distant. He implied that we still feel comprehensibly close to Christian ancestors' history, beliefs, and values. Then, he continued, "Just multiply that two thousand years by ten, and you are here—the time of Lascaux!" In other words, he explained, these "distant" ancestors who made the art we still find moving are not really so far removed from us; they were modern humans, he emphasized, who wore jewelry, enjoyed paintings, and had a religious sanctuary, as he characterized Lascaux—often called "the Sistine Chapel of prehistory."

One example of ancient art that reveals our misunderstanding and imposition of modern assumptions and perceptions is a small ivory head known as the Venus of Brassempouy from France (fig. 1). It is less than two inches high (3.65 centimeters), but the face seems emotive, tranquil some say, though only partially carved. There are clear eyes, nose, chin, cheeks, forehead, a neck, and hair, but no mouth. The "hair" or headwear is carved in a checkerboard-like pattern that suggests an elaborate hairdo or a decorative headpiece. This decorative hair is likely what leads many to consider the figurine female, though it is in fact unsexed. Only what we interpret as stylized hair or head décor suggests *to us*, based on our gendered assumptions, that this is a woman's head; thus

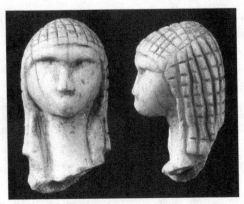

Fig. 1. Front and side view of the la Dame de Brassempouy or Lady
of Brassempouy (sometimes also called Venus); 3.65-centimeter
ivory mammoth figurine dated to 25,000 BP, found in a cave at
Brassempouy, France, 1892.

we named *her* Venus or Lady of Brassempouy—for where she was found—or
Lady with the Hood.[26] There were at least eight human figures found along with
this one in two caves at the Brassempouy site, among the first Paleolithic sites
explored in France. Some may have depicted women, but this one may not.[27]

When I first saw a reproduction of this evocative little head in person in
France, I felt deeply moved, standing and staring for quite some time, circling
the case, reading the museum's description, wondering about it, even though
it was only a reproduction. I felt connected to the representation of a human
head made by people who lived so differently as long as twenty-five thousand
years ago. I had read about and even taught a little about prehistoric art back
in the United States. I had even shown a slide and discussed this very head
in a humanities class. But seeing it in person, in that place full of prehistory,
while breathing the air of ancient limestone caves and rivers, felt different
and profoundly moving. I would not characterize my experience as spiritual. I
did not perceive the little head as a goddess, in spite of "her" goddess name; it
did not move me religiously. Rather, what affected me profoundly was feeling
connected to distant ancestors via this ancient representation of humanity,
a tiny remnant of some of the oldest human art, recognizably and movingly
human. In caves with imprints of human hands, you almost feel like the hands
are reaching out to you—human to human, through *many* millennia (fig. 2). I
found myself transfixed by such remnants of early humans in the Dordogne,
wanting to learn more than the placards told me, to take classes, to talk to
experts, to learn everything I could.[28] Indeed I did a fair amount of studying,
reading, visiting museums, sites, and more over the years.[29]

Fig. 2. *Main négative préhistorique* de la Grotte du Pech Merle (Le Lot, France); negative handprint and dots (example of many similar in cave); discovered 1922. Some images in seven-chambered, two-kilometer cave date to at least 25,000 BCE, though others may be from later (16,000 BCE).

Prehistorian Randall White explains that our contemporary understandings, various as they might be, probably misapprehend most of this prehistoric art, which he thinks is better termed *representations* than *art* in any modern sense. White (2003, 221) suggests our appreciation is a "tragedy" to anthropologists because our focus on what we perceive as art, like identifiably human figurines, usually meant "the total neglect of what lay beneath them on the cave floor," meaning most of the context crucial for interpretation. But emotional responses are common, as Ruth Tringham and Margaret Conkey (1998, 28) emphasize in "Rethinking Figurines": "Because of the strong emotions involved in interpreting human representations," the standard archaeological methods focusing heavily on context and details of life-use to interpret artifacts, are often not applied or asked of "anthropomorphic figurines" by nonexperts. Contexts and specific meanings are "likely to have been varied and varying, more ambiguous than fixed, and differentially experienced, even at any one point in time."[30] Thus, we mostly do not consider these artifacts scientifically enough because of the emotional resonance they evoke. Our very appreciation and excitement taint our understanding. To attempt to deepen understanding and avoid pitfalls of contemporary reimaginings of and appropriative impositions on the distant past, I give space to expert information on a few particular works and their contexts (chapter 1). These ancient, inspiring representations spur completely imagined stories of ancient life, ancient gods, and especially goddesses.

Prehistory is a huge and complex field covering vast swaths of time and space. Most experts agree that there was significant cultural variation in beliefs, lifestyles, tools, stories, music, and other markers of culture over the tens of thousands of years of the Upper Paleolithic era. My travels, reading, and study have merely scratched the surface in understanding what these experts spend their lives examining, but my folklore training teaches me to listen well. Experts know a tremendous amount about the period—details such as what people ate, how they made tools, how they organized living spaces, even how they made the artifacts. Even though they can't know everything, like specifics of stories and beliefs, specialists can help us "to demystify archaeological 'facts,'" to move "beyond the need for certainty" that many appreciators demonstrate, and to find "new patterns in a rich and fascinating body of evidence" (Goodison and Morris 1998, 21). We may marvel at the ways the evocative figurines, engravings, and paintings speak to us today, we may feel close to these distant ancestors, and we may perceive with awe the beauty they left behind. But our feelings and hopes, however profound, don't amount to actually knowing much about the makers, the cultures, the beliefs, the stories, and the perceptions of Paleolithic humans.[31] Our appropriations and reimaginings of the past are unlikely to be accurate except in representing *our* culture and times.

Goddesses from Ancient Greece to Today

As we consider art left by more recent ancestors, such as the ancient Greeks, we may feel we have more ability to understand, interpret, and connect to that art and culture, since these ancestors eventually left written records and we feel their culture is somewhat familiar. Many of us also feel deeply moved by and connected to the art that those more recent (but still distant) ancestors left behind. But our modern conceptualizations and interpretations of the ancient Greeks are often as anachronistic and wishfully imagined as they are historically accurate. Classicists can tell us much about how the Greeks lived, about what they thought and valued, about their art, gender roles, family life, city life, rituals, beliefs, worldviews, and so on (Lefkowitz 2007). But most people ignore experts and probably think they know more about ancient Greece than any historian or archaeologist would consider accurate. Many contemporary assumptions are based largely on popular culture versions of the lives and stories of ancient Greeks, or maybe one or two literary works, probably read in high school or college and likely taught by a nonexpert.

Television shows like *Xena: Warrior Princess* (1995–2001), numerous films over many years, including *Troy* (2004), *Clash of the Titans* (1981, 2010), *300*

(2006), and Disney's *Hercules* (1997), websites, video games, advertisements, poetry, and other media project contemporary interpretations of ancient Greece, mostly suited to and reflective of modern culture. We appropriate whatever aspects suit our purpose or tastes—often making money or projecting a particular worldview in the process. We create our own versions of myths of the ancient past that make sense to us, regardless of whether they would have made sense or even been recognizable to the ancients who inspired them. Modern myths of ancient goddesses or powerful women like Amazons are particularly interesting, as experts explain definitively that they bear little resemblance to original versions. Such stories have long been appropriated, in various ways, including during the last 120 years or so of Western feminist movements. Members of our culture then interpret our reimagined and appropriated versions of Amazons according to personal philosophies or cultural moments. Classics scholar Mary Lefkowitz (1992, 29) describes our consumeristic view of the past as "a kind of pseudo-mystical mixing and matching of symbols and ideas that have nothing in common with each other except the contemporary use to which they may be put." There have long been admirable, powerful female characters based on ancient models in novels, films, comics, and television shows. But we also find many strong women portrayed and perceived as forces of chaos or evil, and many women, including strong ones, are punished or suffer, sometimes terribly. Our contemporary, appropriative approach reflects us, mainly.

Not long after my first trips to the Dordogne, Dan Brown's novel *The Da Vinci Code* (2003) topped best-seller lists, a global phenomenon that spurred many responses and follow-ups, including a feature film (2006) directed by Ron Howard with Tom Hanks and Audrey Tautou in the lead roles, television specials investigating the book's claims, lawsuits about its originality, an official response from the Catholic Church, themed tourism opportunities, and more. This fast-paced adventure/mystery that captivated the world features as a key plot point ancient goddesses and their power and persistence throughout time, even purporting a goddess figure within Christianity. The protagonist of the novel, Dr. Robert Langdon, is a "symbologist" at Harvard, expert on "the Lost Sacred Feminine." Langdon explains his version of the goddess perspective: "Early religion was based on the divine order of Nature. The goddess Venus and the planet Venus were one and the same. The goddess had a place in the nighttime sky and was known by many names—Venus, the Eastern Star, Ishtar, Astarte—all of them powerful female concepts with ties to Nature and Mother Earth" (Brown 2003, 40). He later explains more of the myth to the main character, Sophie Neveu: "Constantine and his male successors successfully converted the world from matriarchal paganism to patriarchal Christianity by waging a campaign of propaganda that demonized the sacred feminine, obliterating the goddess from modern religion forever" (133). This reading of history assumes a prehistory focused on "the sacred feminine," including goddesses, especially the loving mother goddess.

The book depicts the Virgin Mary, Mary Magdalene, and her offspring with Jesus, including Sophie, with whom the hero is romantically involved, as a continuation of the beloved goddess (Brown 2003, 275). Dr. Langdon even explains the Victorian logic for why women were worshiped: "The ability of the woman to produce life from her womb made her sacred" (335). He frequently invokes cryptic symbolism of the sacred feminine, as in pentagrams, roses, and the grail or chalice (39–41, 49, 103, 113–14, 207, 219–20, 257–58, 274–75, 296, 369, 420, 451–52, 464, 479). Langdon solves clues with Sophie, ultimately revealed in the novel to be the descendant of Jesus Christ and Mary Magdalene, the continuation of the goddess in our culture. All through the book, Langdon explains to Sophie the "secrets" of feminine divinity and goddesses throughout history. One character explains that there is a Christian goddess: "Mary Magdalene was the womb that carried His [Jesus Christ's] royal lineage. The Priory of Sion, to this day, still worships Mary Magdalene as the Goddess, the Holy Grail, the Rose, and the Divine Mother," explaining as well that the grail—really a bloodline of godhood—represents this "lost sacred feminine" (275–77, 279).

We learn that Princess Sophie, as she is called by her grandfather, "the premiere goddess iconographer on earth," embodies that secret but enduring goddess within Christianity (Brown 2003, 25). Brown's best seller and its major motion picture spin-off show the ongoing popularity of the goddess myth. Brown embraces all the main tenets of the myth, demonstrating the same imagery and messages as appear in many versions (including dualities, chapter 2; tables 2 and 3). That such a message resounds so profoundly in today's world shows the extent to which our culture responds, positively or negatively, to goddesses and a myth of goddess culture, even one imagined as stretching back many thousands of years. Though Brown's novel has encountered serious contention, it remains one of the best-selling novels of all time and shows the ongoing popularity throughout our culture of supposed prehistoric goddesses.

If we consider such stories of goddesses in popular culture today as myths, sacred stories of the ancient past that offer metaphoric advice on how to live and what matters, what does all this reveal about our culture? Why are goddess myths so popular today, and what do they communicate? Do we hunger for stories that appear to redress millennia of imbalance and focus on strong, intelligent, powerful, capable women? Or do these new myths perpetuate old, though disguised, stereotypes and patterns? Are there any truly imaginative, hopeful, newly conceived and told goddess myths? One perspective I use in answering these questions throughout the book is that of feminism. Feminist theory is often an assumed or stated epistemology of those who praise goddess culture and its myths, but feminism is neither monolithic nor simple. Many feminists, like me, critique goddess myths as ultimately not advancing a particularly feminist worldview or agenda, at least not always and not automatically.

Feminist Theory

Though feminism and feminist theory can be quite complex and variable, at root feminism refers straightforwardly to "the radical notion that women are people," as bumper stickers, t-shirts, and buttons proclaim.[32] Broadly considered, feminism works toward economic, political, and social equality for all humans, regardless of gender. Feminism also values and encourages equal access to education, health care, and other social opportunities, especially for those who otherwise lack such access, which often means women and girls. For many years, feminism was mainly a social and political movement that strove to advance equality for women, given that our patriarchal society privileges men at all levels. In addition to obvious rights—like voting or owning property—that women have lacked, there might be deeper, less obvious ways that women's rights are impinged.

For instance, if all medical studies about heart disease focus on male subjects and their heart health, and if, as scientists fairly recently began recognizing, women's hearts, bodies, and health work differently from men's, then women have unequal access to effective heart health care, putting them at greater risk.[33] Similarly, if social groups such as schools or families value men's potential intelligence and thus education over women's, they will likely conclude it is more important for boys to attend school rather than girls, especially if sending all children to school is not possible. We all grow up enculturated with subtle biases—that men are inherently smarter, more likable, more worthy of regard or attention, more forgivable (for instance when transgressing or acting aggressively)—so we may be prone to favoring boys and men in many situations. Families and social systems might ensure boys and men have more opportunities to study, might be prone to giving them financial assistance, jobs, or raises, might be likely to vote for them and support them in all ways.

Teachers might be more likely to call on boys in the classroom and to give them better feedback. Girls, women, and less masculine boys and men often suffer discriminations of opportunity, attention, or assessment, even when no one has bad intentions or awareness of these biased actions and preferences. So ingrained are our biases and suppositions that in many cases even what may later seem obviously problematic behavior might go unnoticed for many years. For instance, most teachers (at all levels), studies show, unconsciously call on white male students to answer questions, even when equal numbers of men and women and students of various races raise their hands, and even when the professor is a woman or a person of color.[34]

The ways various oppressions, perspectives, and actions intersect reflect systemic problems, which can sometimes remain hidden or difficult to trace or prove. Feminist theory and work has helped bring many such issues to light. Most feminists do not hate men or boys, nor do they seek to overthrow governments, destroy capitalism, or deny anyone's values or rights. We simply assert that all genders should have equal access to rights, opportunities, and sometimes things considered privileges of all kinds, including attention in medicine, education, law, government, and research. We also seek to consider and redress centuries of inequality and oppression and its myriad effects, which are often insidious and cryptic. This understanding of feminism also implies access to information and education for all, a level of social engagement reflecting practices and beliefs to ensure equality across various barriers, and it is something that can be part of all areas of life—from large political arenas, to classrooms, to most workplaces, to everyday acts and choices, to all our literature, media, and popular culture and all considerations thereof.

Feminist theory helps interpret how gender works and is perceived, particularly when we consider how gender inequalities intersect with other social inequalities, including in our artistic expressions. In terms of literature and popular culture studies, feminism is often applied usefully in various ways, and I briefly describe two. First, feminists may *seek to recover and consider art works by women*, and possibly other oppressed groups, that otherwise may have gone unnoticed, unconsidered, unanalyzed, or underappreciated. This can mean shifting away from traditional canons to discover or reclaim artists and artwork, not only to rewrite our histories and broaden our perspectives of all kinds of art, but also to redefine or refocus related academic fields and histories. For instance, even illiterate or untrained women have been producing beautiful quilts, gardens, meals, written works such as journals, and other forms of art for many millennia. But generally, such "domestic" artistic productions are ignored as insignificant, transitory, and unworthy of academic attention. Even published literature or art by women has been largely ignored and sometimes mocked for much of history. Quilts by nineteenth-century women that offer bold, abstract artistic designs inspired by the world around them were considered insignificant and perhaps "messy" or "crazy" and have only recently garnered space in museums.[35] But when male artists started producing similarly bold and abstract designs in the early twentieth century, they were hailed as geniuses, and their canvasses were hung in galleries and sold for significant sums.[36] So reclaiming and regarding women's art of all kinds is part of a feminist agenda.

A second way feminist theory can be especially useful in analysis of art, literature, and film is by *asking new questions of texts*, old and new, by any writers from any gender or century. Questions such as what kind of roles women and men are given in the works, how women and men (or gender more generally) are portrayed, who speaks, who doesn't, and what characters' motivations, opportunities, and so on, are all matter. All such questions can be answered more fully when taking gender into consideration; feminist answers to these questions can be illuminating in rethinking old and new texts and reconsidering our culture. The male gaze, for instance, an influential concept that feminist scholar Laura Mulvey first analyzed in 1975, helps us perceive the way women and the world are depicted in film and literature, and what that implies. Most art is usually constructed, presented, and received from a heterosexual, masculine perspective. A woman (or women) may be on display for men within a film, painting, or literary work, for the consideration of the men behind the camera, canvas, or pen and for the men consuming the work. Attending to the significance of gaze and all the social processes and norms behind it, including the artist's training, perspectives, motivations, and assumptions of audience, can lead to new insight into texts from many genres and times periods.

An example of a *new question of old texts* that has been influential is literary critics Sandra Gilbert and Susan Gubar's (1979) *The Madwoman in the Attic*, which considers the common presence of dangerously insane women characters in nineteenth-century literature, including some written by women. Women in these literary worlds were often confined, they argue, to two roles: either angel, like Jane Eyre by Brontë, or monster, like the first wife of Eyre's employer and beau, Rochester, who screams madly in the attic, later starts a fire that disfigures Rochester and traumatizes Jane, and is ultimately killed. These exaggerated, narrow roles—angel and monster—affected women writers and all society as well, narrowing patterns and perceptions of women's options and potential, reducing us to unrealistic extremes (Gilbert and Gubar 1979).

Another example of new questions and interpretations comes from feminist folklore scholars who help us reconsider fairy tales, which often feature women and girls as main characters. Many fairy tale girls show remarkable agency in shaping their lives, more so than formerly realized. Folklorist Jeana Jorgensen (2017), for instance, analyzes a number of fairy tales with strong female heroes, including Aarne-Thompson-Uther tale 510B, "Peau d'Asne"/"Donkeyskin"/"The Dress of Gold, of Silver, and of Stars [Cap O Rushes]," in which a father threatens incest toward his daughter after his wife dies. The girl figures out a way to escape this fate in all versions. Jorgensen concludes: "Despite varying cultural contexts, versions from Sicilian, Palestinian-Arab, and French narrators align to present a tale showing a young woman escaping her father's incestuous advances and establishing herself in a new household. This may happen with more or less magical intervention, and more or less guidance from a helper figure, showing that at the tale type's core is a resilient and independent woman" (Jorgensen 2017). Such independent, strong women may be recovered and reconsidered via this type of feminist scholarship.

Agency is crucial to feminists analyzing characters in texts, as tracing agency—the ability to act as well as actually acting within a narrative—and its effects can often offer significant insight into gender assumptions, roles, and potential in texts. In the art world, for instance, many male painters are critiqued for portraying mainly unclothed, reclining, static women subjects. Paul Gauguin, for instance, portrays many mostly nude Tahitian women in paintings. They recline, sit, are inactive, and sometimes seem to be yearning— looking wistfully directly at the viewer; perhaps these women mourn a "lost paradise" evoked by the lushly colorful, flowery, and verdant backgrounds in which they rest. Gauguin may have meant to portray the effects of colonization on formerly active indigenous populations. But the prevalence of nude women is common in much art, and often these naked bodies are reclining or seem positioned mainly to titillate the assumed viewer—a man whose gaze is the artist's key consideration. Such paintings that feature women apparently without agency include "odalisque" paintings of "Oriental" women maids or slaves on disheveled beds.[37] Feminist analysis explains how these women are reduced to sexual objects waiting for men's attention: they are symbolically activated by and exist for the male gaze. Women existing mainly to please or be "activated" by men troublingly reflects realities of gender history that continue in current society.

Feminist attention to famous artistic, literary, and film texts' portrayals of women (and of gender generally) reveals how women (and others who are not cisgender men) were often written or directed into spaces where they lack agency or exist statically for the dominant male gaze. The Bechdel test offers a basic way to measure a film's regard for women characters and the relevance of women's roles in film: Does the film feature at least two women characters who talk to each other about something other than a man?[38] That few films pass this test, basic as it seems, reveals much about film history. Later, other critics added additional tests and nuances of how we should consider films from the perspective of gender studies. For example, the Mako Mori test asks whether a film includes women characters who have their own narrative arc and are not just supportive of a man character. We might also ask how prominently women characters figure in the action, whether they are portrayed stereotypically, if there are identifiable LGBT characters or characters of color, and if any such characters have major, nonstereotypical roles.

Feminist theory offers many such gender-focused perspectives and tools, like considering agency, the male gaze, or the complexity of women's roles, to help analyze expressive works. Working toward equality of the genders, valuing all genders as important, offering all genders equal opportunities within society, including within scholarly and artistic realms, have been important goals within feminist movements since the earliest days of feminism, though new and dynamic perspectives are always emerging as feminist scholarship continues and we build upon earlier insights. Scholars delineate "waves" of feminism in modern times. The first wave of feminists, in the nineteenth and twentieth centuries, were suffragettes who fought mainly for women's rights to vote, own property, and hold political office. The second wave of feminism emerged especially during the civil rights movement in the 1960s and 1970s and focused largely on reducing other social inequalities in terms of family, the workplace, sexuality, schools, and legal and reproductive rights. Writers such as Greer Garson, Betty Freidan, and Gloria Steinem were prominent, influential voices. Third Wave feminism, emerging by the mid-1990s, embraced individualism and diversity, urging feminists to focus on layers of oppression, or "intersectionality," which attends to interconnected effects of numerous oppressive institutions on gender, including racism, sexism, phobias about orientation and identity, classism, ableism, and so on. Third-wave feminism also seeks to transcend social structures, including the male-female gender binary, as artificial constructs connected to power dynamics. Fourth-wave feminism, which emerged between 2008 and 2012, recognizes the impact of the internet and social media on feminism and all social movements, further urging intersectional perspectives to examine emerging interrelationships between notions of gender and various power structures, including government and business. It recognizes the power of using social media in helping advance feminist agendas, and is particularly focused on opposing sexual harassment and violence against women, along with the #MeToo movement and concepts like "mansplaining."

Feminism also contains many submovements and ideologies, including, radical feminism, which calls for a reordering of society to eliminate patriarchy; ecofeminism, which links domination and abuse of women with domination and abuse of the environment; and postmodern feminism, which suggests in part that gender is constructed through language. Mainstream feminism is sometimes considered too focused on upper- to middle-class white women and lacking attention to issues of race and class—hence third-wave feminism's rise. Overall, feminism is on the one hand simple and straightforward, working toward equality of genders, but on the other hand, feminist analysis can be complex and varied, albeit usually with a similar root perspective. Feminist perspectives offer many ways to ask new questions and gain new insights into old or new cultural material. Throughout this book I employ the above-described primary methodologies from feminism—considering possibly ignored texts, asking new questions of texts, and focusing on agency and gaze—along with any other aspect of feminist theory that helps us analyze the texts herein. I am less interested in limiting or delineating my feminism based on schools or periods than in employing *any* feminist insight that will help better analyze, understand, and evaluate texts and what they mean to our worldview and lives, particularly in terms of women's lives, given my focus on goddesses. I often consider characters' agency, concepts like the male gaze, portrayals of gender, and intersections of gender with other important, relevant factors.

Goodison and Morris (1998, 13) suggest that "goddess writers," proponents of a view of prehistory as woman centered and as worshiping a great goddess figure (further explored in chapters 1 and 2), have asserted their authority in interpreting the distant past, creating a "new orthodoxy," an "appropriation of feminism for themselves, as if there were not many diverse feminisms, both within and outside of archaeology." Posturing as sole authorities on what constitutes a feminist perspective on the past and the goddess myth "leads to intolerance, a shutting down of imaginative powers and a sense of closure." Even among scholars who agree on a feminist agenda more broadly, differences arise over specific interpretations, insights, and larger messages in any particular example of any sort of cultural production or analysis. Remember that interpretive efforts are complex and multifaceted. Surely there should be room for multiple feminist analyses of cultural expressions, past or present.

Films, television shows, books, and all forms of culture may promote or undermine feminism or intersectionality, overtly or cryptically, knowingly or not. Some cultural productions purport to be feminist while actually coopting one particular idea of women or projecting messages, possibly in subtle or hidden ways, that some might read as anti-feminist—possibly unrealized even by the creators or most of the audience. Even people who claim they wish to support feminism might create art that others could interpret as problematic from a feminist perspective. Feminism is complicated, dynamic, and emergent according to specifics of any given cultural moment and has been debated and negotiated by various scholars, artists, politicians, and citizens for many years. There is no single, agreed-upon, best feminist theory, topic, idea, character, or art. I believe that everyone who calls themself a feminist should be taken at face value, though individual definitions or methods of application might vary. But when people claim they are writing or perceiving feminist characters, I assume that purported feminism can be found in that work somewhere. Still, I also recognize that there might be other levels of how characters, events, and perspectives in art can be interpreted as problematic or incomplete from other feminist perspectives. All interpretive efforts are complex and variable, and simply intending a character or a myth to be feminist does not ensure it is so from all perspectives. My feminist textual analysis considers characters' full human potential, regardless of gender or other markers of identity, along with texts' overt or hidden structures and messages.

Proponents of the goddess myth and movement often passionately argue that various aspects of their faith, the practices related to it, the assumptions behind it, and many reflections of it in contemporary media are feminist, with feminist impulses, and working toward feminist goals. Many perceive goddess-centered reflections as pointing the way to a brighter future for all humans, resting on the "myth's transformative affects and effects. . . . The reclaiming of this past and the reworking of its symbols comprise a political, emotional, spiritual, and psychical vision that not only describes but also generates a resistant, nonpatriarchal consciousness and an alternative path of *becoming* for both women and men" (Caputi 2004, 10). Particular texts built upon or inspired by this vision or myth might fulfill such promises on some levels, but on other levels, I argue they are overly optimistic and may miss or overlook some of what the myth communicates. For one thing, those versions that accept the prevalence of goddesses in an ancient past do not attend to contemporary feminist archaeologists.

The goddess movement, identified with any number of neo-pagan and earth-based spiritualities, is purportedly the fastest-growing religion in the United States and is hailed by believers and supporters as feminist, empowering, ethically superior, and offering new possibilities—often known by terms like *neo-pagan*, *Wicca*, and *New Age spirituality*.[39] But many versions of this story are not as new, exciting, or promising for women as hopeful readers believe. Still, in contemporary popular culture we cling to the myth of a goddess-centered, possibly matriarchal prehistory and demonstrate persistent fascination with related prehistoric images or ideas of women. But most of these goddesses are completely reconceived, newly imagined by and for contemporary people—us. Scholars of prehistory are rarely consulted or heeded in specifics of such new myths. Many films, television shows, literature, and popular novels reimagine, reinvent, and re-present bits and pieces of the distant past, appropriating prehistoric women and goddesses or images of them, and interpreting them according to contemporary assumptions, styles, and formats. Writers and directors create goddess myths for their own purposes, reflecting worldviews that may or not purport to be feminist. Our versions of goddesses serve more as a feedback loop within our culture than reflection of a superior past.

———————

Scholars rarely examine or discuss such contemporary goddess narratives in light of scholarship on myth, and often their analyses disagree about the presence, level, or effectiveness of feminism in these new myths. Lefkowitz (1993, 262) writes that in spite of lack of evidence from past religious traditions for their beliefs and practices, "it was inevitable that today's women would need to develop a new mythology of their own and that they would turn to paganism for models.... The goddess modern women have chosen represents themselves more accurately than she represents any goddess or goddesses in the past." Lefkowitz's skeptical appraisal of goddess "cults" today mirrors my skeptical analysis of specific myths (268). Eller (2000), Goodison and Morris (1998), as well as ten other women archaeologists in their edited volume, and many other scholars question the feminism of goddess culture and resultant myths. But none of them scrutinize in-depth the many popular culture versions of goddesses. By examining this pervasive myth *as* a myth of contemporary popular culture from a feminist and folkloristic perspective, we discover how this myth reflects our culture's still problematically sexist issues, biases, and stereotypes about women and all humanity. We also find a few recent examples that appear to break new ground in overcoming old stereotypes, promising a more feminist myth or at least more realistic views and hopes of women's lives within our culture.

Part I

The Goddess Myth as Myth

Chapter 1

Origins, Prehistory, and Attending to Science
Overview of Goddess Culture

In much literature and popular culture, our culture regularly imagines and represents goddesses and associated cultures, like matriarchies, often claiming or presuming ancient antecedents. These *new myths*, not based on and rarely informed by pasts that experts perceive, tend to uphold long-held stereotypes of gender symbolically reflective of our predominantly patriarchal world. Still, many communities and individuals (and expressions thereof) today practice or evince various forms of goddess worship, invocation, and inspiration, or simply acceptance of a purported past when goddesses ruled. Organized or communally practiced goddess-focused beliefs and cultures that thrive today include Wicca, the goddess tradition, goddess spirituality, spiritual feminism, and neo-paganism (Allen 2001). There are variations and nuances among iterations of these practices and discourse (the myth, related rituals, etc.). Many other scholars offer thorough information about details, variations, and nuances of goddess culture and worship, including fieldwork of specific neo-pagan or goddess-focused groups.[1] Wiccans, various neo-pagan or New Age spiritualists, feminists, and many people generally demonstrate an implicit belief that our prehistory was dominated by goddesses, regularly including a great mother goddess, conceived often as a sort of unified woman god, thought to incorporate or subsume locally named goddesses and at times a kind of substitute or parallel for the Judeo-Christian God.[2] The goddess is "linked with movements and disciplines as diverse as Christianity, feminism and eco-feminism, environmentalism, witchcraft, and archaeology. In each of these the Goddess phenomenon is taken as a given rather than one speculative interpretation" (Meskell 1995, 75). Some believers claim ancient origins: "The

Goddess serves as a vehicle for women's groups and activists to reinforce legitimization of their position by means of an ancient antecedent" (Meskell 1995, 75). Such an antecedent is unprovable and probably unnecessary, as feminist goals could be conceived and worked toward without proof of a matriarchal or goddess-centered past.[3] In spite of a persistent and growing body of scholarly work skeptical of such claims, our culture embraces and imagines a worldview of goddesses as prevalent and primary in prehistory, though these goddesses assume many guises (not always positive) in myths created for our world.

The prehistoric period when the goddess myth situates its origins is often assumed to have been a superior, even utopian time, or alternatively backward and chaotic.[4] Archaeologist Marija Gimbutas (2001, 3, 215), influential in inspiring neo-pagan, goddess-centered cultures, beliefs, and myths, writes, "In Old Europe ... it was the feminine force that pervaded existence," and her editor affirms her work's effects: "philosophies—describing a world where men and women might live in harmony with one another and with their environment—found a home in the hearts of thousands of people." Trained in the 1930s and 1940s in Europe (mainly in her native Lithuania, with some postdoc work in Germany), Marija Gimbutas helped deepen and inspire the goddess movement in the second half of the twentieth century, based on training in old-school-thinking of early twentieth-century archaeology. Working at Harvard and then as a professor at UCLA, she directed some excavations of Neolithic sites in Macedonia and Greece. She wrote prolifically, often in support of interpretations of goddess-centered prehistory, especially in later books (1982, 2001), positing a "Goddess-oriented Old Europe."[5] As her popularity grew among goddess culture proponents, she increasingly compared ambiguous images stretching across many millennia and cultures, often to serious criticism.[6] As the science of archaeology developed, by at least the 1950s, many scholars questioned such generalized, comparative readings of a homogenous prehistory based on matriarchies and goddesses.[7]

Although goddess believers hail Gimbutas's achievements as a scholar and scientist heartily, many other scholars take issue with her methods and conclusions.[8] Gimbutas was critiqued by peers and later scholars for her intuitive leaps in interpreting prehistoric religious beliefs.[9] For instance, she "began seeing representations of the Goddess, and of female reproductive apparatus (wombs, Fallopian tubes, amniotic fluid), in a huge array of Stone Age artifacts, even in abstractions such as spirals and dots" (Allen 2001, 9). Like many scholars familiar with Gimbutas's work, goddess scholar and NYU professor Johanna Stuckey sees Gimbutas as "going off the deep end" because we can't prove anything about prehistory in terms of specific beliefs and stories, but

Stuckey also sees what many agree is a positive aspect of the work: "the myth of goddess culture is a useful one. 'There's a sense of empowerment'" (qtd. in McDonald 1996, 50). Interestingly, Gimbutas didn't consider herself a feminist and at first found it unlikely and funny that she became a feminist hero, but she eventually embraced the community that made her popular.[10]

However contested her methods and insights may be, Gimbutas's theory of a "matrifocal, sedentary, peaceful, art-loving, earth-and-sea bound . . . Old-Europe" (qtd. in Tringham and Conkey 1998, 23), stretching from the Paleolithic to the end of the Neolithic—40,000 to 3,000 BCE—has inspired many other best-selling and influential works promoting the goddess movement.[11] Generally, the mythic goddess's prehistoric period is portrayed by believers, in boldly utopian terms, as peaceful, nature centered, and worshipful of women, particularly for their functions like menstruation and childbirth (Marler 2003). Eller (2000, 41) describes the movement as diverse, which it is, but also finds "a number of themes appear repeatedly in feminist descriptions of prehistoric matriarchal societies: peace, prosperity, harmony with nature, appropriate use of technology, sexual freedom (including reproductive freedom), and just and equitable roles for women and men." Most incarnations of goddess culture (which are variable in our world) present themselves as pro-woman and pro-nature, and women and nature are perceived as deeply linked.

The "'goddess' is often described as having three faces (virgin, matron, crone) or as having a double role of creator/destroyer. . . . She is linked with the moon, contrasted with a male sun; identified with the earth, contrasted with a male sky. The end of the story tells of the takeover of her matriarchal society by warlike Indo-European males (c. 3500 BC), and carries a strong moral sub-text with women as the 'goodies' and men as the 'baddies'" (Goodison and Morris 1998, 12). This "cult" (as Lefkowitz [1993, 268] calls it) or religion (as Peach [2002, 350] characterizes it) is neither monolithic nor always generalizable in specifics, but most goddess worshippers today tend to enact rituals that celebrate women's feelings, sexuality, individuality, and spiritual power; New Age spirituality; and "present-day concerns" including "feminist activism, lesbian separatism, and so forth."[12] At their best, practices like Wicca give their "practitioners a sense of connection to the natural world and of access to the sacred and beautiful within their own bodies" (Allen 2001, 11). Lefkowitz (1993, 267) describes these "present-day interpretations" as a "female version of the structure of Christianity, except that the Holy Spirit seems simply to have disappeared"; she believes the faith reflects "resolutely Christian values," for instance insisting that "witchcraft can only be used for good." Again, proponents see their faith as a force for good in the world.[13]

Numerous scientists today demonstrate that in reality little or no evidence exists of our distant ancestors' beliefs and that we can glean limited details of cultural perspectives in prehistory: "most archaeologists acknowledge the ontological difficulties in accessing ancient mentalities through the material record" (Meskell 1995, 75).[14] There may have been periods or subcultures with matriarchal, egalitarian, goddess-centered, or ecological tendencies, as indeed there are in our current, predominantly patriarchal culture. There may even have been some fully matriarchal or goddess-centered cultures, but there is no definitive evidence of a widespread, long-lasting, goddess-dominated, female-oriented, mainstream culture.[15] Given that the word *utopia* means "nowhere" in its original Greek, conceptually recognizing the implicit impossibility of a perfect society, it shouldn't surprise us that humans likely never achieved anything close to feminist utopias.

Yet many goddess believers and people generally resist or ignore expert insights, and our culture still embraces the goddess myth, at least in casual ways, as reflected in our literature, popular culture, and worldview. Proponents of goddess culture often discourage or criticize questioning such "consciousness" (of a goddess-oriented past or its superiority), even though experts offer many reasons to question the essentializing, reductionist interpretations of actual, rich, complex archaeological records and insights (Tringham and Conkey 1998, 22). The many voices celebrating a goddess-centered prehistory are not all in accord and do not present a unified vision or voice, and archaeologists agree that we must make giant leaps in assuming what the actual images of women might have meant to the prehistoric people who left them behind or when assuming that our distant ancestors and their beliefs were connected over vast distances and time periods.

Symbolic prehistoric art was first studied in modern times more than 150 years ago, when prehistory became another arena in which to debate the nature of culture, humanity, and the origins of life. Discoveries especially in Europe led to questions about the dawn of humanity and social evolution. For instance, some scholars in the nineteenth century doubted whether humans could even have existed before six thousand years ago because of biblical dates. Others who accepted the ancient dates attributed to the caves and prehistoric artifacts doubted that humans thirty thousand years ago or even fourteen thousand years ago could have had any meaningful culture (White 2003). Cave paintings were sometimes overlooked or literally unperceived.[16] Sometimes observers missed or misunderstood the art because of preconceptions about this so-called primitive art being necessarily devoid of a sacred context—it could only be art for art's sake because the people who made it could not have had a complicated culture, it was erroneously thought. This idea lost favor and impact in the face of more and more art that was found deep in caves, where no casual appreciation or use for it could be conceived. More systemic and widespread ethnology in many parts of the world also helped provide data to demonstrate other cultures, even so-called primitive ones, as sophisticated in terms of having artifacts, arts, belief systems, myths, complex thinking, moral codes, and technologies (based on local environments and resources).[17]

Since at least the 1950s, the majority of archaeologists and prehistorians agree, based on mounting evidence examined with increasingly sophisticated techniques that enable fuller contextual understanding, that the mother goddess theory posited in the earliest years of the field of archaeology lacks any credibility or relevance.[18] Instead, experts posit widely varying cultures with multiple gods and goddesses, with no single overarching pattern, and probably no female-centered or egalitarian culture sustained over millennia or a wide geographic area.[19] White (2003, 220–21) believes that representational art likely originally gave humans an evolutionary advantage and explains the great variability in artifacts and cultures that produced them:

> Since at least 40,000 years ago, all modern humans everywhere have practiced material forms of representation. We have seen how, evolutionarily, representation in material media must have been advantageous. However, we should not imagine that these systems of representation were everywhere inspired by the same perceived needs and cultural bodies of ideas. An 18,000-year-old female statuette from Grimaldi is not the equivalent of a 30,000-year-old painted rhinoceros from the Grotte Chauvet or the music of a 34,000-year-old flute from Isturitz . . . [as there are] profound cultural conceptions underlying the choice of particular media, in particular human contexts, in particular places, at particular times.

Archaeologists urge learning as much about cultures and contexts as possible and not making assumptions when analyzing or comparing images. Those who have attended to such details and specific cases concur that there were likely many diverse worldviews and myths, including ideas about gods, goddesses, and various social organizations.[20] Archaeology "has made astounding strides in the past thirty years in its pursuit of knowledge about human life and culture in the distant past," attests White (2003, 31), and armed with such increasing understanding, prehistorians, archaeologists, classicists, and most contemporary scholars of the past find no evidence for unified, continuous, or long-lasting matriarchal, goddess-centered cultures or utopias.

Thus, the goddess myth that many people in our society assume to be true is based on a highly unlikely and largely intuitive, anachronistic interpretation of prehistory. No definitive evidence exists for a long-standing and widespread women-centered, goddess-focused prehistory, nor for the dominance of what Lefkowitz (1993, 266) calls a "unitary goddess"; evidence instead suggests great variety of cultural expressions, beliefs, social arrangements, and gendered deities. Gimbutas's champions defend her work (even in the face of criticism by women experts) as recognizing such variety, quoting her: "It is true that there are mother images and protectors of young life, and there was a Mother Earth and Mother of the Dead, but the rest of the female images cannot be generalized under the term Mother Goddess. . . . They impersonate Life, Death and Regeneration; they are more than fertility and motherhood" (Gimbutas qtd. in Marler 2003). But more recent feminist archaeologists, considering the whole of Gimbutas's writing, see a pattern of "a misrepresented picture of the past and our human heritage by dismissing or misconstruing the archaeological record" (Meskell 1995, 84). Other experts likewise perceive "that Gimbutas does diverge from archaeological practice with her arguments by assertion, that increasingly lack even the minimal 'linking arguments' between the archaeological materials and the interpretations that are made of them. . . . For example, Gimbutas suggests that the female imagery all shows a certain 'cohesion,' but this is not explained" (Tringham and Conkey 1998, 23–24). Lefkowitz (1992, 29, 33) agrees that many (especially nonexperts) engage in "pseudo-mystical mixing and matching of symbols and ideas that have nothing in common with each other except the contemporary use to which they may be put" and that an "overwhelming interest in unity is the fundamental problem." Serious questions remain about Gimbutas's and her followers' methods and conclusions, though she is accepted by many who embrace goddess culture and her ideas remain influential.

One early famous proponent of the goddess and her powers is American writer, teacher, and activist Starhawk (Miriam Simos). Widely acknowledged as a main inspiration and self-described "pioneer" for the neo-pagan, Wiccan, radical feminist "revival of Goddess religion," Starhawk proudly recognizes Gimbutas's influence, including at Belili.org, a website devoted to her work.[21] Starhawk lauds Donna Read's films (some by Belili Productions) that celebrate a goddess culture inspired by Gimbutas's universalizing theory. Read's film *Goddess Remembered* (1989) opens thus: "The spiritual journey of earth's peoples began with the idea of a goddess, universally called 'the Great Mother.'"[22] The film compares representations of women from different cultures and times, including, in the opening scenes, these images:

1) Venus of Laussel: dated (in the film) to thirty-five thousand years ago. This Paleolithic artifact from France is engraved on a limestone block (about eighteen inches tall) and was found with other engravings, all of which had fallen from the ceiling, where they were originally carved; it is more commonly dated to twenty-five thousand years ago.

2) Maltese "Fat Ladies" (as they're commonly known): large (up to two meters each), corpulent standing or sitting sculptures of unclear gender from Malta that the film dates to seven thousand years ago but are more commonly dated to 3200–2500 BCE.[23]

3) Minoan "snake goddesses" (a title our culture imposes): figurines of bare-breasted women, some holding or decorated with snakes (and more), from Minoan culture on Crete (c. 1600 BCE); eleven to thirteen inches each and made of faience.

Throughout, the film compares and conflates varying ancient images of women like these, from different places and many thousands of years apart, as definitive evidence of an enduring "Great Mother Goddess." These representations from prehistory seem to speak to us today and offer clues to our ancestors' lives, but Read's film boldly generalizes and interprets specific representations from disparate cultures and times. Each artifact has a particular context and various possible meanings that experts explain in numerous sources (like some examined herein), which the film ignores. Many representations of women from varying times and places during the long period (more than thirty thousand years) of prehistory shown throughout Read's films are treated as evidence of most of prehistory being goddess-centered. The film suggests a continuum of representations of the goddess, though each particular image is strikingly different in size, detail, form, and material. Believers celebrate these disparate pieces from various cultures dating tens of thousands of years apart as dynamic evidence of the goddess's mystery, depth, and variable nature. While comparing, conflating, and celebrating representations, the film affirms (as do believers) a singular, unified goddess essence. Many believers, such as Monica Sjöö and Barbara Mor (1987, 425–27), describe what they term "ecstatic" energies and a "dynamic . . . Winged Illumination" that they perceive in "'undivided'" and "original gynandrous consciousness," believing the "greatest harm patriarchy has done to us is to stifle, coopt, and deform our power of imagination" that they experience in the art connected to female-centered goddess spirituality. Such "power of imagination," as creative, respectful of nature, selfless, and peaceful, evinces a profundity that is only increased by variety of form and context, they believe.[24]

Members of our culture commonly appropriate and reimagine whatever aspects of the past will advance their particular message, creating contemporary visions and messages of perceived art, including in terms of how it inspires us. Treating ancient artifacts as art (in a modern sense) is itself an assumption (White 2003), and as we boldly imagine specifics of cultural context, beliefs, and myths, the results reflect and inspire our own cultures' values and worldviews. These new myths that we create, including almost all of our uses and presentations of so-called goddess art, are thus representations by us, for us, primarily drawn from and inspiring our biases, patterns, worldviews, and hopes. White (2003, 61) explains that when a major exhibit of Paleolithic art he curated opened at the Museum of Natural History in New York City in 1986, excitement it generated led to anachronistic expression: "a ten-foot-high statue of so-called 'Venus of Willendorf' . . . dominated a storefront in Manhattan's East Village." Since we cannot know what the figurine symbolized to the people who made it, nor how it was used, this modern, *much larger* image takes the original object pretty wildly out of context and even out of text itself (considering how much smaller the original is), appropriating it to express assumed overlaps between the original and modern sensibilities and values. Perhaps the figurine resonates with contemporary artists as a symbol for modern people, but the actual form and probably the imaginative flights it inspires likely differ dramatically from originals.

The actual statuette from Willendorf is about five inches tall and is estimated to have been carved more than twenty thousand years ago. Most of us know little about the context of this statuette, how it would have been considered or used long ago. It might have been used in rituals (though even then it might not have represented a goddess); it could have been a toy; it might have been sacrilegious; it could have been transitory (where the making of it mattered more than the object); or it could have had idiosyncratic meaning or use. Yet the object is embraced as an icon by and for some contemporary people, assumed to represent a link between aesthetic and other values of contemporary humans and very distant, foreign ancestors. As White (2003, 61) explains: "The appropriation and re-presentation by late twentieth-century New York artists of 25,000-year-old images from the Ice Age cultures of Europe laid bare a multitude of epistemological questions, and revealed assumptions about 'art' deeply held not only by the modern people we know as artists, but by the vast majority of ordinary people who make up Western civilization." White highlights a common phenomenon of contemporary humans appropriating ancient images: we perceive and use cultural artifacts as we will, out of context and for our purposes. Since we consider them relevant to us or our art, bold changes to size and imagined, modern interpretations and assumptions of artistry are not surprising. Contemporary perspectives inform these appropriative processes, as they did for early archaeologists.

The very use of terms like *Venus* or *mother* to describe figurines, first done in the nineteenth century, already shows significant imposition of our assumptions, values, and culture onto the representations (White 2003, 54–55).[25] White calls the term *Venus*, as used in regard to such figurines, "inherently tainted and interpretively vacuous" (55). Some archaeologists named figurines of women (Venus or otherwise) based on shape variations, which they connected to race. Édouard Piette, in 1867, considered steatopygous figurines and images, those with large hips, bellies, and thighs, as "grotesquely obese," and he called them Venus as "representations of African women," meaning "Southern African (Bushman) types," while slimmer figures (more appealing to tastes then and considered less "ugly" or "grotesque") were considered "Egyptian-like" (White 2003, 54–55)—in other words Black and white.[26] Notions of more- or less-advanced races influenced the naming and interpretation of figurines in disturbing ways. Such racist and hegemonic theories were overturned by experts, though they lingered for many years in some quarters, as did associated concepts, like the term *Venus*. From its inception, then, the appreciation and study of prehistoric art reflected and influenced our culture more generally while also attracting various popular theories of the day. Ruth Tringham and Margaret Conkey (1998, 24) remind us that "figurines . . . do not speak for them themselves. . . . They have to be interpreted to have meaning in any century."

Outdated notions of race and cultural evolution that we map onto ancient art and often attribute to groups of others were revealed as inaccurate, largely by fieldwork, in the late nineteenth and early twentieth centuries, as anthropology and folklore became rigorous academic disciplines whose practitioners routinely carry out ethnology. The experience of living immersed in other cultures proves those cultures (with volumes of data and many years of experience that helped reshape the whole field of ethnology and related social theory) to be complex, artistic, moral, and so on. Our understanding of prehistory and other cultures has grown greatly, yet even today, some visitors and students exposed to these sites and artifacts find their preconceptions and philosophies challenged.[27] Prehistory has particular touristic appeal to many because it feels mysterious yet also familiar and powerfully moving to us today. Scientists demonstrate ways we all map preconceptions, biases, and hopes onto the art.[28]

We suppose we are reclaiming ancient "goddess" characters, and then when we fictionalize our ideas of those imagined, appropriated beings in our art and popular culture, we typically either romanticize or vilify them (as all good or clearly evil). This process may be a natural human reaction to ascribe meaning and to fictionalize experiences and ideas, including glimmers of the past. Rarely do most of us dig deeper and attend to what contemporary experts of past cultures explain, revealing our biases and readiness to assume, appropriate, and interpret. Examining and considering even a few individual works of "art" or representation from prehistory through expert lenses reveals much. An overwhelming majority of prehistorians today emphasize that these many objects and images vary dramatically over time and place and that each must be studied in its particular context to be interpreted in a scientifically meaningful way. White urges us to avoid mapping our assumptions about art itself onto prehistoric peoples or their representations. What we call "art" likely had different contexts, meanings, and "cultural logic": "When we look at a prehistoric representational work we should not be so arrogant as to think that we can understand it with the aesthetic tools of our own culture" (White 2003, 220).

Particular representations from prehistory may be only partial—such as torsos, vulvas, or other body parts, with varying styles and degrees of detail, some requiring significant interpretive effort to even be perceived as female. Many experts demonstrate through careful examination of actual images that "most of the imagery of human-humanoids cannot readily be identified as male or female" (Tringham and Conkey 1998, 27). Some claim as goddesses many ambiguous symbols, such as lines, dots, geometric shapes, and various animals or natural representations.[29] Experts today contest such claims.[30] Some aspects of context are easy to grasp and help demonstrate why context matters: "figurines are found in every kind of context—refuse pits included.... It could demonstrate that these figures are not sacred at all; or they may have multiple meanings which change as a figure is made, used and discarded" (Meskell 1995, 82). Since the multiple contexts of prehistoric peoples—how they lived, what they believed—vary from each other and from today, it is unlikely that our modern assumptions or interpretations are relevant unless we immerse ourselves in what we do know of prehistory, though even then we'd have contextual and interpretive limitations.[31]

Meskell (1998, 54–55) notes how we "have consciously moulded the images" from prehistory—she specifically studies Neolithic culture—based on our culture and wishes "into something familiar and desirable" because some of us "need ... visions" for our own hopes. She urges us not to "rest on the foundation of the golden age of antiquity" for our own "aims for social change," which instead "should be based on a fundamental humanity" (55). Meskell and many experts perceive and embrace ambiguity, diversity, a range of possible interpretations for any given artifact or site. She characterizes a "fervour" and "a very real *archaeology of desire* for a number of groups" today that "search for a utopian model" as a "template for change" (60–62). This "*archaeology of desire,*" which she italicizes, highlighting its significance, accurately describes much of the goddess culture stimulated by Gimbutas and reflected in pop culture and literature today. Contemporary, often personalized visions of these artifacts, and what *we want them to mean*, dominate, often in defiance of what archaeologists explain. Many concur that our desires need not be mapped onto the past for any goal, including positive change.

Ancient art is better understood as diverse and complex, with emergent meanings dependent upon particular contexts, which archaeologists understand better the more they study them. The same is true of contemporary art and cultural artifacts—good scholarly analysis of any cultural production requires attending to context. Scientific methodology encourages engaging with the "messiness" of things, as Meskell (2017) describes it, "messiness" meaning multiple associations, layers, complex situations, and so on. By engaging messiness, thus resisting appealing, simpler, assumed "truths," and by recognizing objects' complexity and "fundamental embeddedness and their myriad historical residues and entanglements," we may hope to better understand the past and perhaps the present (Meskell 2017). *Not* attending to messier, more complex archaeological insights, many non-experts in our culture think of a standard, homogeneous and widespread—across time and space—representation of woman, or a continuum of various female images, that we interpret as goddesses or a unified "great" or "mother goddess."[32] Let us then engage some messiness by delving deeper, considering briefly a few key "goddess" representations, what experts reveal about them, and how they are misunderstood.

Prehistory and Goddess Culture Appreciations and Appropriations: Paleolithic Goddess Figurines

Upper Paleolithic "artwork" often appeals to us and spurs goddess myths. The 1940 discovery of Lascaux and similar sites in Europe changed our understanding of the origins of art and prehistory.[33] Representational designs are carved, incised, and painted on rock, ivory, bone, and other materials in ways that seem variably realistic, stylized, or strange. Most commonly depicted are animals, signs (dots, lines, rectangles, crosses, fleches), and sometimes humans (typically stylized); many caves feature human handprints made by blowing pigment around a hand to leave a negative imprint (fig. 2), and some scientists speculate these are women's hands.[34] Tourists enjoy but also endanger the art by visiting it—hence the original Lascaux and many other formerly toured caves are now closed to visitors, though some have visitable replicas.[35] Visitors and appreciators naturally wonder about the makers and their cultures, often resorting to fanciful speculation that inspires contemporary stories and whole subcultures of goddess myths and imagined pasts. The art evokes fanciful fantasies more often than it leads to seeking out best scholarship about the past.

So-called Venus figurines and representations of women generally are often assumed to have religious associations—thus "goddesses"—but particular examples of the source artifacts differ considerably and were likely made, used, and understood differently from how we imagine they were. When examining representations of women with careful scrutiny, we can quickly perceive a great range of forms styles, and materials, often portraying women in startlingly different ways—from each other and from our ideas of "goddess figurines."[36] Some representations appear to emphasize fertility or sexuality, possibly pregnant bellies or vulvas;[37] others focus on slender, possibly adolescent female figures;[38] and often only parts of women, such as heads, torsos, or vulvas are represented.[39] While fleshy figures might seem to represent pregnancy or fertility, and while vulvas represent sexuality pretty obviously according to contemporary semiotic communication, we cannot know this was true for past humans—mapping our semiotics and epistemologies onto the past is a hermeneutical problem. Many representations are stylized, and some previously identified as women are not unambiguous, and experts now contest that many are women. Many representations of humans, animals, and signs are probably connected to ritual activities,[40] such as celebrations, hunting, harvests, mythic enactments, rites of passage, sexuality, fertility, or any number of other qualities and activities that may have had any number of possible meanings to those who made and used them.

Not only should we resist the urge to assume a logical, obvious meaning to the images, but there is no image that is singular, common, or homogeneous among those found, in spite of the fact that many people conceive of a preponderance of fleshy "Venus" or "mother" figurines existing in prehistory. Women are represented in tremendously varied forms, sizes, shapes, materials, and styles. And so are men. Some steatopygous figurines emphasize large breasts, bellies, and buttocks (like the so-called Venus/Woman of Willendorf [fig. 6] or Venus of Laussel [fig. 5]). But many others represent thinner, young-seeming women's bodies (e.g., Vénus Impudique [fig. 4], Venus of Galgenberg, and one Venus of Petřkovice); some representations of women are headless or have tiny or featureless heads, sometimes along with small arms and feet (Willendorf); some are faceless (Willendorf); others are just heads, like Venus of Brassempouy, which is also apparently thin, and possibly not even representing a woman (see introduction). Figurines and engravings depict various gestures or positions, often emphasizing buttocks or genitalia, as in Venus of Neuchâtel, or engravings of vulvas at places such as Castel-Merle or Combarelles in France. Representations of women existed in great variety.

Many artifacts include various additional decoration and symbolism, such as headwear or hairstyles, notches, dots, or other symbols or details such as facial features or props. Facial expressions, hairdos, and props, including clothing, chairs, and animals, increase during Neolithic and later times. Many representations (not only of women) bear traces of red ocher, meaning they were painted and probably decorated in other ways, possibly with things like grass, wood, or shells that have long since decayed. The many thus far discovered figurines, engravings, and pictographs from prehistory are neither homogeneous nor monolithic. Very different cultures, sometimes tens of thousands of years and thousands of miles apart, represent women in a striking variety of form, material, style, and context. Yet many in our culture consider them as evidence of a continuing primary, variable goddess, believed to have dominated religiously and culturally for tens of thousands of years.[41] Almost all evidence invoked from prehistory, such as the figurines or later representations and stories referencing women (like Amazons), and even Neolithic geometric designs at places like New Grange, Ireland, are at best ambiguous and do not prove matriarchy, nor a woman-forward nor goddess-centered culture.[42]

Venus of Hohle Fels

Possibly the oldest yet found representation of a human (though recently discovered), the so-called Venus of Hohle Fels or "Venus of Schelklingen" (fig. 3) was carved of mammoth ivory and found near Schelklingen, Germany, in 2008; it "dates to between 35,000 and 40,000 years ago, belonging to the early Aurignacian, very beginning of the Upper Paleolithic, associated with earliest presence of Cro-Magnon in Europe"; it is the "oldest undisputed example of a depiction of a human being yet discovered."[43] This oldest dated Venus is more oddly proportioned than our common idea of goddess or Venus figurines, with "ballooning breasts and elaborately carved genitalia" (Curry 2012). The large breasts are not proportionate to the buttocks, and the vulvic notch is more deeply carved than in most figurines. Some have called it "prehistoric porn" and insist it is "art" of "the essence of being female . . . imbued . . .

Fig. 3. Venus of Hohle Fels or Venus of Schelklingen, six centimeters, mammoth tusk, Aurignacian, 35,000–40,000 BP, unearthed in a cave in Germany, 2008; oldest undisputed representation of a human being.

with larger meaning," while other experts counter that we cannot know this.[44] Tringham and Conkey (1998, 25) argue that similar interpretations "reflect the primacy of the notion of 'Woman' as both an erotic and aesthetic ideal, and contemporary pornographic views of the female body as sexual object." They also suggest that our impulse to consider large breasts, buttocks, or stomachs as indicative of motherhood—let alone idealization or deification of it—is "problematic," since we can't even know what "'motherhood' might have meant some 20,000 years ago in these particular societies" (25). We cannot not know what this depiction of a woman meant, and the assumptions of sexuality, motherhood, and goddesshood are all questionable. The disproportionate breasts and deep vulvic carving could indicate a carver without skill (a mistake), could have been intended as an exaggeration to emphasize gender or as a joke or parody, or could be read in various other ways.

Fig. 4. Venus of La Laugerie Basse or La Venus Impudique or the Immodest Venus; eight centimeters, ivory; first sculptural representation of a woman found in modern times, 1864.

La Venus Impudique

The first figurine given the name Venus (fig. 4) was found in 1864 at Laugerie-Basse in Dordogne, France (Norman n.d.). It is called La Venus Impudique or the Immodest Venus, a name earned because it seems to visually contrast the "*Venus pudica* ('modest Venus'), [an] appellation used to describe statue types of the Classical Venus which often show the goddess attempting to conceal her breasts and pubic area from view" in ancient Greek and Roman statues (Norman n.d.). This thin, almost boyish or adolescent figure with no noticeable breasts has a notch to represent a vulva but seems nothing like the fleshy "mother goddess" most people have in mind as *the* prehistoric representation of woman or a Venus figurine. There are actually many slender or less full-figured representations (non-steatopygous ones) of women, without large breasts, bellies, or thighs (e.g. Venuses of Galgenberg, Neuchâtel, and Eliseevichi, among others). From the earliest days of our modern appreciation and study of figurines, like this earliest discovered "Immodest Venus," we established a pattern of imposing modern, Western ideas, categories, and even names onto them, to enfold them into aspects of our culture and history. Why should we assume a naked figurine of a woman was any sort of goddess or that she might be considered "immodest," a concept dependent on recent mindsets and mores? Ironically, this first "Venus" is one of the least stereotypically goddesslike prehistoric representations of women, lacking physical features later associated with beauty or goddess qualities, such as large breasts or buttocks. We can call her a woman, and indeed many more recent textbooks refer to such images as "woman" instead of "Venus," but we cannot know much more about what she was meant to represent than that gender, and even gender categories and considerations should be a subject of inquiry in terms of prehistoric cultures.

Fig. 5. Venus of Laussel, limestone bas-relief painted with red ocher, forty-six centimeters, 25,000 BP, found in Laussel rock shelter in France, 1911, holds a bison horn or cornucopia with thirteen notches.

Venus of Laussel

There are many figurines with large bellies, breasts, and thighs, apparently obese and possibly pregnant (e.g. Venuses of Willendorf, Dolní Věstonice, Lespugue, Gagarino). Some, especially the Venus of Laussel (fig. 5), are often interpreted as being connected to fertility because the woman's hand rests on her large belly, just below large breasts, which could indicate pregnancy. Her other hand holds a bison horn with thirteen notches carved onto it, which could represent thirteen menstrual cycles or moons in a year—details commonly assumed, by us, to represent fertility or abundance. But, interestingly, like at most sites, this is not the only representation of a human found at the site: "the Great Shelter at Laussel has produced five bas-reliefs representing women, one adolescent and a representation of two opposed figures," plus various other images, including animals and a male with hunting instruments and posture.[45] This image of a possibly pregnant woman was not found in isolation and may not have been the most important image at the site, but it is the only image most people know from the site and is one of the most reproduced pieces of evidence of a goddess (and especially a mother goddess) being worshiped in prehistory.

Since the blocks of limestone on which all these images had been carved fell to the cave floor (a common event in limestone shelters like this one) before modern discovery, much of their context was lost, including how the representations may have related to each other. The Venus of Laussel still bears some traces of red ocher (common on many artifacts of the period), which some interpret as representing blood, and thus menstruation or child-birth. Many non-feminine representations are also painted with red ocher, so that problematizes a quick conclusion of blood, pregnancy, and fertility. Again, assuming this woman represents a goddess or even fertility is a mod-ern interpretation based on limited, out-of-context information. Expert opin-ions differ about the purpose of the full array of representations found at the site. The most famous, singled-out representation, engraved on rock fallen from the ceiling (fig. 5), and the other fallen blocks depicting other women and probably a male hunter lead many to question the goddess conclusion.[46]

There are enough images of other women and designs among the Laus-sel ruins that many experts interpret the collection of images, which in situ might have represented a "scene," or a story, as *not* representing a great mother goddess, nor any single goddess, but a more complicated scenario involving multiple women, a man, and animals.[47] Motherhood or fertility might be part of the scenario, as might other ideas. Large breasts and bellies have no defini-tive sexual or motherly meaning—no baby or child is depicted, as is common in later depictions of motherhood and motherly goddesses. Yet many recent interpreters, ignoring or unaware of the plurality of images found at the site and mostly relying solely on the most popular Venus with a Horn image, con-fidently assert that the woman represents fertility and the mother goddess and that she is connected to all other ancient representations of women, god-desses, and mothers, which they believe a dominant type in prehistory. This very image is one of the pieces shown at the beginning of Read's film *Goddess Remembered* as evidence of an ongoing, ancient mother goddess legacy, which assumes these distant ancestors worshiped a "mother goddess" and that she would have been similar to our concept of a mother goddess. This interpreta-tion also embodies and spurs assumptions of definitive power of female fer-tility and thus women's place as revered and powerful. Such representations

Fig. 6. Venus of Willendorf, Oolitic limestone carved figurine with traces of red ocher, estimated 25,000 BP, found in Austria, 1908; four views, as shown at the Naturhistorisches Museum in Vienna, Austria, January 2020.

may represent fertility or abundance, but we cannot conclude so definitively, and we cannot know if this image represents a goddess, nor what type, if so; nor can we know if her culture glorified male figures and activities like hunting. The scene and the most famous image in it are all intriguing, but only a little research of what's known of the context and what experts can tell us reveals how questionable the conclusion is that goddesshood and evidence of a goddess-dominant tradition are associated with this image.

When one peruses many other such representations of Paleolithic women (online, in books, at museums), one finds not only wide-ranging depictions of female forms but no clear or unified, predominating pattern of representations of gender generally. As noted, in most Paleolithic representations of humans, there are no women with children or babies, as is typically the case of goddesses revered as mothers in later cultures.[48] Nor is there other evidence suggesting divinity in the images, like objects, gestures, or props that later cultures typically include to indicate goddesshood.[49] If the symbolism is present to indicate the status of the beings depicted, we cannot decipher it.[50] There are also numerous images of men throughout this period, also ranging from particular body parts, like a phallus, to full, often stylized figures, sometimes with props. There are not more women than men depicted, and a plethora of variation exists in representations of both women and men.

Venus of Willendorf

Probably the most famous Paleolithic Venus is that of Willendorf (fig. 6). She wears what may be a shell cap, which some speculate to have carried significance—shells coming from the faraway Mediterranean. She also bears traces of red ocher, probably a valued trade item. Some art historians describe the Willendorf figurine's body as "rounded perfection" in what they perceive as "key areas . . . which would be most important in the preliminary phases of love-making," while other areas—arms, feet, face—are relatively ignored.[51] But contemporary feminist archaeologists analyze such statements to show that "scholarly discourse about these Upper Palaeolithic female images relies upon—and effects—a hierarchical and gendered subject-object relationship: that is, the appropriation of a female body by a masculine subject" (Tringham and Conkey 1998, 26).[52] Assumptions of the importance or naturalness of the male gaze seems applied to the past here (by male scholars). Most often, Tringham and Conkey argue, art history texts about all such figurines impose "twentieth-century sexist notions of gender and sexuality" (26). Whatever the images meant to our ancestors "must be made the object of investigation for debate, not assertion" (3), Tringham and Conkey urge us to remember. There may have been female deities or reverence for childbirth or fertility back then, and perhaps this figurine represents such. But we cannot know so, and our desires and impulses should not dictate our understandings and interpretations. These Upper Paleolithic representations of women intrigue us, but they are not ours in any but an appropriative sense, which also typically represents sexist and other contemporary ideologies, including racism.

Conclusions about Paleolithic Figurines

Jill Cook (2017), a British Museum curator of the 2013 exhibit "Ice Age Art: Arrival of the Modern Mind," believes that Paleolithic figurines are not about sexuality or enticing men. To demonstrate her interpretation, she too points to the great variety of representations of women from this distant past, representing all stages of women's lives, "some slim, young, sexy ones," and older ones past childbearing "who were a bit overweight," and none with "the posture or gaze" of the "classic kind of Venus . . . rising from her bath" who "directly connects with" the viewer. By contrast, Cook says, "these [Paleolithic] ladies have a downward gaze; they're not trying to give you the come-on. Their arms are tucked in, often on their swollen bellies; their knees are always clenched tight together."[53] Cook disagrees with the common idea that these sculptures were about the male gaze and pleasing Paleolithic men.

One common theory is that much such art was seen as holding magic connected to hunting or fertility.[54] Another popular theory is that the representations reflected dreams or hallucinogenic states of mind, possibly connected to rituals.[55] Particular objects like the Hohle Fels Venus (fig. 3) suggest to some "that the corpulent figurines symbolized the hope for a well-nourished community" (Curry 2012). These efforts to represent their world remain an early form of human communication that was excitingly innovative, socially bonding, society forming, and reflective of huge technological innovation, probably spurred by competing for land and resources (White 2003). Representations must have had some evolutionary advantage, White believes. The art suggests "organizational and adaptive implications" that likely gave our ancestors greater social and cognitive skills necessary for survival and cultural development (White 2003, 16).[56] Probably the prevalence of art in this region at this time suggests its more general significance to our species. Various shared cultural representations, from personal adornment to icons and visual images, were likely used to "construct and define a multitude of social categories . . . and social solidarity"; in other words, the art helped humans bond together as a successful social group (15). Considering specific examples reveals expert insight that urges us not to approach ancient representations in conclusive, modern-oriented ways but rather to be open to complexity and inquiry, considering what these communicative productions might or might not have meant to our ancestors in ways that are emergent and shifting as we study and build context.

Whatever the art meant to people living in "social and environmental contexts that no longer exist on earth today" (White 2003, 17), it probably was quite different from what most of us, living in such exceedingly different contexts, imagine. Many archaeologists, who themselves debate the art's meaning, agree on lack of certainty: "University of Illinois archaeologist Olga Soffer doubts that we'll ever know the true nature of these creations, and cautions against speculating about prehistoric imagery in terms of '18th-century Western European art'" (Curry 2012). Most experts believe "a multiplicity of meanings and motivations lay behind Paleolithic representations" (White 2003, 54). There is no single generalizable or conclusive explanation, just as there is no homogenous image, but all interpretive efforts of the various representations require careful consideration of objects *in context*, based on expert research and insight, which is why I focus on these few particular examples.

Many interpretations are possible for such ancient representations, but it remains the case for most figurines that there is "very little traditional contextual information" to help interpretive efforts, and what context is known is often ignored; the fact that "most figurines have been found in trash pits in a broken state," according to Tringham and Conkey (1998, 28), is rarely known or acknowledged. That context alone—being found broken and in

Fig. 7. Seated Woman of Çatalhöyük, Turkey, 6000–5500 BCE (Neolithic); head, part of left arm, and left feline head are restored, Museum of Anatolian Civilizations, Ankara, Turkey. Baked clay figurine, approximately eight inches, unearthed in 1961 by James Mellaart, who considered it to represent a fertile mother goddess.

trash pits—might suggest very different interpretations from reverence, or having been cherished, but then again, breakage or placement in trash pits might have occurred after centuries or millennia of different treatment. Much of the deeper significance of ancient art may remain unknown to us, but by attending to experts of the Paleolithic era, which spans tens of thousands of years over a large geographic region, we can comprehend tremendous variation in form and potential meaning.

Neolithic Goddess Figurines

Mother Goddess from Çatalhöyük

The rich variation and complexity of depictions of women only increase as we start comparing Paleolithic representations of women to those from later historical periods. Certain famous Neolithic representations labeled as "goddesses" carry the imposition of our assumptions and hopes quite blatantly and fabulously. For instance, the famous mother goddess figurine from Çatalhöyük, Turkey (fig. 7) found by British archaeologist James Mellaart in 1961 in a grain bin represents a seated woman. The woman depicted has different physical details from Paleolithic figurines, including kneecap lines, detailed feet, and props such as a chair with feline heads on the armrests. Numerous other representations from the period have been found at Çatalhöyük as well, including many depictions of men, but *most* images and figurines depict animals. Numerous small animal figurines are made of barely fired clay, often crudely formed and found in garbage pits, or in walls, floors, or abandoned structures—possibly tokens or charms. The Çatalhöyük "goddess" is often cited as evidence of a goddess culture continuing through the entire Paleolithic and Neolithic periods, an idea now understood as scientifically suspect, yet there are no obvious shrines (Meskell 1998). Still, these figurines and their interpretation excite the goddess community and "have attained iconic status" in spite of their shady provenance and contexts (Meskell 1998, 46).

Mellaart, who first excavated the Çatalhöyük site, imposed his generalist vision and modern interpretations on the material, as when calling the Anatolian figurines "slim girls in topless 'bikinis,' their hair done up in pigtails" (Meskell 1998, 46, quoting Mellaart's 1975 *The Neolithic of the Near East*, 115). Mellaart was eventually accused by fellow archaeologists in his day of manipulation of his evidence, including to fit his mother goddess bias. Because of accusations of fabrications, fraud, dealing in the black market, and focusing only on representations that fit his theories,[57] he was ejected from Turkey, and the site was closed for thirty years.[58] More recent research at the site reveals that less than 5 percent of images found there are of female forms, and the other 95 percent, of more than three thousand images found thus far, are of animals. Meskell's analyses show that many "objects of experience"—the animals—were "quickly made and quickly discarded," apparently by everyone (Meskell 2017). There are also murals depicting men clearly in the process of hunting.[59] Meskell's and others' work here requires us to rethink our categories, for instance, being open to the idea that the act of *making* the objects was perhaps more key than the objects themselves. We must seek clues to context and avoid "liberating" objects from their context, Meskell (2017) urges, reminding us that how we think of such objects today likely has little to do with how they were thought of or used in the past. Our interpretive efforts are enhanced by recognizing numerous complex situational associations of all such objects at any given site.

Meskell (1998, 47) sees Mellaart's interpretations as clumsy, based on rushed excavation at the site, and meant to advance "the grand narrative tradition of archaeology in the 1960s," which helped in the "institutionalization of the 'Mother Goddess.'" Many have accepted the "notion that the 'Goddess' held universal religious sway through time and space" and saw selected female figurines from the site as precursors to Minoan and Mycenaean cultures from nearby Greece (47). Mellaart's interpretation, including that this site further demonstrates widespread worship of a great mother goddess, "will always be *our* fiction," Meskell states, meaning a myth for today that she considers inspired "by Gimbutas's universalizing gynocentric narrative" (49). In contrast to this narrative, Meskell finds no obvious shrines at Çatalhöyük and notes that "many of the human figurines are defaced and damaged, as were … heads" from some depictions on walls, suggesting possible links with death (59). She argues that even if they were associated with fertility and rituals, "ritualized fertility should not be conflated with the presence of a 'Mother Goddess,' since they can be mutually exclusive concepts" (60). In spite of a lack of evidence for matriarchy or a mother goddess in this culture, she perceives "a very real archaeology of desire for a number of groups," including Gimbutas and those who "search for a utopian model" through "the invention of tradition" out of a "veiled" and "shrouded" prehistory (61–62). Mysteries appeal to us, as these ancient images appeal to us. Once interpreted as fitting a narrative that many approve and even revere, that appropriated interpretation of the past takes hold for many today, and thus many find it hard to perceive other possibilities, and thus often neglect basic research about given sites, like this, even when strong evidence exists and is easy to find and understand.

Minoan Snake Goddesses

Among the most famous Neolithic representations of women considered goddesses and often used as further evidence of a long-standing goddess tradition are the so-called snake goddess figurines found by British archaeologist Sir Arthur Evans, who led the excavation of the five-acre Palace of Knossos on Crete starting in 1900 (remains circa 1500 BCE). The faience figurines of glazed earthenware have often been considered by goddess supporters as among the most stunning and exciting examples of ancient depictions of and evidence for prehistoric goddesses generally or of the great goddess in particular (fig. 8). These representations of women include details like facial features; elaborate clothing and body décor, such as bared breasts with dresses tightly cinched at the waist; and props such as snakes and cats. They also typically have much slimmer bodies than steatopygous figurines, yet many consider them reflective of the same goddess continuum. Their large, exposed breasts seem titillating, and their stomachs are trim, appealing to a modern aesthetic of women's bodies.

According to curator and art historian Kenneth Lapatin (2002, 60), Evans found fragments of the figurines, along with many other fragments, implements, bones, and shells, at previously overlooked cists covered with gypsum slabs during his fourth campaign at Knossos in 1903: "Because Evans thought their previous contents had been transferred from a damaged shrine and deliberately buried in antiquity, he called the pits 'Temple Repositories,'" and

Fig. 8. Minoan "Snake Goddess" figurines, c. 1500 BCE (Bronze Age), excavated in Knossos, Greece, 1903, by Arthur Evans; reconstructed pieces of faience figurines found in a pit or cist in the "palace" at Knossos, interpreted as goddess and priestess by Evans.

considered the "beauty and interest" of the contents as surpassing any other finds. But the found fragments constitute at least five figurines: "When the material was sorted, it became clear that the fragments of at least five faience statuettes had been recovered. Two were soon restored" (61). One heavily restored figurine received much attention: "The statuette immediately became famous and is to this day one of the most frequently reproduced pieces of ancient art.... But familiar as this figure has become, it is rarely noted that the 'original,' now on display in the Herakleion Archaeological Museum, is badly damaged; it was discovered without its head and most of the left arm," which Evans hired an artist to fashion (62). Not only is one of the most famous images of the goddess significantly reconstructed by twentieth-century artists, but what we know of the context—being found with four or more other such female figures, some of which are larger—does not readily suggest a solitary, singular, or great goddess. These are certainly dramatic female figures, and like much at Knossos, they appeal to modern tastes. But nothing of this little contextual information suggests an ongoing tradition of a unitary goddess.

Two of the reconstructed figurines, labeled by Evans as the goddess and her priestess, receive much modern attention, generated by Evans's own enthusiasm for the objects and how he treated them: "From ruined fragments he carefully staged a ritual scene" (Lapatin 2002, 76; fig. 9). The other figurines—when noticed at all, since Evans didn't give them much attention—are usually considered attendants. Other partial figurines are also headless and usually ignored (Goodison and Morris 1998), even though they are present in an altar tableau constructed by Evans from various fragments found in the cist. He set up the altar according to his imagination, and it changed over time. For instance, he "pasted a small stone altar over the 'snake bones' and

Fig. 9. Altar constructed by Evans using objects found in the "temple repository cists" where figurine of "snake goddess" was found in 1903.

added the restored head of the Snake Priestess" (Lapatin 2002, 77). His "altar," already a staged scene based on his imagination, included many objects, such as seashells, found where the figurines were dug up, and "in the center of the assemblage, between the reconstructed faience snake handlers, he places a Minoan marble cross, which he associated with the primary symbol of Orthodox Christianity and whose 'special religious significance,' he wrote, 'can hardly be a subject of doubt'" (Lapatin 2002, 76, quoting Evans's *Palace of Minos*). Even while recognizing similar, though all very damaged, additional female figurines, Evans's interpretation insists upon a single goddess with priestess and attendants and a Christian cross, perhaps meant to indicate her unitary goddess status. Why not perceive multiple such figurines found together as reflecting multiple goddesses, since multiple goddess representations are found throughout this part of the ancient world? Evans's views and interpretations were likely inspired by his personal life and existing written works by Friedrich Wilhelm Eduard Gerhard (1849), Johann Jakob Bachofen (1861), Jane Ellen Harrison (1903), and perhaps most influentially Sir James George Frazer (1890, 1906; Lapatin 2002). Evans likely sought and manufactured a "truth" of artifacts at his site based on his beliefs.

Many such late nineteenth- and early twentieth-century scholars posited a universal theme of a mother goddess in ancient religion, which was variously explained. Frazer thought that in "primitive modes of thought" there was always a "Great Mother and her younger male consort, the Dying God" (Lapatin 2002, 72–73). Thus, Evans imagined that "a Minoan priest-king may have sat upon the throne at Knossos, the adopted Son on earth of the Great Mother of its island mysteries" (qtd. in Goodison & Morris 1998, 113). Evans was the first to argue for a regional religion that "centered on a Great Goddess attended by a dying and rising god who symbolized the agricultural cycle" (Goodison and Morris 1998). But "another strand of scholarship has long argued that the Minoans—like their Near Eastern and Egyptian neighbours— were polytheistic, worshipping a number of gods and goddesses" (113). Lapatin (2002, 89) likewise suggests that "it hardly seems *probable*" the Minoans would have been monotheists, when all their neighbors and the evidence we have suggests polytheism. Our conflation of multiple goddesses in traditions we know about, such as ancient Greece, suggests Evans's interpretation reflects modern tastes and theories and ignores the more likely explanation of multiple, differentiated goddesses, common in other contemporary cultures in the region (Lapatin 2002). Goodison and Morris (1998) give details of numerous other female figurines of different styles also found on Crete, including many "poppy goddesses," who most likely represent goddesses, since goddesses of the time are typically depicted with upraised arms, which those figurines have. But poppy goddesses are more commonly accepted as plural and differentiated, not representative of a single "mother goddess," suggesting a pluralistic pattern as likely in various stages of Cretan history.[60]

Even though we have evidence of a plurality of goddesses on Crete, and very little evidence exists that these evocative snake goddess figurines were perceived or worshiped as a solitary goddess during the time they were made, and even though there are few such figurines compared to many other images of women on Crete, these rare and appealing snake goddess artifacts at Knossos have become some of the most often cited and popular evidence of women's roles in the ancient world. The figurines are believed to represent evidence of the varied continuum of a unitary, powerful, pervasive goddess tradition and related social systems. Poor scholarship and methodology, even when identifiable as from a different, biased era, can lead to modern appropriative tendencies in understanding prehistory, which in turn easily lead to interpretations of the past mostly pertinent to and reflective of our culture.[61] Rarely do contemporary fiction, films, or television represent the past thoughtfully, and we shall see that contemporary goddesses and related cultures continue to mostly reflect our own culture.

Goddess Art Today

The Knossos snake goddesses' popularity has also spurred something of an industry in forgeries, imitations, and a kind of feedback loop of goddess evidence. Evans himself bought or enthusiastically endorsed the validity of a number of pieces in styles similar to the figurines he found at Knossos. But Lapatin's (2002) careful research shows that many such objects have unclear provenance, and he considers them modern fakes that earned money for local artisans on Crete. Once an imaged past is posited and "authorized" by an acclaimed (at the time) expert, others "find" or create evidence to substantiate that view, especially when it becomes popular and serves contemporary culture.

Contemporary artists openly reference these presumed (or created) past goddesses, including Judy Chicago in her multi-media exhibit *The Dinner Party* (1979). Chicago's installation artwork features a triangular table of thirty-nine place settings (with hand-painted plates, cutlery, chalices, napkins, place runners, and other details like a tile floor inscribed with another 999 names). Each main setting has a "guest of honor," meaning "historical figures" referencing goddesses or goddess-like figures from throughout history, arranged in three wings, staring in prehistory and extending to recent times (Georgia O'Keeffe is the most recent artist represented). She includes settings in wing 1 for "Primordial Goddess," "Fertile Goddess," and "Snake Goddess," along with ten named goddesses, artists, and historical figures. Her explanations draw upon work by Gimbutas and others from that era of goddess culture. Chicago (1979) explains the place setting that represents a snake goddess from Minoan culture:

> The snake motif is apparent in the images of gold snakes on the back of the runner and in the snake intertwined in the letter "S" on the runner's front ... echoes the Cretan figure, with a flounce that mimics that of the goddess' skirt. . . . The plate is rooted in vulvar (or central core) imagery found throughout The Dinner Party, and is largely based on the color-scheme of Cretan Snake Goddesses statues. Echoing their gold and ivory tones, the plate contains four pale yellow arms growing out from a center form, "whose egg-like shapes represent the generative force of the goddess.[62]

In the "Primordial Goddess" setting, she dates these "Primordial Goddesses" to as far back as 2,500,000 BCE, especially the "Upper Paleolithic 30,000 to 10,000 B.C.E," and explains, "the goddess, as the divine creator, was mirrored in each woman's body," which she says reflects "cycles of the female body, such as menstruation, pregnancy, birth, and lactation" as part of a "tradition of the Mother Earth Goddess," like Gaea (Chicago 1979). Referring specifically to the Çatalhöyük goddess (in the "Fertile Goddess" setting explanation), she says, "Many scholars and archaeologists have used the excavated site to theorize about an early matriarchal society in which the primary divine being was the

Fertile Goddess, a model for subsequent goddess worship traditions." Chicago's vision of goddess-centered prehistory still has popular appeal as a permanent exhibit in a feminist "Herstory Gallery" of a major New York city art museum, even though experts referenced in this chapter perceive such generalized and conclusive aspects of Chicago's message as inaccurate, generalized, and conclusive. This art, and many other such work by contemporary artists, along with kitschy and touristy items inspired by ancient goddesses, may be moving for us, may be powerful or evocative, may be commercially successful, or may evoke feelings of connection to our distant ancestors or lifeways, but that reflects the power of the human spirit and our creative imaginations more than the actual past.

Conclusion

Examples of supposed prehistoric goddess representations extend from more-than-thirty-thousand-year-old Paleolithic to less-than-two-thousand-year-old Neolithic images of women. Current scientific insight demonstrates the complexity and diversity of representations that vary tremendously in form, detail, expression, style, and likely function and meaning. Each representation was found in a distinct, multivalent, complex, "messy" context, and each can be analyzed and somewhat demystified based on those contexts. Experts offer more information than most of us accept or realize that can help us move beyond simple, reflexive goddess generalizations. These few examples demonstrate that images of women each have distinctive qualities and implications, reflecting fascinating, diverse cultures from which the images emerge, each amazing, differentiated, and involving variable contexts suggesting varying meanings. We can't completely reconstruct everything about any single figurine or image, let alone generalize about all ancient representations of women, but we can learn much that is fascinating and compelling by listening to experts who help us demystify and appreciate the dynamic variability and rich possibilities of early human cultures and their representations.

Our ancestors left artifacts and representations that we appreciate as moving and provocative, they probably had myths and shared religious systems around the same time, and they likely understood metaphor and symbolism in profound ways. This does not mean our ancestors lived exactly as we do, nor that we conceive of the world in similar ways. But potential understanding of our ancestors, and of ourselves, improves if we accept ancient people's capacity for complex intellectual and representational expression and work.

Emotional responses to the figurines lead many today to underappreciate or ignore contextual details and explanations that *are* available for much prehistoric art. Prehistoric cultures in "Old Europe" and the Mediterranean, "where claims for a Goddess have been most insistent and where there is, therefore, a case to answer" for what many have argued or assume that this art means. By attending to feminist archaeologists we discover fascinating and thougthful analyses amounting to "a picture of staggering diversity" (Goodison and Morris 1998, 16). Why are these "staggering" insights into the various cultures who made and used complex and diverse ancient forms of human expression not as attended to or perceived as being as worthy of celebration as the inaccurate, monolithic goddess concept? Our appropriated, imagined, recent goddess myth is far more popular than scientific explanations and remains a widespread assumption about the past, perhaps because it offers an easier to grasp, fantastic, generalized "answer" seemingly of and from the past that appeals to many today, speaking our language.

One reason we insist on such appropriative interpretations may be our "consumeristic" culture, which mixes and matches "symbols and ideas" for our own purposes (Lefkowitz 1992, 29). The contemporary goddess worldview, including its self-reflexive impulses, can be traced to nineteenth-century men who first posited the possibility of a single goddess with multiple manifestations (Gerhard 1849) and that all cultures began as matriarchal (Bachofen 1861), as chapter 2 shows.[63] Lefkowitz (1992, 33) sees twentieth-century Jungian goddess enthusiasts as "reminding us" of "the central importance" of goddesses to "virtually all ancient religions," and laments that "they insist on speaking of the Goddess, because such a usage implies that a unitary deity as a 'natural' form that divinity might take." Her careful study of ancient Greek culture reveals that "multiplicity and diversity were defining features of the divine," and current anachronistic goddess cultures often "harm women" by reducing them to "creatures of mere sexuality" (33). In ancient Greece and Rome, Lefkowitz (2007) finds most modern conceptions and representations misguided, ignoring or misperceiving significant strengths of actual women we know about from these patriarchal cultures.

Rather than appreciating expert insights on past cultures, many people focus more on outdated, popular, nonscientific, generalized, and thus easier and probably comforting views that fulfill what they wish to find in the past. The implicit assumption that this one unlikely reading of the past can help inspire or forge a future to which we may aspire is actually ephemeral, limited, and bound to disappoint, given how myth works. Let us honor archaeologists and other experts who offer information to redirect our visions of the past along more scientific routes. Accumulated research and more sophisticated archaeological methods offer insight every year about probable Paleolithic and Neolithic life and culture. These insights do not support a monoculture of the goddess but are nonetheless fascinating and illuminating about our species. Interestingly, nineteenth-century men scientists founded this myth, while many contemporary feminist scientists debunk it, partly due to its origin and partly due to changes in science based on accumulated knowledge and improved techniques.

Ancient representations of women fostered a worldview that has inspired many portrayals and ideas of goddesses that persist today. The continued appeal of goddesses is due partly to how well the concept and its expressions *sell* in our culture, whether as fabrications and exhibits for museums, galleries, performances, souvenirs, kitsch, art, dance, travel, and workshopping, or literary and popular culture reworkings of fictionally reimagined characters inspired by our skewed, appropriative vision of the past. But all such efforts remain largely unaware of and minimally informed by the insights of archaeologists who document and explain a richly complex past. As is often true in our culture, many prefer easy, appealing answers and myths that we *feel* work, rather than complexity and science, perhaps since the latter requires patience, time, and effort and may offer only partial, emergent, dynamic, messy understanding. Straightforward, definitive answers that appeal to our own values and visions are much easier to embrace and perpetuate. Most of our popular culture reflects distorted, limited, or wish-fulfilling visions of the distant past. We appropriate an imagined, hoped-for past as inspiration to create contemporary culture that reflects worldviews, memes, and myths of, for, and by us, today. This is our myth, and it works as a myth, for our culture.

———

As we have attended more closely to experts in archaeology who demystify authoritative, optimistic-seeming "facts" about the past, so too shall we use analytical tools to scrutinize and deconstruct today's myths. Since at least the 1970s, scholars have employed feminist theories to critically question the goddess myth as not necessarily advancing a feminist agenda. The now-old goddess myths are not the only story of our past or future, despite their influence and seduction. Reimagined pasts usable for contemporary contexts are alluring to some, but why should they be so authoritatively insisted upon when new, more contextually inspired readings of the past that are just as fascinating and more revealing of human nature, emerge annually, often from the hard work of our sisters in the field? It can be satisfying and comforting to retell old stories, even misguided ones, but ongoing feminist inquiry and fresh and innovative feminist myths await as well. Open inquiry urges listening to the best work of feminists in any field, and a promising vision of a feminist future with stronger, inspiring women, even goddesses, need not rely on old stereotypes, outdated research, and problematic epistemologies. Understanding the goddess myth more deeply is the first step toward analyzing how versions of the myth work in our culture.

Chapter 2

Mythic Expressions of Goddess Culture and Mythology

Outdated and inaccurate ideas of a goddess-centered, matriarchal prehistory that persist today stem from nineteenth-century patriarchal roots. Religion scholar Philip G. Davis (1998, 344, 343) traces "the Goddess movement's false claims to ancient origins" and explores "its actual roots in the Western esoteric tradition. . . . The Goddess, in short, represents the imaginary feminine ideal of Romantic men." Romantic poet John Keats's 1818 poem "Endymion," for instance, embraces a goddess perspective: "Four thousand lines about young love of Endymion and the moon goddess Diana. It's a kind of hymn to the Beauty, Love, Moon, Muse, and even the chanting of ancient Greece as the 'golden age' of humanity" (Keats 1818). Conceptions about the primacy of a mother goddess and likely matriarchal societies grew along with archaeology becoming an academic discipline in the nineteenth century (Lefkowitz 1992, Davis 1998, Goodison and Morris 1998, Eller 2000, 2011). Eduard Gerhard was among the first scholars (in 1849) who "analyzed classical symbols" to suggest "that the various goddesses of the ancient Greek pantheon might have been manifestations of a single primordial Goddess" (Eller 2011, 34). "Influential" mythographer and historian Johann Jacob Bachofen, who wrote the lengthy 1861 treatise, *Das Mutterrecht* (*Mother Right*), was "the first scholar seriously to suggest that females were dominant . . . before their powers were usurped by men" (Lefkowitz 1992, 29). The mother goddess perspective was further espoused and developed in various ways by influential nineteenth-century "fathers of anthropology," such as Sir E. B. Tylor and Lewis Henry Morgan, and other scholars such as Sir James Frazer, Jane Ellen Harrison, and Sir Arthur Evans. Scientists of the psyche such as Sigmund Freud, Carl Jung, and

Erich Neumann further embraced and popularized the myth in the twentieth century (Goodison and Morris 1998, 7). Eller (2011, 69, 100) perceives "bold . . . sweeping conclusions" of late nineteenth-century anthropologists, including about goddesses and matriarchy: "The political use of matriarchal myth was a natural fit in the wider social context of the late nineteenth century."

Many theories posited that fertility cults and female-centered religions existed earliest in human societies and then declined as "more advanced male-focused religion" developed (Goodison and Morris 1998, 7).[1] Contrary to how the myth is now told by hopeful proponents—that this earlier matriarchal period was superior—these early men found the later dominance by patriarchy to be a triumph of reason and culture over emotion and nature. Scholars of Bachofen's time assumed the maternal relationship must have been the most important to what they considered less intelligent, "primitive" cultures. Sherry B. Ortner (1974) analyzes much of this history in her article "Is Female to Male as Nature Is to Culture?" Not only is woman associated with reproductive (i.e., "natural") functions, but her body "dooms her" to being dominated by natural forces, including emotions and creative processes. By contrast, men were thought to transcend their bodies to create culture: woman "is still seen as achieving less transcendence of nature than man" (Ortner 1974, 84). Indeed, Bachofen's theory may have appealed to many male scholars precisely because it ultimately produces "imagery [that] continue to purvey a relatively devalued view of women" (87). Lefkowitz (1992, 30) perceives that in spite of this, "Bachofen's account of human development is unproven and unprovable, but it has had a powerful appeal to certain women and certain lovers of myth." While seeming to some to exalt women as awesome objects of veneration, this theory was originally conceived as confirming women's limitations and inferiority.

Lefkowitz (1992, 30) credits Carl Jung (Freudian founder of analytical psychology) with promoting spiritual and psychological possibilities of goddess culture and archetypes in the twentieth century: "Jung and his followers . . . developed the notion of a female archetype they called the Great Mother." In the mid-twentieth century, Marija Gimbutas, James Mellaart, and others trained in this school of thinking and continued advancing old theories, with some twists (such as eventually claiming matriarchies are superior), after most archaeologists had begun questioning them. But the theories were mainly advanced by Victorian men, stemming first from the Romantics, who linked natural forces to women, positing a period of female dominance, including among deities, as part of a social evolutionary view of human culture (Allen 2001; Davis 1998; Eller 2011; Goodison and Morris 1998; Lefkowitz

1992; Meskell 1998). This previous period was considered inferior by all the earliest scholars, which may be why they are not often cited as origins of goddess culture. Archaeologists like Evans, Mellaart, and Gimbutas manipulated evidence or engaged in heavy speculation to fit such theories (chapter 1). Some even ignored or discarded evidence that didn't support a preconceived mother goddess reading (Allen 2001, 7–8; Goodison and Morris 1998; Meskell 1994; Lapatin 2002). One answer as to why many today believe that goddess images were most common in prehistory is that so many wanted to find them, and so a tradition emerged of expecting them, creating them, or manipulating and interpreting evidence to "find" them. Archaeologists show that *no more than 50 percent of prehistoric images of people depict women*, so the assumption of women's or goddesses' primacy back then is faulty and unlikely (Goodison and Morris 1998). In examining nineteenth-century arguments, Joan Bamberger (1974, 265, 280) asserts that "Bachofen's matriarch is a far cry from today's liberated woman," perceiving any "romanticization of womanhood" as problematic from a feminist perspective, as we'll also see in pop culture goddess myths.[2]

Aspects and Aspirations of the Goddess Myth Today

We find works inspired by a goddess-centered perspective in a huge variety of fields—theology, art, psychotherapy, mythography, cultural history, religious studies, literature, and more—most of them according to Goodison and Morris (1998, 11) varying between "careful and cavalier." One freelance European editor and author of books on "symbolism, mythology, religion and spirituality," Clare Gibson (1998), published *Goddess Symbols: Universal Signs of the Divine Female*. A full-page image that opens the beautifully illustrated, glossy book depicts the Venus of Willendorf; one of the last images in the book is an uncredited photographic essay of a pregnant woman (titled "2 stages of pregnancy, then baby at breast"). The book includes ancient sculptures and images, European medieval and Renaissance art, ancient Egyptian art, twentieth-century Mexican murals, much nature photography, Native American art, and more, as just a small sample of the many cultures conflated as carrying on universal goddess traditions that are all conceived as a part of a general continuum through vast swaths of time and space. These many lovely images from many time periods and virtually all cultures, including our own, are appropriated, blended, and celebrated as evidence of a universal, ongoing goddess culture, meant to offer hope and inspiration for a better future (Gibson 1998).

Copious similar works documenting, celebrating, and promoting god-desses that conflate and appropriate imagery, cultures, assumed conscious-ness, invented myths and worship, and usually environmental ethics seem popular with consumers and publishers. There are hundreds of thousands of hits on Google and Amazon for "goddess books." Additionally, there are popular goddess-themed handbooks, journals, therapy books and resources, retreats, vacations (with tours of famous goddess sites, often incorporating rituals, dances, etc.), websites, artwork, and many products for sale, such as T-shirts, bumper stickers, jewelry, amulets, and goddess-shaped soap. There are also many related organizations, including the many neo-pagan and new age groups who honor or worship goddesses. Many voices proclaim passion-ate and hopeful feelings about the worth and strengths of goddess spirituality.[3] There are various goddess traditions, practices, beliefs, expressions, and move-ments, and I don't claim to present an ethnographically informed discussion of specific goddess cultures, nor comprehensive details of any single version thereof. But since the main focus of the rest of this book is popular culture and literary versions of goddesses, as conceived more generally (not from within a faith tradition), detailed understanding of any one goddess culture is not necessary, and many others have already provided such studies. Other experts have also distilled similarities that can be gleaned among different specific groups. The aim here is to perceive the most common, shared aspects of the various systems and practices based on goddess-centered beliefs.

Problems with the Myth

Given the plethora of positive sentiments, testaments, and hopes attached to this movement, one might wonder what could be wrong with goddess prac-tices, beliefs, movements, theories, or metaphors, even if they are based in inaccuracy or at least an unlikely reading of the past. Indeed, criticism of the movement is a much-contested issue. Proponents feel strongly that this faith or movement works for good, especially the good of oppressed women, and defend it vigorously, while others such as feminist archaeologists, reli-gion scholars, and historians spend considerable time and effort critiquing or questioning it. One problem many skeptics perceive is that this perspective's origin rests in the outmoded social evolutionary perspective, which in itself is considered distasteful and harmful in social studies today (Goodison and Morris 1998). This theory considers "primitive people" as less intelligent or less culturally "advanced" than modern Western civilization, relegating past or less technologically advanced humans to "other" status, meaning not *us*. A part of the original theory, now valorized as celebrating women's nature as mothers, assumed that prehistoric people did not understand the reproductive process and saw female fertility as an "awesome mystery," a notion long since discredited (Allen 2001, 8).[4] Critics point out that too many proponents rely on early authorities of archaeology, rather than examining primary evidence carefully and in context (as in chapter 1).[5] These founders were mainly men with Victorian, Romantic, sexist views of women, or racist ideologies, which many who embrace the myth likely overlook (due to perceived benefits) or don't know.

Lefkowitz (1992, 33) laments not only that "the Goddess's present-day cultists are not faithfully rendering the ancient models" but that the myth's "present reconstruction," which is not an understanding of the past, "will surely harm women, by simplifying and demoting them to creatures of mere sexuality" and ignoring "some of the qualities that women share with the rest of humanity, such as individuality, independence, and intelligence."[6] Gimbutas posited, "'The main theme of Goddess Symbolism is the mystery of birth and death and the renewal of life, not only human but all life on Earth and indeed the whole cosmos, [recalling a] . . . gylanic [freeing, dissolving], nonviolent, earth-centered culture' . . . which celebrates the life-giving powers of the female . . . and female sexuality" (qtd. in Lefkowitz 1992, 32). Starhawk "emphasizes inner development, spiritual and psychological . . . prescribes ways in which adepts, usually women, can merge themselves with the archetype [the Great Mother], and then emerge from it with stronger, more fully integrated personalities" (Lefkowitz 1992, 31).[7] Gimbutas's work "places a distinctive emphasis on sexual definition and development" (Lefkowitz 1993, 264). However appealing to some, these qualities are reductionist and limiting.

Many goddess culture ideas rest in an essentializing "appeal to universals" that is "disquieting" to many scholars, as though "human societies all started the same way following a single blueprint, and all women have been essentially the same since the beginning of time [which] reduces our options, as if there were only one predetermined 'archetypal' path for women to follow" (Goodison and Morris 1998, 13). Reducing women to such essential, biologically grounded functions—for instance as sexual beings or mothers—as part of "the Goddess 'consciousness'" in such a way that "it is used implicitly as a device that may be taken for granted and not questioned" (Tringham and Conkey 1998, 21) is problematic, universalizing and homogenizing things like gender roles, and "ignoring the agency of prehistoric men and women, as well as their variable roles, identities and practices . . . [instead seeing them] as set and fixed" (23). At root, this reductive and over-generalized view is also a product of patriarchy, as Goodison and Morris (1998, 20) point out: "Sexual mother, concubine and entangling female embrace are all male fantasies." Our distant ancestors are now thought to deserve more credit for having agency and sophisticated thinking than many formerly believed, and we may imagine other options for women than sexual or motherly bodies.[8]

Many are also troubled that women in goddess myths, including some contemporary reimaginings of them, follow stereotypical patterns, as shown by Joan Bamberger in 1974. She considers both the myth of prehistory and similar, more recent "myths of matriarchy" in indigenous South America: "The final version of woman that emerges from these myths is that she represents chaos and misrule through trickery and unbridled sexuality" (Bamberger 1974, 280). She also shows that the myth characterizes woman unrealistically "to remain either goddess or child" but not "as the coequal of man" (280). As we consider how the goddess is manifested and interpreted in actual uses and versions in contemporary popular culture and literature, we shall find her shaped in ways that misunderstand, essentialize, sexualize, remove agency, and stereotype all women's nature and roles in society.

Starhawk recognizes the controversy over Gimbutas's research but maintains that the "experience" of the goddess tradition remains "valid" and powerful. She responds to Charlotte Allen's critical article with a bold claim of how much good this movement does regardless of its origins and whether or not Gimbutas's version of the past is true:

> Archaeologists may never be able to prove or disprove Marija Gimbutas' theories—but the wealth of ancient images she presents to us are valuable because they work—they function elegantly, right now, as gateways to that deep connected state. We may never truly know whether Neolithic Minoans saw the spiral as a symbol of regeneration—but I know the amazing, orgasmic power that is raised when we dance a spiral with two thousand people at our Halloween ritual every year. I may never know for certain what was in the mind of the maker of the paleolithic, big bellied, heavy breasted female figure that sits atop my computer, but she works as a Goddess for me because my own creativity is awakened by looking at her every day. (Starhawk 2003)[9]

To demonstrate the validity of experiences of goddess worship, Starhawk spirals around emotionally moving terms such as "deep connected state," "amazing, orgasmic power" (of thousands of dancers), "creativity . . . awakened," "engages strong emotions," and "mobilizes deep life energies." Such moving and appealing testimonials for how positively these religious practices work to save the planet and empower women abound among believers. Those involved *feel very deeply* the truth and good of their practice or faith.

Positive descriptions, testimonials, and language from goddess enthusiasts reflect regard for "sacred nature"—the environment—as connected to an intuitive, sexually charged "essence" of the female, which is opposed to a patriarchal, rational, culture-based, scientific worldview. Such views establish a contrast between skeptical scientists, typically seen as male (representative of culture), and hopeful artists, or intuitively inclined "scientists," typically characterized as female (representative of nature), which Sherry Ortner (1974) boils down to culture versus nature. Many women, like Starhawk, Carol P. Christ, Rosemary Ruether, Jane Caputi, and others claim the myth is deeply influential in a positive way. More recent skeptics perceive it as troublingly problematic, mythically reflective and supportive of the status quo of our patriarchal culture (analysis of specific goddess myths in later chapters also reveals this). One big question in this debate is why many goddess-believing feminists cling to unprovable and unlikely notions of women from prehistory that essentialize femininity as biological and nature-based and in opposition to cultural and scientific masculinity.

Worried about the reductionist aspects of the myth, many feminist scholars (such as Goodison, Morris, Meskell, Eller, and Lefkowitz) suggest that we could and should move beyond it to embrace a truly feminist future, not one that essentializes gender in any way, let alone according to an unprovable view of the past. Goodison and Morris (1998) point out that critiques of anyone who questions goddess culture, or specifics of its myth or evidence, serve often to close off and shut down some inquiries and voices, like those of feminist archaeologists today. The actual archaeology and histories that experts offer today seem to me more exciting and promising than the utopian goddess myth, yet, as noted, many prefer the romanticized, conclusive version; thus it remains difficult to move beyond the myth for our culture as a whole, partly because of gatekeeping by goddess supporters, based on deeply held feelings of the myth's positive aspects.

Some more recent feminist scholars also question aspects of women's spiritualities that are rooted in second-wave feminism (1960s–1970s), critiquing them for being too narrowly focused on upper-middle-class white women. Alvarez (2015) quotes a PhD candidate in women's spirituality: "If you know a trans person—especially if they are gender fluid or gender fuckers, someone who is neither male or female, but something else—it forces your mind to break outside of these gender categories. And there's a divinity in that." In other words, god is better conceived, some gender studies scholars believe, as beyond gendered categories. Another of Alvarez's (2015) sources "speculates that 'there is something ineffable and mysterious in this universal force that is beyond gender or sex.'" From this perspective that any concept of god should be beyond definitive gendered assumptions, recasting god as female is as limiting and problematic as considering god as male—replacing one gender bias with another.

Many scientific, feminist, skeptical critiques offer more complex, more open, and some might argue better approaches to prehistory and to current spiritual practices and ideas. Yet even when only a hundred or so years old, myths can have power and tenacity, appealing emotionally and viscerally to believers—hence the believers' fervent defenses and attacks of questioners. The term *myth* is often invoked for beliefs and stories involving goddesses. Often those who invoke the term neglect to actually explain what they mean by *myth* or fully explain or apply the genre. Theories allow us to do our work as scholars, though our best efforts come with self-awareness of the theories and methods we employ. We now understand and discuss traditional myths and other such texts as emergent and intricately connected to performance situations or specific contexts of their cultures, along with cultural assumptions of the scholars.[10] But our goddess myths are more reflective of *our culture* than what we can access of the past. Our goddess myths, in terms of content and context, for instance how we discuss and respond to the myth, tend to reflect binary oppositions or symbolic dualities. To understand how the *myth* of goddess culture works and influences contemporary culture, let us focus on myth generically. Let us also consider specific discourses and practices of goddess believers.

A Generic Understanding of Mythology

From ancient Greek μῦθος (*mȳthos*, meaning "word, story, speech, tale, conversation"), myths are words strung together to narrate a plot. Originally meaning stories of any kind, the word *myth* in English became so associated with Greek stories of gods (as from Homer), that many started to reserve it for stories considered "sacred narratives." Early nineteenth-century German folklorists Jacob and Wilhelm Grimm (1882–83) wrote that "divinities form the core of all mythology" (qtd. in Bascom 1965, 20), reflecting part of their "sacred" nature. My decision about which contemporary examples to discuss herein is largely guided by this most simple sense of the term *myth*, as most texts herein contain goddesses (divinities), named as such therein, or characters who could be argued as divine or godly in a serious way, not just metaphorically, or the characters live in goddess-informed cultures. *Sacred* in mythic definition can mean connected to ritual or religious ceremonies, containing sacred characters, like gods and goddesses, or being *believed* as literally or metaphorically truthful, which includes being considered deeply, spiritually meaningful and serving to shape worldview and values; thus, myths have truth and power in human lives, even when not considered literally "true." Most folklorists distinguish myths from other commonly collected narratives such as folktales and legends. Generalized scholarly definitional parameters of myth might be narratives that are believed as true, or that have a truth factor, perhaps metaphorically; that often function to direct social norms or values; that offer symbols and metaphors for how to live; that may explain how things came to be (i.e., are etiological); and that are often considered to have a particular structure, such as nature allegories, binary oppositions, or anthropocentric modalities.

Although these are common ways myth is understood by mythologists, many myth scholars agree that there is no single, all-encompassing definition, at least no universally agreed-upon one, and I concur that limiting myth by defining it too specifically can be problematic.[11] Probably because there are so many myths from so many cultures, myths can and should be analyzed according to their particular contexts and theoretical interests. Genres are categorizations imposed by scholars seeking ways of classifying and analyzing material they study and so are extremely useful as analytical tools. But genres are fluid, emergent (according to particular contexts and cultures), and often messy guides (or tools), rather than absolute, neat, and fixed realities.[12] Various scholars see myths as explaining rituals, as nature allegories, as charters for social behavior, or as models of the human mind (Kirk 1970, 78–83).

Many great social theorists from the nineteenth and early twentieth centuries (Freud, Frazer, Jung, linguist and mythologist Friedrich Max Müller) analyzed myths, usually collected by others, as evidence of posited universal truths—a priori grand theories about human nature. Myths were theorized by many Victorian scholars as survivals of previous times, perhaps decayed or reflective of "primitive" ancestors who took them literally. Some saw myths as evidence for social evolutionary theories of the nineteenth century. Victorian scholars such as E. B. Tylor (1871) believed that humans in all cultures progress through stages of evolution from "savagery" to "barbarism" and finally to "civilization."[13] Such hegemonic legacies of a colonial past no longer seem reasonable. Scholars now recognize the complexity, thoughtfulness, and beauty of many other cultures that may once have been considered inferior to our own, such as Paleolithic "cave men."[14] We appreciate our ancestors' abilities to manipulate their environments toward their survival, and we appreciate their art, even though we may not fully understand it. We also recognize that our current theories and some of our culture may seem as foolish or be as misunderstood by our descendants as some of our ancestors' conceptions of the universe sometimes seem, or may have seemed, to us or previous scholars.

Many twentieth-century ethnographers, such as Claude Lévi-Strauss, Franz Boas (and his students), and Dell Hymes, used deductive methods in analyzing myths (partly as a mean to understanding cultures). Each theory may help analyze some myths, some perhaps more persuasively than others, but no one theory is universally accepted or used, and all can be "misleading" (Kirk 1970, 83). Nonetheless, in various circumstances or contexts, various theories can be illuminating. Thus, mythologist Gregory Schrempp (2002, 2012) and others discuss certain typical patterns in myth, defining it broadly, as outlined.[15] Late twentieth-century folklorist Alan Dundes (1984, 1) also evokes the sacredness of myth: "A myth is a sacred narrative explaining how the world and man came to be in their present form. . . . Myth may constitute the highest form of truth, albeit in a metaphorical guise . . . [and will] refer minimally to a narrative." As noted, myths are often considered sacred stories of ancient times believed to be true. Other scholars, however, contest that myths do *not* have to be sacred or necessarily tied to narrative (Hansen, Kirk, Schrempp, etc.). Classics scholar and folklorist William Hansen argues that the sacred element of myths is a recent attachment to definitions, perhaps beginning with the Grimms and then solidified by anthropologist Bronislaw Malinowski, who also tied them to rituals. But in his studies of ancient Greek myths, Hansen (2002, 21) notes that not all myths had a sacred element: "an analytic definition of myth as a kind of sacred story is problematic." They were not necessarily connected to religious beliefs but were often secular stories, he perceives.

Schrempp (2012, 15) describes the primordial setting assumed as typically mythic: "stories of supernatural beings or heroes set in ancient times and telling of cosmos- and society-shaping deeds and events." He also explains that myths often include "structures . . . that form the backdrop—the worldview—of such stories" (15). He discusses as well myth's anthropocentric tendencies and more colloquial uses of the term, as in untruth, or as something that carries "a kind of psychological primordiality, or ultimacy, and may yet carry hints of the numinous and the timeless" to provide "societies and individuals with an ultimate moral ground, a validation and justification of an accepted or prevailing way of life and scheme of values" (16). Thus, while myths do not have to have a sacred element, they often share a world-forming or worldview-forming function, often important in religious contexts. Schrempp considers perspectives on myth that do not require narrative frameworks, contradicting Dundes's and others' basic definition of myth as narrative: "I am sympathetic toward many non-narrative approaches to myth" (16). He also notes that myth can represent a whole "set or totality of elements integrated around a compelling theme and comprising something like a worldview . . . [such as] 'Elvis mythology' or 'Star Trek mythology'" (17).

Malinowski completed ethnographic work in the South Pacific in the early twentieth century, affirmed that myths must be sacred and also discussed how they *function* as a charter for social action. Functionalists see myths serving as charters for social action—functioning to hold societies together. Many other myth scholars also discuss this aspect of myths, including anthropologist and folklorist Paul Radin, who considers myth distinctive because of its function and implications as determined by certain individual society members. The myth-makers explain symbolically how to live, Radin (1949, 370) argues: "A myth is always explanatory. The explanatory theme often is so completely dominant that everything else becomes subordinated to it." Myths serve to explain and encourage worldview and good action within society. Many other theorists of myth concur that it has a functional dimension, but some argue that is not the only or most primary point of myth.

Structuralist Claude Lévi-Strauss postulates that myths serve to mediate conflicting or dualistic elements of society and life, which is a sort of function, but perhaps at a less easily discernable level than what functionalists meant. Lévi-Strauss ([1955] 1974, 83) recognizes "a basic antinomy pertaining to the nature of myth" and to human nature and believes that recognizing this antinomy "may lead us towards its solution." Binary oppositions or dualities provide a structure of myths than can help classify and scientifically decipher their meaning, according to Lévi-Strauss, through structural analysis. Antinomy or contradiction is often evident in the form of dualities or binary oppositions, such as hot/cold, raw/cooked, night/day, which Lévi-Strauss emphasizes appear in "bundles" in myths (87). Looked at as whole structures, myths reveal a typical pattern: "mythical thought always works from the awareness of oppositions towards their progressive mediation" (99). By tracing structures of dualities and their "mediation," we can decipher deeper meanings of the texts. The symbolic mediation of binary oppositions in myths offers inspiration for culture and a way for culture members to heal, flourish, or accept their reality, according to this theory. The hero in this theory mediates between puzzling dualities, offering balance and confirming the world we have as livable.[16]

As myth gives meaning and purpose to even the most seemingly disparate and fragmented elements of culture, so it affirms life processes of change and refashioning. Lévi-Strauss's idea that mythic symbols and images tend to be dualities suggests we often find binary oppositions in myths, and these dualities are often confused during chaotic stages of the primordial period, early in a myth. But the bricoleur or hero helps us perceive progress of mediating these dualities toward recognizing the order of our world, which involves livable dualities.[17] Dualities, or binary oppositions, are often considered troubling at first within the myth, but usually the mythic plot progresses from chaos (lack of order, or nothingness) to cosmos (order), to affirm the rightness of the universe, our cosmos, as we experience it. As the making of society proceeds and the structure of the universe is established, the order and "rightness" of dualities, or the structure of our world as we know it, is affirmed— however confusing or troubling these dualities may be at times, including in the myth's plot. According to Lévi-Strauss, the hero bricoleur tinkers with the pieces of our world or culture until order is affirmed and we are assured that our cosmos is good.[18] Structuralism posits that one purpose of myths is to explain the structure or cosmos of the universe, which the hero affirms is good and livable, which connects to myths' movement from original chaos to cosmos—the actual, experienced order of the universe.

Myth's very complexity, endurance, and rich symbolism, conveying our most powerful symbols, metaphors, and deeply meaningful messages, makes it worth attending to. The fact that scholars continue to discuss various possible definitional and theoretical frameworks of myth demonstrates its ongoing vitality and importance. Analyzing myths is as complex, emergent, variable, dependent on context, or "messy" as is studying prehistory or any aspect of culture. Realizing the fluidity of narrative forms stretches throughout the history of folklore scholarship and into the present day.[19] From the perspective of performance theory, distinctions between generic forms and their meaning and function should remain fluid, dynamic, to be discovered (Bauman 1991).[20] Applying scholarly tools of mythologists helps analyses of particular versions of contemporary goddess myths. Taking into consideration all such discussions, these general conceptual frameworks gleaned from ways of defining myths help, not as definitive conclusions, but as opening paths for analyses.

General Conceptual Frameworks of Myth

1) Myths are cosmogonic narratives, connected with the foundation or origin of the universe (and key beings within that universe), though often specifically in terms of a particular culture or region. Given the connection to origins, the setting is typically primordial (the beginning of time) and characters are protohuman or deific. Myths also often have cosmogonic overtones even when not fully cosmogonic, for instance when dealing with origins of important elements of the culture (food, medicine, ceremonies, etc.).

2) Myths are narratives of a sacred nature, often connected with some ritual. Myths are often foundational or key narratives associated with religions. These narratives are believed to be true from within the associated faith system (though sometimes that truth is understood metaphorically rather than literally). Within any given culture sacred and secular myths may coexist.

3) Myths are narratives formative or reflective of social order or values within a culture (e.g., functionalism).

4) Myths are narratives representative of a particular epistemology or way of understanding nature and organizing thought. For example, structuralism recognizes paired bundles of opposites (or dualities—like light and dark) as central to myths.

5) Mythic narratives often involve heroic characters (possibly proto-humans, superhumans, or godly) who mediate inherent, troubling dualities, reconcile us to our realities, or establish the patterns for life as we know it.

6) Myths are narratives that are "counter-factual in featuring actors and actions that confound the conventions of routine experience" (McDowell 1998, 80).

Many other functions and implications have been attributed to myth. As McDowell (1998, 80) indicates, myths often involve extraordinary characters or episodes that seem impossible in our world, but "the extraordinary feats and traits of mythic protagonists are possible only because they attach to a primary and formative period in the growth and development of civilization"; thus their various aspects or dimensions are best considered as "organically intertwined." In fact, the contemporary connotation of myth as "a falsehood," often understood as being in opposition to science, probably stems from recognition of the sixth attribute of myth in isolation. Myths also seem in opposition to science because they are not testable, which is the case at least for origin myths. Cosmogonic myths—origin narratives focusing on the beginning of the world, people, animals, or customs—are set in the distant past, usually in a primordial place, an earlier, other world. This primordial setting precludes their being repeatable or logical in our world.

Although the prevalence of mythological details in our discourse keys us to its importance, we typically insist upon distinguishing ways of thinking about the world, and today we think of myth as lesser than science. The general public persistently, though not in all cases, uses the word *myth* to describe something untrue or unworthy of serious consideration. The Greek word *mȳthos* or "story" suggests potential untruth (versus truer *logos*), but the perceived unworthiness of mythic stories stems from valorizing as superior a scientific, rational perspective. As Doty (1986, 8) explained, the "crucial" and "special" messages of myths connect them to truths, rendering them as "big stories" that shape and reflect our lives. The persistence of myths throughout our culture reveals their worth even to scientists, whom Schrempp (1992, 2012) shows create myths of their own.[21] Early scholars in myth theory created myths to paint pictures of early human life and conceptions of the universe. Discussions of myth and much else that we consider valuable or important can thus also become mythic—special stories that influence how we understand people and the world, that is, our worldview. Mythic and scientific explanations of the cosmos may be parallel in many ways. Yet because of their differences from science, myths may be considered less significant or dismissed as whimsical, useless, or primitive—hence the often derogatory or false connotation of calling something untrue "a myth."

Some people today lament a perceived decline of myths and their power. One potential of myth is to provide moral guidance and comforts that helps enrich life. Those who feel the power of the goddess myth in their lives defend it for just such reasons. Because of such emotional resonance, many people remain interested in myths and seek to revive or revere them. Additionally, myths continue to intrigue us because of their rich symbolic, metaphorical, and narrative appeal—art that makes us appreciate life. In our postmodern world, many people believe myths exist in new, combined, or revived forms. One of the functions of all art may be reconciling us to paradox—the most fundamental of which is life and death itself—something at which myths excel, if Lévi-Strauss is right. Another perceived function of myths is to suggest or affirm fundamental patterns of life and the universe—again, something people still find appealing to contemplate, even in mythic moments of contemporary artistic and scientific modes. The specific

Table 1. Characteristics of Myth

KEY CHARACTERISTICS OF MYTH (FULFILLED BY GODDESS MYTH)
SACRED NARRATIVE ○ Connected to ritual or religious ceremonies (neo-pagan Practices) ○ Worldview-forming (true throughout our culture) ○ Deeply, spiritually meaningful (main attribute hailed by proponents)
COSMOGONIC (about origin of world/cosmos) ○ Set in distant past or ancient times (prehistory) ○ Primordial period or world (when things were fundamentally different)
BELIEVED AS TRUE ○ Evidence of actual perceived truths offered (by believers) ○ Beliefs persist regardless of science ○ Metaphorically truthful (connected to spiritual importance)

FUNCTIONS TO DIRECT SOCIAL NORMS/VALUES
○ Connected to worldview forming aspect and belief (metaphorical)
○ Metaphors and lessons/values for how to live
○ Goddess myth values see goddess culture as
  • More ecological
  • Better communities
  • More Peaceful
  • Utopian (potentially)

ETIOLOGICAL (Explains how things came to be the way they are) *In goddess culture some main etiological explanations include* ○ Why we have war ○ Why we are patriarchal and "anti-woman"
FOLLOWS PARTICULAR STRUCTURE ○ Binary oppositions (nature = good; culture = bad, etc.) ○ Nature allegories (related to Etiology); explaining world ○ Anthropocentric modalities
NOTE: These are some of the main ways that myth is typically defined, though there is no universally agreed-upon single definition or set of defining characteristics of myth, according to myth scholars.

characteristics of myth listed in table 1 are intended as general, to-be-dis-covered, and applied-as-appropriate, case by case. They are not to be applied or assumed relevant in each and every analysis of any myth. Consider this a kind of accumulated analytical wellspring, which may be helpful in various ways, for various cases. Taking into consideration most myth theory, the above table, which is neither comprehensive nor prescriptive, should be helpful in considering the goddess myth.

Even when myths are no longer associated with religious rituals, belief systems, or primordial moments of creation, big stories of heroic characters who mediate, contemplate, perceive, and celebrate the troubling paradoxes, wonder, complexity, and hoped-for meanings of life will always compel us and can, I believe, still be found in our culture—and so may be called myths. Stories that involve impossible, powerful heroes, even gods or goddesses, that move us profoundly, that reflect and inspire cultural wisdom or wondrous and deep patterns of existence can all be considered mythic. As we analyze modern myths, we find that like all art, they can be interpreted in various ways and have hidden messages and implications, that are to be discovered case by case, analyses of which can best be attempted by those who best understand the context and complexities of the culture from which they emerge, along with their own scholarly assumptions. Versions of the goddess myth that our culture still creates, re-creates, imagines, imposes, appropriates, celebrates, and in some cases condemns reveal much about contemporary lives, beliefs, and cultural patterns.

Goddess Culture as Myth

Many modern myths inspired by goddess culture fit numerous aspects of the genre of myth as defined above. First, goddess culture's view of the time when goddesses originated—the origin—is situated in a distant past or primordial period, "ancient times" (Schrempp 2012, 15). Gimbutas calls this time "Old Europe," dating from the Neolithic period (7000–3500 BCE), but also interpretable as stretching back through the Upper Paleolithic period. Donna Read's 1989 film *Goddess Remembered* opens by proclaiming a primordial goddess-centered time: "We know that thousands of years before the Bible was ever written, creation stories centered around a Goddess. The reverence our ancestors once felt for the primal power of the female is reflected in those dimly lit times of the prehistoric ages, when the power to give and nurture was supreme. Only recently, for six thousand years ago is recent in the age of humankind, has the Earth and the female perspective been ignored." Scholars do *not* in fact "know," as Read claims, that long ago "creation stories centered around a Goddess." But this opening narrative or myth of the film confirms how distant the goddess myth situates itself—stretching to long before the Bible, long before patriarchy, which this film conceives of as starting in the West around six thousand years ago. There is a concomitant assumption of this time as existing long before any male-god-centered myths or cultures.

Read's idealized primordial origin differs from other versions, but the sense of a goddess-centered origin in the distant past usually predominates.

New Age goddess culture practitioner and writer Zsuzsanna Budapest (1989, 54) describes contemporary goddess worship as a "Dianic Tradition" and identifies the "True Beginning" of goddess culture: "worship . . . comes to us from these earliest Stone Age Times."[22] *Dianic* refers to the Roman goddess of the hunt, Diana, associated with the moon, nature, and wild animals—having power to talk to and control animals, similar to Artemis in Greek myth (Bell 1991). Budapest (1989, 54) explains the Dianic tradition: "In the True Beginning, before the Judeo-Christian Genesis, The Goddess was revealed to her people as the Soul of the Wild. She was called Holy Mother, known to be a Virgin who lived in wild places and acted through mysterious powers. Known also as Artemis, She was worshipped in the moonlight, and young nymphs and maidens were called to serve in Her rituals." Note the evocative words in this description, "Soul of the Wild," "Holy Mother," "virgin," "wild places," "mysterious powers," and "moonlight," which help establish the kind of nature-based, motherly, wild, and dark aspects of the goddess—all reflected on the left side of table 2. Budapest sees this Artemis/Diana goddess as an archetype: "Dianic Tradition (referring to the goddess Diana, not the Dianus of Margaret Murry)" (Davis 1998, 340).[23] Davis (1998) traces Budapest's inspirations to earlier, mostly male creators of contemporary Wiccan (or witch) practicing cults. In other words, the specifics of neo-pagan beliefs and practices that Budapest describes and teaches were first imagined by men. Yet Budapest's Dianic tradition of "feminist spirituality" expresses lesbian separatism (Davis 1998, 340).

Goddess believers often suggest that mysterious and cryptic origins of beliefs and practices, like Wicca, related to goddesses and women's power, stem from "survivals" of ancient paganism in Europe (Davis 1998).[24] For instance, English self-educated cult enthusiast Gerald Gardner helped create modern Wiccan and neo-pagan traditions by attesting to finding and learning from hidden practitioners in twentieth-century England (Davis1998). But he likely invented and recycled everything he practiced and shared, and other neo-pagan and New Age founders and practitioners keep recombining various such modern inspirations, though they often claim ancient origins. Scholarly analysis debunks such claims: "Goddess spirituality is very much the child of American second-wave radical feminism," under the further influence of Margot Adler, Victor Anderson, Gwydion Pendderwen (Thomas deLong), Miriam "Starhawk" Simos, and Zsuzsanna Budapest, with Starhawk extending "the Goddess beyond the confines of Wicca into the broader stream of contemporary feminism and political activism" (Davis 1998, 338, 340). Davis demonstrates an interdependent feedback loop among practitioners, including writers Merlin Stone, Riane Eisler, various Jungians (like Joseph Campbell and Erich Neumann), Marija Gimbutas, Carol P. Christ, and Mary Daly, who rely on each other as sources that confirm each other's hypotheses.[25] An ancient provenance for any specific beliefs and practices is untraceable and unlikely, but it remains a common claim in many versions of the myth and related practices.

Gimbutas situates the cosmogonic myth in a primordial Stone Age utopian "gynaecocracy" (a term she evokes a few times including 2001, 123, and that her followers further embrace). She explains her revised title ("goddesses" listed ahead of "gods," to prioritize their primacy) and highlights how "Old Europe" reflected a women-forward culture: "a pre-Indo-European culture of Europe, a culture matrifocal and probably matrilinear, agricultural and sedentary, egalitarian and peaceful. It contrasted sharply with the ensuing proto-Indo-European culture which was patriarchal, stratified, pastoral, mobile, and war-oriented" (Gimbutas 1982, 9). The matrifocal, peaceful culture continued in Gimbutas's story until the Kurgans from the Russian steppe swept into the Mediterranean region in waves, imposing their warlike, patriarchal ways (Gimbutas 1989, 2001).[26] Gimbutas (1982, 9) states that "this period of the female deities" is "more accurately" described as "the Goddess Creatrix in her many aspects," and doesn't explicitly refer to it as a matriarchy. She is careful to explain that "in old Europe the world of myth was not polarized into female and male as it was" later, and that "all resources of human nature, feminine and masculine, were utilized to the full as a creative force" (237–38). But she also asserts that "the pantheon was dominated by the mother. The role of woman was not subject to that of man" (237). Her positive descriptions of a "matrifocal," "matrilineal" Old Europe in which mother goddesses dominate implicitly contrast patriarchy, leading many into conceiving of it as matriarchal (Gimbutas 1982, 9; 2001). Her description of "Old Europe" as appealingly "egalitarian and peaceful," among other admirable traits, overtly contrasts it "sharply" to the later patriarchy.

Many believers and expressions of the myth consider a goddess-centered prehistory as peaceful and egalitarian to the point of utopia, a fantastically superior time, and that imagined ancient past is cast as inspirational and helpful for our world. Read's 1989 film echoes Gimbutas and deepens goddess culture ideas of prehistory with conclusive, generalized statements, for instance as a time focused on mothers and nurturing, when cultures were peaceful, female-centered, cooperative, agricultural, and respectful of nature,

that is, harmonious: "We know women developed agriculture and the domes-
tication of animals," that women made the first laws, guarded truth and justice, "insisted upon truth and kindness," invented agriculture and writing, and
inspired early religious practices; "for our oneness with each other and all of
nature lies at the heart of goddess worship." Skeptics perceive this reverent,
appealing view of a goddess-centered prehistory as unprovable and unlikely,
but the film suggests that such "truths" are still discoverable: "If we listen to
the echoes—they have much to say." These specific words are spoken as scenes
of a woman dancing with snakes before a sunrise is shot from the opening of
a stone shelter—all evoking a primordial, Stone Age origin, conflating Paleolithic stone shelters and Neolithic "snake goddesses," and imagining prehistory as a mythically goddess-centered primordial origin. The film also gives
voice to a number of goddess-culture-believing women, including Starhawk,
Carol P. Christ, Merlin Stone, Charlene Spretnak, and more. No skeptics nor
contemporary feminist archaeologists, some of whom were debunking these
theories by the seventies, are interviewed. The film and its sequels, *The Burning Times* (1990) and *Full Circle* (1993), are beautifully filmed, lush celebrations of a longed-for myth that also evokes a hoped-for, superior future. The
films celebrate the myth as real with romantic cinematography of nature,
much ancient artwork, and voices of numerous women believers extolling a
superior, possible way of life that is overtly contrasted to today's patriarchy,
described as placing fear—of women's sexuality, nature, and death—at the
center of a negative worldview and way of living, in effect giving the past a
sacred tinge while evoking dualities.

By casting the primordial past as *sacred* in nature, invoked in rituals and
religious ceremonies, and confirmed as superior, this myth is also affirmed as
true, at least metaphorically, as Gimbutas (1982) argues.[27] Much "evidence" is
presented by believers, for instance the work of Gimbutas, to prove the myth's
veracity, though as demonstrated by Davis (1998), much such "proof" is circu-
lar.[28] The need to affirm the myth's sacredness connects to a will to believe it
and to ignore or criticize recent scholarship (e.g., by skeptics and archaeologists). Gimbutas's followers attest to core messages of the myth as value laden:
"balanced, egalitarian cultures, the cultivation of an earth-based spirituality
and the desire to create more balanced and human societies are at the core....
This movement that embraces nature and the body, experienced by many as a
dynamic process of spiritual and cultural renewal" (Marler 2003). The myth is
also thus considered directive of how to live—fulfilling functional definitional
parameters of myth, to reflect and stimulate foundational values of and for
believers. Marler, Read, and others describe their story as a charter for social

action, mythically offering guidance through symbols and metaphors for how we should live.[29] Perceived "sacred" "truths" they attest to influence and reflect the worldview of believers and practitioners. Once we deconstruct these concepts, we will see that the myth shapes *and reflects* our general cultural worldview and values, possibly more than reflecting and shaping worldview in the way its believers hope.

Structural analysis particularly helps reveal contemporary cultural patterns this myth reflects, including a plethora of dualities or binary oppositions. Kirk (1970, 78) notes of myths generally: "binary analysis is one obvious mode of thought"—in other words, many cultures' myths are full of dualistic symbolism (binary oppositions). Myths typically work to resolve or "mediate" dualities: "problem-reflecting . . . [of] an underlying structure of relationships . . . to construct a model by which contradictions in men's view of the world can be mediated" (7, 78). But like others, Kirk cautions that no one theory be considered absolute and all can be "misleading" (83). Thus, we should not expect to "find any or all of these properties in the myths of any culture," reminding us to always attending to context and take each myth as a unique case to be discovered (83). If the context of the goddess myth is the culture of believers, writers, directors of versions of the myth today, and scholars who study it, we still find structuralism applicable and useful, since at all such levels in various relevant discussions and versions we perceive fundamental and significant dualities.

Believers sometimes deny such a dualistic framework, emphasizing the goddess's holistic, cyclical, unifying features and claiming therefore that the myth cannot symbolize binary opposition. Though the myth is told in various forms in our culture, binary oppositions abound in the form of metaphors in most versions and explanations. Narrations, reception, and scholarship of this myth are full of dualities such as patriarchy and matriarchy or peace and war. Scholars' responses and interpretations diverge dramatically. Starhawk (2002, 274), for instance, explains patriarchy as "power-over, from domination . . . ultimately the power of the gun and the bomb, the power of annihilation that backs up all the institutions of domination," versus "power-from-within," which she says "can be called spirit" or "immanence" or "Goddess because the ancient images, symbols and myths of the Goddess as birth-giver, weaver, earth and growing plant, wind and ocean, flame, web, moon and mil, all speak to me of the powers of connectedness, sustenance, healing, creating." She openly dichotomizes male "power-over" and female "power-from-within" as contrasting yet linked principals, that is, dualities, that we must deal with: "how do we overthrow . . . the principle of power-over? How do we shape a society based on the principle of power-from-within?" (274).

Most neo-pagan and modern goddess myths contain value-laden, sacred discourse rife with implied and overt dualities, even when duality itself is denied as the opposite of believers' worldview. Gimbutas is quoted on Belili's website: "The Goddess in all her manifestations was a symbol of the unity of all life in Nature. Her power was in water and stone, in tomb and cave, in animals and birds, snakes and fish, hill, trees, and flowers" (Starhawk and Read 2003). This strongly roots goddess culture as nature centered, establishing a framework to help differentiate it from contemporary Western civilization, which destroys nature and to which goddess culture is overtly contrasted. Goddess culture links nature and women regularly, as though women-based, goddess-worshiping cultures are more ecological, partly because according to some versions women are inherently more "natural" beings. Women being lesser, or greater, than men and being somehow more "natural" are common modern tropes criticized by Ortner and others. All human beings are animals, as intimately a part of and connected to nature as all other animals, and no human being would be considered by scientists as more or less natural than another. But since nature is contrasted with civilization (or culture) in many worldviews, like the Romantic and Victorian ones that inspire goddess and matriarchal theories, and since men were considered the masters of the highest levels of civilized existence, women were then conceived of as below men, as closer to nature. Recasting this ordering of one gender's deeper connection to nature as a positive rather than a negative attribute does not make the premise any less absurd or harmful. Conceiving of any gender of humans as more or less natural is scientifically invalid and meaningless, yet it is common in goddess myths and worldviews.

Calling the goddess (and her myths) a "symbol of unity" may highlight her presumed ability to serve as the "hero" mythically, as one who can mediate oppositions represented in the symbolic dualities of the myth, which would in structuralist terms make her a mythic hero. But goddess proponents don't generally offer such analysis. Still, the language in telling and discussing the myth draws attention to the presence therein of fundamental binary oppositions, as seen in Margot Adler's (1986, 374) explanation of what attracted her: "Neo-Paganism seemed to be a religion that would celebrate . . . the interrelatedness of all living things and their environment . . . that would heal into synthesis all oppositions: primitive and civilized, science and magic, male and female, spirit and matter." Many agree with this hope of synthesis, but many versions of the myth belie the image of synthesis by evoking or (as here) *listing dualities* and purporting alternate, oppositional worldviews, one nature-centered and healing, and the other not. The Belili website also summarizes a contrast of positive, peaceful, egalitarian goddess culture with what comes later: "Egalitarian and peaceful, 'Old Europe' existed for thousands of years without war. . . . Widely acclaimed by feminists, by women and men in the growing earth-based spirituality movement, by artists, dancers, novelists, and by many historians and archaeologists. . . . If her [Gimbutas's] theories are correct, then peace, reverence for the earth and the honoring of life are not only human capabilities, they are the very underpinnings of European civilization itself" (Starhawk and Read 2003). The mythic time was superior because it was dominated by "more natural" and more artistic beings—women, who seem impossibly capable of utopia.

Goodison and Morris (1998, 15) label this idealized aspect of the myth "a static 'Golden Age'" that fails to recognize that human life is dynamic. Indeed, the goddess myth implies that change is implicitly bad, for it was change, in the form of the oppositional patriarchy, that brought an end to this idyllic golden age, as in Read's (1989) film *Goddess Remembered*, where "The Golden Age of Greece," "the dawn of civilization," and "man's time" (history) included a "rewriting of the myths" as devolution:

> For the man, it was the beginning. For the woman, it was the end. [A cymbal clashes softly and drums play in the background through the rest of this narration.] The Greeks announced that history would now begin and proceeded to obliterate or pervert the twenty-five thousand years that had gone before. Athena was redefined [a flute and other instruments join in the music track]: Once the Goddess of Wisdom and Love, she became the Goddess of War. The violent and the erotic became linked as they never had before. Man, said Man, had always been the natural master of the earth. He was now also the procreator: Athena sprang, fully armed, from the brow of Zeus. Eve was born from Adam's rib. Female inferiority forever was proclaimed by the book of Genesis.

The soundtrack's clashing cymbals emphasize figuratively the described clashing dualities of the sexes, of beginnings and endings of respective cultures, and of inferior patriarchy versus superior matriarchy. The narration also suggests that "female resistance" to this change "gave rise to legends of Amazons. But the man soon asserted his total domination, and so it has been for 3,500 years" (Read 1989). The film not only overtly evokes abundant dualities but asserts as fact things about which we have no evidence, essentializing gender as a definitive, encompassing duality.[30] Women and their matriarchal cultures are essentialized as peaceful, loving, more natural, more sexually wise, generally superior. Men and patriarchy, in contrast, do not revere the earth, women, or sexuality, but rather are connected to war, hierarchy, and domination. We find similar patterns of binary opposition and stereotyping portrayed metaphorically in most popular culture and literary version of the goddess myth as well.

Budapest, Adler, and many other goddess proponents deny duality as key to feminist goddess beliefs, but implicitly and sometimes explicitly, these myths pit patriarchal religions and culture against matriarchy and goddess culture in identifiably dualistic fashion. Jungian analyst and author Clarissa Pinkola Estés (1992, 22) follows this pattern in *Women Who Run with the Wolves*, which became a best seller by portraying women's "instinctual lives, their deepest knowing" as a wild woman archetype. Estés overtly connects such "knowing" to gender: "to deny motherhood is to deny women. Patriarchal religion is built on this denial," and "in Paganism ... women's values are dominant ... pleasure-oriented, joy- and feasting-prone, celebrating life ... working in harmony with Mother Nature," contrasted to "male energy [that] pretends to have power by disclaiming the female force" (3). Conclusive statements based on generalized gender assumptions like these equate women with motherhood, potentially excluding men from nurturing roles. Estés's list of wild, natural characteristics of women, contrasted with "those who are their detractors," men, shows typical reductionist, absolute gender categories, conceived of as binary, fighting against each other, inherently different.[31] The qualities she connects to women (and wolves) are emotional, nurturing, motherly, intuitive, pack-oriented, devotional—reductive stereotypes of women that Victorian men would have completely agreed with, though they would have perceived them as negative rather than positive qualities. Recasting a negative, essentializing stereotype and conceiving of some humans as more "natural" based on gender is regressive and troubling. We are a species of this planet, all of us humans, biological beings with equal access to and potential connections, regardless of gender, to the rest of nature.

Applied Aspects of Myth

1) Primordial: setting the myth in a previous, primordial, period, one from the Stone Age and especially preferable for women
2) Sacred: central ideas and narrative considered sacred (perhaps metaphorically) and evoked in various rituals and mythic expressions
3) Functional (social charter): serving as a beacon for how we should live, including

Table 2. Major Dualities in the Myth of Goddess Culture

WOMAN / MATRIARCHY	MAN / PATRIARCHY
Art loving (female creators)	Competitive (male creators)
Body	Mind
Cooperation/joy	Power/control
Creator	Destroyer
Domestic	Public
Earth	Sun
Innocent victims	Cruel exploiters
Instinct	Science
Intuition	Reason
Moon	Sun
Nature	Culture
Nurturance	Contest
Peace	War
Primitive	Civilized
Sexuality	Rationality
Static/sedentary	Dynamic/mobile

- a) Achieving equality or higher status for women
- b) Achieving better environmental ethics and relationship to nature
- c) Achieving sexual ethics
4) Worldview-forming: pointing the way to a better feminist future that might recapture some aspects of a glorious, golden age—often via inspirational narratives
5) Dualistic: contrasting all previous aspects with more troubled, present patriarchy
    - a) Misogyny and many sexist policies that result in worse lives for women
    - b) Severe environmental crises, abuse of nature
    - c) Poor ethics in terms of sexual relations and many other aspects of our world
    - d) Troubled politics[32]

Table 3. Scholarly/Worldview Dualities of Goddess Culture

MATRIARCHAL WORLDVIEW	TRADITIONAL WESTERN WORLDVIEW
Artistic/poetic/symbolic thinking	Empirical observations/logical inferences
Becoming god (goddess in all)	Fellowship with god (god distinct)
Believers	Scholars
Body	Mind
Domestic	Public
Golden Age (harmony)	Imbalance (in nature and gender)
Grassroots movement	Organized religion
Hopeful artists	Skeptical scientists
Immanence (spirit in all, to be discovered)	Transcendence (divine separate)
Myth	Truth
Psychic or spiritual truths	Scientific truths
Religion	Science
Romanticism (intuitive, nature-based)	Reason (rational, intellect-based)
Romanticized views of women	Vilified views of women
Sins of men	Sins of women
Social change	Status quo
Unstructured (personal, unmediated)	Structured (hierarchical, authoritarian)
Utopian	Dystopian

Dualities and other mythic aspects as documented in believers' words appear in table 2.[33] In versions of the myth from a few influential proponents, we readily perceive such dualities, both explicit and implicit. Most mythic presentations of goddess culture, including those we shall examine from popular culture and literature in the remaining chapters, also fulfill and project these dualities.

Similar binary oppositional patterns exist in much of the scholarship discussing and analyzing the myth, its possibilities, and its limitation or errors. Many scholars embracing, using, or critiquing aspects of the goddess myth are polarized in their approaches, language, and schools of thought. Whether scholars agree with the myth or its vision of a golden age of women and goddesses, or whether they critique it as bad scholarship, we find their discussions fit dualistic patterns (table 3). Writers and filmmakers inspired by the myth also tend to fall into patterns that reflects many of these dualities (from tables

2 and 3), though part of this is because of the same kind of feedback loop that informs many specific beliefs and rituals.

Specific examples of scholarship that leads to, includes, or encourages these kinds of worldviews with a dualistic framework may discuss:

1) Utopian versus skeptical attitudes toward a prehistory dominated by goddesses or matriarchy (Peel 1990);
2) How any theories related to such perspectives reflect the Age of Reason versus the Romantic historical periods (Davis 1998);
3) How systems of thinking build and reflect emphases on nature, immanence, poetry, and spiritual truths or the contrast (Davis 1998);
4) How patriarchy has brought about a "split in modern consciousness" that goddess culture might heal (Adler 1986, 375);
5) The tensions between structured versus unstructured religious experience (Adler 1986, 437);
6) How matriarchy or goddess culture itself represents immanent utopia versus the lived, contemporary dystopia, at least for women (Christ 1997, Grey 2001, and more).

As we examine works of literature and popular culture in coming chapters, we see how they tend to reflect the terms and attitudes of these dualities as well. Works in chapters 3 and 5, by women writers, fall more on the matriarchal side; works in chapter 4, television and film mostly by men, fall more on the patriarchal or traditional Western side. Goddess myth ideas and iterations result in many terms or attitudes on the matriarchal side of the duality. Dichotomies of the goddess myth and scholarship thereof stay fairly stable across many disciplinary perspectives and approaches to the material. But the myth is also variable. Many types of women—scholars, artists, worshippers, tourists, writers—contribute to, are deeply immersed in, or even just brush up against this movement, religion, myth, or worldview. Archaeologists, psychologists, art historians, mythologists, religious studies scholars, historians, writers, artists, and popular culture figures all engage with goddess culture and new myths featuring goddesses that range from cliché repetitions of mythic tropes from more than a hundred years ago to more nuanced versions inspired by recent intersectional feminist perspectives, politics, and global events. Though many examples of goddesses in popular culture and literature share a consistent, dualistic bent in their symbolism, language, and images, we also explore a few more promisingly original, intersectional, complex modern myths (especially in chapter 6).

Conclusion

In some ways, the goddess myth itself undermines its efficacy as a way to advance a feminist agenda by reflecting and projecting problematic gender stereotypes, as becomes clearer in analysis of the myth's underlying structures and concepts in its many incarnations and even vague impressions articulated in contemporary film, television, and fiction. Most works involving references to goddesses are created not from a deeply informed, insider perspective of actual past times or goddesses (nor any scholarship thereof), but by members of our society, influenced by hundreds of years of beliefs trickling down through our culture.

———————

Creative versions of the goddess myth reflect contemporary, inaccurately imagined, newly created, or appropriated versions of goddesses and related women-centered cultures—some do so very deeply, others for relatively brief moments. Writers, directors, and many in our culture incorporate and speculate upon perceived echoes of this imagined past in various ways relevant to contemporary culture. Fictionalizations set in the contemporary world or anachronistic speculative pasts tend to follow two main patterns: goddess and matriarchy are vilified as destructive forces of chaos (chapter 4), or romanticized as superior, a longed-for past that we might hopefully reclaim or use as inspiration (chapter 5). At either end of this goddess spectrum, we find reflections of current, misogynistic, patriarchal, discriminatory patterns, though sometimes we must dig a bit below the surface to fully perceive them. Fictions are always relevant to and reflective of purposes and visions of their makers. Contemporary goddesses and related cultures are at best loosely and imaginatively connected to any known past. But amazingly, they live vibrantly and popularly in our present. However shining our goddess myths may seem, they mostly embody self-reflexive fantasies or project contemporary wish-fulfillment, working as our myths.

Part II

New Goddess Myths in Literature and Popular Culture

Chapter 3

Literary Myths of Matriarchy

To better understand how the myth functions outside neo-pagan and New Age circles, in more mainstream cultural contexts today, let us examine how some acclaimed literary writers have incorporated goddess culture worldviews in their works. Many feminists in our culture, dismayed by our culture's long history of belittling, mistreating, ignoring, or relegating women to the margins, hope goddess culture might redress such imbalances, which is why the myth remains appealing and why some fine literary minds have fictionalized goddess cultures. Leslie Marmon Silko and Alice Walker embrace the goddess myth in complex, intersectional feminist ways, though also without fully formed goddess characters. Because their settings and characters reflect our world more realistically (less speculatively than the rest of the works I consider), including our culture's gender-based problems, these works are more like mainstream literature, and they are fairly hopeful, even with thornier stories, compared to most contemporary goddess myths. These imagined women carve out spaces for themselves to tackle difficult issues and live hopefully.

Native American writer Leslie Marmon Silko's *Gardens in the Dunes* (1999) and African American writer Alice Walker's *Possessing the Secret of Joy* (1992) both offer potentially hopeful treatments of goddess themes and potential matriarchies in twentieth-century settings. These women writers also incorporate an awareness of women's second-class, often despised status in patriarchal cultures and religions, as well as how gender intersects with other issues of ethnicity, class, and so on. Silko's work traces interconnections and relationships among women in a variety of religious contexts, referencing mystical women like the Virgin of Guadalupe, a Mayan blue woman, and European pagan images of the Great Mother, none of whom emerge as a primary focus but all of whom provide inspirational backdrops for the story of a Native American girl traveling with an upper-class white woman religion scholar. Silko's many women characters in this work survive and thrive through vital and affirmative connections to the land and gardens, which unite and inspire her characters in communities that emerge as miraculous just by persisting amid patriarchy. In Walker's novel, the main character, Tashi/Evelyn, is scarred literally and figuratively by her patriarchal African culture's practice of female genital mutilation. By investigating a myth at the root of this practice, Walker's characters discover a goddess myth (inspired by twentieth-century goddess culture) that ultimately gives them hope.

Even while building beautiful and compelling literary worlds, Silko and Walker recognize the hardships women in our world face. Facing brutalities of patriarchy, their women characters band together to carve out relatively small spaces for women within patriarchy. I call these imagined communities "matrices of matriarchy"—moments and small communities of women that somehow, possibly in secret or in unnoticed, seemingly insignificant ways, find spaces to survive or even thrive as women-centered, though not without bruises and limitations. These matrices are probably the best forms of matriarchal culture achievable in our world, given what we know of history. These fictional works show such women drawing inspiration from "goddess light," goddess myths, goddess worship and building small communities that remember or imagine an older time of goddess reverence and women thriving, even while the characters are beaten, scarred, punished, and marginalized in realistic and resonant ways for today's women. The metaphorical truths of these myths are that women can hope for miracles of matriarchy and goddess culture but must live in a punishing patriarchy, as do these women. The BIPOC characters in these novels are marginalized and discriminated against in multiple ways, yet they persevere persistently in their hopes and visions. It's as though being so beaten down, belittled, and ignored gives them space and inspiration to perceive or imagine other possibilities.

In chapter 6 we discuss hopepunk as a perspective these works evince— basically the characters find hope and work to make the world better in spite of great oppression. Silko and Walker write characters who do whatever they can to build community, as do more recent writers such as N. K. Jemisin, Tomi Adeyemi, and Madeline Miller. We admire these thoughtful, hopeful fictional worlds where women endure even as they face troubling, apocalyptic times. Much great literature and myths offer not only observations of the human condition but speculation about how to hope and find beauty in the face of oppression or despair. Myths are most prevalent during trying times—offering comfort and hope during crises. Post-1960s writers such as Silko and Walker, who experienced the second wave of feminism, offer literary explorations of oppressed women's lives but also offer modest, workable hope. Their literary interpretations are a sort of mythic high point of goddess culture, though still with enough realism—connections to the patriarchy we know—to make it relevant and realistically hopeful, similar to works in chapter 6. Silko and Walker offer hopeful glimmers of women banding together in matrices of matriarchy and resistance.

Silko's Landscape of Miracles and Matriarchy

Silko sets her novel *Gardens in the Dunes* in 1900 and employs the style and subject matter of Victorian novels.[1] The characters, including young southwestern Native American sisters, a wealthy educated northeastern woman, and others, encounter various religious and gardening practices, with an underlying emphasis on building community and family. Using a typical quest motif, in fact a typically Victorian one (Dickensian even, with an orphan story), Silko nevertheless rhetorically undermines the Victorian trope by using it to create fictional communities of women who challenge the patriarchy, including its misuse of the environment. Silko subverts the patriarchal story mode with matriarchal content and messages. The term *matriarchy* is usually employed to indicate a society where women control politics, economy, and/or culture. Thus, matriarchy cannot fully exist within a patriarchy, where men are in control. But one function of art and myth specifically is to explore and reconcile us to paradox. A duality where patriarchy and matriarchy coexist might seem impossible, as miraculous indeed as gardens in sand dunes. Paradox, most obviously one of landscape, is a controlling metaphor of the novel reflected in the title. Silko's women do not rule society and in fact suffer greatly under the oppressive patriarchy. Still, they find and support each other to build communities that constitute matrices of matriarchy within the patriarchy. That their communities, and gardens, thrive *is* the miracle, at least from within the perspective of the dominant patriarchy.

Silko's women help each other and the land to survive. Nature emerges as a source that may be shaped in various ways, but only flourishes in this novel with the care women provide, even while it heals and helps them in turn. Silko's exquisite prose is infused with dream sequences and "consummately beautiful sentences" (Aldama 2000, 458). Her lyrical style is especially evident in descriptions of nature: "The huge night-blooming Victoria lily dominated the center of the pool with perfumed white blossoms as big as teapots; it was early enough that the flowers were still open, crowding the smaller blue water lilies that required full sun to blossom" (161). It feels appropriate that the style sparkles in descriptions of nature, since the story draws profound connections between the environment, women, and their ability to build their communities through caring for the land and its fruits. The controlling metaphor of the novel is that nature is beautiful and good.

Working with nature through gardening is one of the primary ways Silko's characters survive the patriarchal system that controls, harasses, and seduces them. It also allows them to build and maintain communities of women. Gardening has long been metaphorically connected to both women and concepts of paradise in Western religions. Demeter or Ceres from Greco-Roman mythology bears the titles "goddess of the earth, of agriculture, and of fertility in general" (Bell 1991, 156). Many other cultures also link agriculture and fertility to female deities. Isis, Inanna, and Cybele are powerful women goddesses from the ancient Near East associated with fertility and agriculture: "Like Inanna, Isis and Demeter, she [Cybele] was regarded as the founder of agriculture and law" (Baring and Cashford 1993, 295). Many such mythological women are also either punished, like Demeter's daughter Persephone's abduction, or they die or suffer in some way, for instance Inanna's descent into the underworld and Gilgamesh's mocking denial of Ishtar (Baring and Cashford 1993; Spretnak 1992).[2]

The premier woman in the Judeo-Christian tradition, Eve, fits the patterns of women as inferior to men and of women "goddesses" or heroes connected to gardening and fertility. As the first sinner, Eve is despised for causing our ejection from Eden—a perfect garden. As a result of her actions women become bearers of children (fertile) outside of "paradise" (a perfect garden), and humans are simultaneously made into tillers of soil (working for their food). In this Western vision of man's relationship with nature, Adam and Eve must struggle against the land outside Eden, scratching at the soil in toil, with goals of controlling and taming the wilderness. Specifically, God tells Adam and Eve in Genesis: "Cursed you are. . . . Dust you shall eat. . . . cursed is the ground because of you; in toil you shall eat of it all the days of your life; thorns and thistles it shall bring forth to you" (Genesis 3:14). The "curse" toward man and the land, along with the expulsion of people from the lovely, verdant nature of paradise (now guarded against all humans by an angel) and the negative descriptions by God himself of post-Edenic nature—with "dust," "thorns," and "thistles"—all reveal much about the Western worldview in regard to gardens and nature. Our very metaphors contain notions of "taming" or "conquering" "the wilderness." In addition to conceiving of nature as something to battle, we also have a Western tradition of considering nature as beneath us, something that exists for our use (and abuse). This attitude is believed by the goddess community to have overturned previous, pagan attitudes regarding nature: "By destroying pagan animism, Christianity made it possible to exploit nature in a mood of indifference to the feelings of natural objects" (White 1996, 10). Our Western sense of disconnection from and superiority to nature surfaces in the actions and mindsets of most of the male characters in Silko's work.[3]

Silko (1999, 14) opens her novel in an Eden-like homeland to which her main character, a Native girl named Indigo, hopes relentlessly to return, a desert landscape that holds miraculous, ancient, terraced gardens: "Grandma Fleet told them the old gardens had always been there. The old-time people found the gardens already growing, planted by the Sand Lizard, a relative of Grandfather Snake, who invited his niece to settle there and cultivate her seeds." Typically, dunes and deserts evoke images of an inhospitable, mostly barren landscape like that to which Adam and Eve are banished. Yet contrary to both our assumptions and the instructions of God to Adam, Silko's dunes *are* the garden, the paradise that shapes and binds her women characters. Here the snake in the garden is not evil, but the progenitor and guardian, who passes his knowledge on to a woman, "his niece." This opening offers Judeo-Christian motifs—a heavenly garden, a snake that gives fruit and knowledge to a primeval woman, the establishment of gardening, and a paradise that is temporarily lost. Unlike the Eden myth, however, this gardening takes place by current humans in their original site, which exists in this world. This Sand Lizard garden is described as "heavenly," "blossoming," "fragrant," "magical," "refreshing," "wonderful," "delicious," and "intoxicating" (all in the first paragraph), and the place evokes in Indigo and her sister, named Sister Salt, who are naked and rolling down the dunes in the opening scene, feelings of effortlessness, "ease," warmth, laughter, and belonging (13).

This wonderful place is a "miraculous" paradise, yet unlike Eden, it is neither lost nor entirely the work of god. In the Western tradition, a post-Edenic garden reflects inherently man's control of nature, which reflects the "'will of civilization to overcome nature and achieve unconditional human mastery over the earth'" (Merchant 2003, 50). Silko's (1999, 15) garden results from a blend of nature and nurture; it is terraced and reflective of generations who have tended it since the first woman "cultivate[d] seeds" there; one of the lessons taught to the Indian women who tend the gardens in the dunes is to leave some fruits to seed themselves each harvest. Throughout, women gardeners cooperate with rather than control or use nature. This cooperative care of nature is the means to their matrices of matriarchy—a paradise from within this feminist rhetoric. We always see Indigo at her happiest when she is in gardens. Even in the throes of homesickness, she finds comfort from nature: "The dawn flooded the porch with golden green light that lifted as she stepped into its radiance and pulled her toward it. She bounded down the front steps and felt the dampness of the grass through her slippers. She ran into the light pouring between the giant trees near the house along the vast lawns. To run and run over the soft earth while breathing the golden fresh air felt glorious" (160). Nature soothes and inspires Indigo, especially when she can share it with her family (opening scene). Women regularly experience nature as soothing and inspiring throughout the novel.

Gardens involves three primary women characters, two Natives, Sister Salt and Indigo, and Hattie, a white would-be scholar of religion and a proto-feminist from a prominent East Coast family. Hattie's proposed thesis topic on the "female spiritual principle in the early church" plans to examine evidence from Gnostic texts of "high status for women and the feminine influence in early Christianity" but is rejected by the patriarchal university system at Harvard's Divinity School (Silko 1999, 100–101; Ross 2001, 35). Devastated by this utter rejection of her research, "Hattie felt she had been dismissed as a suffragist," Hattie suffers deep depression, diagnosed as "female hysteria, precipitated by over stimulation," that she is expected to overcome by marriage to horticulturalist Edward Palmer, whose involvement with forces destroying nature is finally his undoing (Silko 1999, 101, 229). While Edward dreams of orchid cultivation and fortune in the Amazon (very male, Western goals of profit and fame from using nature), Hattie attends to Indigo, whom she all but adopts when she finds the young Indian girl in her husband's greenhouse one day. Indigo, rather than Edward, helps to "cure" Hattie. The younger of the Sand Lizard sisters hides in the greenhouse to escape the abusive boarding school nearby. The key women characters throughout the novel come together over gardens and cultivation.

Hattie's harsh treatment by the patriarchy threatens to destroy her, as she is eventually assaulted, raped, robbed, left for dead, and then considered shamed. But Hattie survives and gets some revenge by burning the town where her attacker lives and where the white people disapprove of her as an independent woman who helps Indians. Hattie then staggers to the camp where Indigo and her community of Indian women are dancing and singing rituals of the Ghost Dance.[4] Though Hattie seems close to death, the Indian women promise to dedicate their ritual to her. When they return from a night of dancing, Hattie is awake and tells them "how she woke feeling so much better and then noticed the beautiful glow outside the lean-to, so much like the strange light she saw before" (Silko 1999, 469). A previous view of this supernatural light comes during a strangely prophetic dream, and both are "miraculously" healing.

When Hattie's father arrives to this scene to "save" her, he disrupts the harmonious community of women, evident in the outrageous noise his visit provokes, "the parrot squawked loudly and the monkey screamed; the baby woke and began to cry. Hattie burst into tears" (Silko 1999, 470). Hattie finds comfort in the healing light that has soothed her throughout the novel and in humble women's Indian camp. But her father cannot conceive that she is in her right mind to want to stay there. Hattie's preference to stay with the Indian women rather than return home is considered unstable: "Hattie managed to break free of her father and left the lawyer holding the empty coat; but the soldiers dismounted and helped them subdue her. . . . Hattie struggled with her captors," but she is removed, leaving Indigo weeping for her (471). Hattie nonetheless creates for herself a happy-ish ending, at least from Silko's point of view, by rejoining her Aunt Bronwyn, the eccentric woman in England who tends gardens, eschews the popular culture of her time, and instead uses her money to support archaeological digs that investigate pre-Christian (presumably matriarchal) pagan cultures in Europe. These very gardens brought Hattie joy and "enlightenment"; thus, this is a happy ending. Hattie also maintains contact with Indigo, sending letters, cash, and promises of continued support and love. Women disdained and considered misfits by society at large build a community of love and support, capable of enduring even terrible assaults.

Like Hattie's struggle against patriarchy, Indigo and Sister Salt's encounters with the white world are full of exploitation, often senseless violence, and misunderstanding. The sisters' mother and grandmother raise them in the gardens in the dunes but must travel to nearby Needles, California, during winter months to sell goods, collect seeds, and participate in messianic religious gatherings (Ghost Dances), where their mother is lost one year when the government raids the event. When the grandmother dies the subsequent winter at the gardens, the girls leave the dunes in search of their mother but are quickly seized by white men. Sister Salt is deemed too old for boarding school and gets shipped to a reservation-like ghetto, where she does laundry for dam workers and earns some money through sex work (which she doesn't consider shameful). Although her money is eventually stolen, she is less concerned with that than with maintaining the community of women she belongs to at the camp and with caring for herself and the son she bears there. Meanwhile, upon her seizure, Indigo is placed in a harsh environment of assimilation—at boarding school—until she escapes to Hattie.

While Hattie loves and nurtures Indigo, many others in her privileged, white world, including her husband, Edward, find Indigo annoying, or at least an improper object of Hattie's attention. They indulge Hattie and suffer Indigo. While Hattie finds in Indigo a daughter to love, Indigo never relinquishes thoughts of home or the gardens and lessons of her grandmother about tending them. Indigo's feelings for Hattie are strong, but as a builder of community, she remains loyal to her first family and consistently dreams of a reunion: "She missed Sister and Mama; were they together now? Hattie was very kind to her but she missed her sister and mother so much" (Silko 1999, 283). Sister Salt is similarly focused on an ultimate reunion. And once she has toured the world, seen gardens by other women, and learned to listen to Indigo, even Hattie finally realizes the need to help Indigo rebuild her community: "suddenly she realized they must help the Indian child return to her sister and mother! This was all wrong! How foolish she had been!" (249). The use of exclamation points confirms that Hattie has come to believe sincerely in the significance of Indigo's community. Hattie's encounters with the exciting light help her literally "see the light" of the importance of community.

But before they return to the dessert, the makeshift family travels to New England, England, and Italy, partly for Edward to seek means to begin a citrus farm to save his floundering finances. Like so many women in the novel, Hattie's Aunt Bronwyn cultivates her garden in England passionately, with "plants from all over the world" and stones from pagan times that Bronwyn claims still hold power (Silko 1999, 240). For Indigo, the adventure yields one primary result: "a wonderful opportunity for gardening ideas—Indigo had a small valise full of carefully folded wax paper packets with the seeds she'd gathered" (240). She also expands her "family" by deepening her relationship with Hattie and by gathering animals.

Even while Hattie and Indigo come to understand and deepen their commitment to community and gardens during the voyage, the dominant man, Edward, seems annoyed by their efforts and realizations. Indigo receives gifts of seeds and instructions everywhere she travels. But Edward, who wants to profit from foreign gardens secretly rather than being happy with the seeds and cuttings he too is offered, is constantly annoyed at what he thinks of as a pretense of the child's commitment to both her "family" and gardening. He bristles at the attention Indigo receives: "He found himself a bit irritated at the *professoressa*'s attention to the child, especially her generous gifts of packets of seeds and corms from her hybrids, although he could see that she made an identical bundle for him and Hattie. It seemed a bit ludicrous for Laura to pretend the Indian child would ever plant the corms or seeds, much less perform the pollination process for hybrids, even if she did take notes on all the necessary steps. Of course, Laura could not be expected to know anything about American Indians" (Silko 1999, 303). This condescension is misplaced, as Edward's schemes for profit gardening are the illegal, ludicrous, even dangerous ones, whereas Indigo's efforts yield multiple blessings back home. Edward's horticultural efforts all ultimately fail, and he has only a chimera of any human community, and that finally kills him. Meanwhile, both Hattie and Indigo survive in the communities and gardens they cultivate. Several of the men in the novel strive for fame and riches, in plots typical of the genre of Victorian novels, where men survive and thrive as heroes through their industry, ingenuity, aspirations, and partly by lucky birth or circumstance. Such characters' efforts typically win riches and glory, which the patriarchy considers success.

Virtually all men in this novel emerge as inadequate heroes, far less effectual and interesting than the women. Silko's version of Victorian storytelling thus offers women heroes with different, original story arcs. While their struggles (being separated from family, struggling against oppressive forces, going on long, arduous quests) are superficially similar to their men counterparts, their narratives challenge the primacy of masculine heroic quest narratives. The women's rewards are not to achieve riches or fame in the Western sense; rather their quests are to be allowed to exist outside the patriarchal system, to tend their gardens, build their communities, and live according to their own visions. By allowing these women to find each other and build communities, Silko creates a subversive, virtually miraculous, though limited, hidden, and still oppressed matriarchy. Her women remain strong-minded, adventurous, intelligent, caring, and loyal even in the face of dismissive attitudes, exploitation, assault, and rape.

All of the key women characters share a passionate devotion to gardening, and all that gardening shows goddess connections. Tending gardens becomes a mundane yet miraculous conduit for women's survival. Gardening serves as a metaphor for women's community and healing. Women's devotion to gardening, for food, beauty, and comfort, helps them build worlds that endure to nurture body and soul. After Indigo feeds her family from fruits of her world seed collecting, she thinks, "How strange to think these small plants traveled so far with so many hazards, yet still thrived while Edward died. Grandma Fleet was right—compared to plants and trees, humans were weak creatures" (Silko 1999, 447). Edward, the Victorian gentleman who considers himself

superior to Indigo, dies miserably and without success at any of his horticultural or other dreams. But though Edward mocks the very thought of Indigo's
gardening, she succeeds at it while also rebuilding a community. Hattie likewise becomes a devotee of gardens, dreaming of them often and writing to
her father: "'I wish you had been with me to see the *professoressa*'s black gladi-
olus garden with the "madonnas" in their niches,' she wrote. 'The rain garden
serpent goddesses were quite wonderful. They won me over entirely'" (424).
The women's successes underscore the men's failures at gardening, community, and life. Gardens grow from and help maintain matrices of matriarchies
that are miraculous when viewed in light of the arrogant assumptions and
domination of the patriarchy.

More obviously miraculous events connected to landscape also occur in
the novel, primarily in the form of visionary dreams. For instance, a mysterious, miraculous "shining light" soothes and helps the women characters—especially Indigo and Hattie. Indigo experiences the light during her
participation in Ghost Dance ceremonies. She sees the messiah as "white" and
"shining" and thinks, "No wonder he called himself the morning star!" (Silko
1999, 31). Throughout the novel this light is especially important to Hattie, for
whom it represents revelation and comfort. She's inspired by studying Gnostic
gospels, where illumination is a key tenant, as in one sect's greeting, "May you
be illumined by the light," part of the feminine element in early Christianity
(97). Her studies become real when Hattie sleepwalks to a pagan stone in Aunt
Bronwyn's garden that she previously dreamed of, where she is "illumined":

> She saw something luminous white move through the foliage of the corn plants
> and the tall sunflowers. Her heart beat faster as she heard the soft rhythmic
> sound of breathing approach her. She felt a strange stir of excitement and dread
> at what she would see when she stepped through the gateway. The luminosity of
> the light was astonishing: was she awake or asleep? How beautiful the light was!
> Her apprehension and dread receded; now a prismatic aura surrounded the
> light. It was as if starlight and moonlight converged over her as a warm current
> of air enveloped her; for an instant Hattie felt such joy she wept. (248)

This great joy that makes her weep also inspires, for this is when Hattie
decides to return Indigo to her family (249).

Hattie receives various tantalizing clues explaining this vision throughout her journey, and each quickens her heart. The light seems connected
with an ancient mask, animal figures, objects from the matriarchal gardens
of Aunt Bronwyn and Italian *professoressa* Laura, and with Christ and the

Virgin Mary—in Italy and at the Native Ghost Dances. While looking at an apparition of Mary in Corsica, for instance, Hattie realizes the light as specifically *miraculous*: "So this was what was called a miracle—she felt wonder and excitement, though she saw the flow of colored light on the wall for only an instant" (Silko 1999, 320). Whenever she dreams of, recalls, or hears mention of the light, she feels "peace" (327), "well-being and love" and "happiness" (406). "The glowing light" is "more real now than her manuscript or her marriage" (372); the light spurs her healing not only from the assault but from her brutalization in general at the hands of the patriarchy, which dismisses her. During her convalescence at the Ghost Dance, Hattie experiences the light as bliss, and it seems responsible for her healing: "The crushing pain was gone and her head felt clear; all her senses were alert for the first time since the assault ... the light outside became brighter and more luminous—she recognized it at once and felt a thrill sweep over her. How soothing the light was, how joyously serene she felt" (469). Here her illumination seems most complete, though we are left assuming she will learn more about the light when she lives with Aunt Bronwyn after the novel ends.

Notably, Edward also experiences a sharp, supernatural light. But for him it is "blinding" and causes headaches and other great pain (Silko 1999, 90). He in fact becomes addicted to laudanum and slides into his downfall and ultimately his death as a result, partly, of the torment he perceives this light and things associated with it to be. But to Hattie and Indigo, and presumably anyone who is open to it (though in this novel that only includes women), the light is comforting, inspiring, healing, and miraculous. Throughout, the light is directly connected to religion and nature, especially matriarchal religious traditions, like those Aunt Bronwyn and Laura study and revive, and the traditions that Indigo and Sister Salt were raised upon. Both women's visions conceive of nature as a consistently good, nurturing, healing force of messages and "illumination."

There are also miraculous stones and figurines of all sorts in the European gardens tended by Bronwyn and Laura. One of the more intriguing specific symbols connecting the pagan tradition (of Hattie's vision) and the Sand Lizard tradition is the snake who is connected to gardening and nurturing women. In Laura's gardens especially, there are "masks and terra-cotta figures of goddesses that were half snake or half bird" (Silko 1999, 284) as well as "concentric circles ... the all-seeing eyes of the Great Goddess; and the big triangles represented the pubic triangle, another emblem of the Great Goddess" (291). There are many animal figures, including snakes, among the ancient figures, usually explicitly connected to women. Stories Laura relates even mention a traditional luminous glow. The *professoressa* explains as best she can to the curious Indigo, who is especially intrigued by the snakes so similar to her own culture's traditions: "Laura said when she was a girl her grandmother always kept a black snake in the storeroom to protect it from mice and rats. Indigo smiled; yes, Grandma Fleet always thanked the snakes for their protection—not just from rodents but from those who would do you harm. At the spring above the dunes lived the biggest snake, very old—the water was his" (299).

Such positive attributes retained regarding snakes in Europe is intriguing in light of the obviously contrary view of snakes among the dominant (Christian) culture, where they are satanic, an evil force in paradise responsible for our rejection from the Garden of Eden. This goddess culture view of snakes as a protective, positive force seems contradictory, and is addressed by Silko in considering the figure of the Virgin of Guadalupe, who "crushes the snake" under her feet in most popular images of her. The word *Guadalupe* translates (from Nahuatl and Spanish) as "she crushes the serpent," which needs crushing as both the devil (from the Christian point of view) *and* as a representative of the Aztec hero "Quetzalcoatl, the Plumed Serpent" (Demarest and Taylor 1956, 78). Hattie appears to have learned some of this lore: "Hattie drifted off to sleep recalling the pictures and statues of the Blessed Virgin Mary standing on a snake. Catechism classes taught Mary was killing the snake, but after seeing the figures in the rain garden, she thought perhaps the Virgin with the snake was based on a figure from earlier times" (Silko 1999, 304).

When she later dreams of gardens, Hattie connects all these themes: "Perhaps she would return to England or Italy—she dreamed about the gardens often. Aunt Bronwyn's old stones danced in one of her dreams, and in another dream, Laura's figures of the snake and bird women sang a song so lovely she woke in tears" (392). The positive potential of snakes, as connected to goddess culture, has miraculously survived, the novel suggests, in spite of the more negative, popular attitude of snakes as satanic. Hattie prefers the goddess culture view to the traditional one, seeing it as connecting to the Gnostic gospels (from her thesis research), illumination, and the Great Mother (450), confirming as well Grandma Fleet's wisdom that Indigo shares: "Grandma Fleet always said snake girls and bird mothers were everywhere in the world, not just here!" (455). The snake has for many cultures been a figure of eternal life and resurrection.

One more miracle in the novel is the unlikely restoration of the sisters to their garden, provoking the happy tumble through the "paradise" of their home seen in the first paragraph of the novel. The sisters return revitalized, with a baby, many new plants, new animals, and a strong extended family. A new snake in their garden welcomes them home:

> Early the other morning when she came alone to wash at the spring, a big rattlesnake was drinking at the pool. The snake dipped her mouth daintily into the water, and her throat moved with such delicacy as she swallowed. She stopped drinking briefly to look at Sister, then turned back to the water; then she gracefully turned from the pool across the white sand to a nook of bright shade. Old Snake's beautiful daughter moved back home. (Silko 1999, 477)

The sisters leave the gardens in despair, experience violence, greed, and hardships of all kinds in the outside, patriarchal and non-Native world, and return against all the odds to health, beauty, and continuity of their culture. Like the eternal rhythms of gardens returning to bloom or snakes returning to life, these women survive and persist, to build new, hybridized, but persistent communities that are promisingly matrifocal, though small and nondominant.

Victorians epitomize the hubris of "civilized" patriarchal beliefs that nature exists to be "tamed," "harnessed," "controlled," and used, preferably for profit. Attitudes of controlling the landscape led to environmental degradation that continues today and resulted in the subjugation of Native Americans. The ingenious, productive, world-changing gardens of Native Americans were often considered and described as "messy" by Europeans—evidence of their "savagery" (Wessel 1976). Native people were actually efficient, successful gardeners, giving the world many of our most important crops today—corn, tomatoes, potatoes, peppers, chocolate, and more (Weatherford 1989). Silko's novel highlights the destructive potential of the Western (non-Native, patriarchal) mindset especially in showing its effects on women and Native people, including those removed from their land and forced to work for whites. One sign of the Western attitude toward nature in this novel is the dam that changes and harms the earth for men's profit and "progress." This dam attracts mostly trouble, destruction, and competition.

By opening and closing the novel with views of a traditional garden tended by Native women, a garden and women who flourish miraculously in spite of all the odds and forces against them, Silko offers a hopeful vision. The novel suggests that women's connection to the landscape, in terms of understanding it, cultivating it, and preserving it, is far more profound than any other force in their lives, including the patriarchy. Women survive and endure by gardening and by remembering the lore of their matriarchal, goddess-centered pasts. Silko adds another dimension to the goddess myth, not only that Old Europe

was matriarchal, more balanced, and preferable, but also that indigenous peoples of the Americas were still living in ways similar to the imagined people
of Old Europe, including being environmentally ethical, and so could teach
us something about tending our planet and communities. Silko's non-Native
characters Hattie, Bronwyn, and Laura do not find or reveal all the mysteries
of goddess culture, and Hattie will not be allowed to complete her thesis on
the role of women in religion. Yet from another perspective, in another light,
the novel offers a metaphorical realization of Hattie's thesis.

Silko's rhetoric of gardens, snakes, goddesses, and matriarchy inspires the
women whose lives she creates, and as a novel written for a contemporary
audience, it also confirms the position that a matriarchal past is rhetorically
reflective of contemporary women rather than of our ancestors. In other
words, it doesn't matter if matriarchy or goddess dominance existed or exactly
what the past looked like. We can build our future from the seeds we have,
from this novel's perspective, by tending gardens and building communities.
Silko's tapestry of women, landscape, and luminous potential shows nature
giving us all life, even in the most difficult circumstances, suggesting women
may grasp any miracles of life and potential, even within patriarchy. We can
all "see the light" and like the sisters, Hattie, and the old snake, "move back
home," however we rebuild or envision that home (Silko 1999, 477).

Silko's novel has political implications in terms of the environment, social
justice, and treatment of Native Americans and women in our culture, historically and today. There are often valid political motivations for embracing or
drawing upon a goddess perspective, for instance trying to change practices,
mindsets, or laws that are harmful to women. Silko does not shy away from
the abuse women receive at the hands of the patriarchy, nor does she suggest
resistance is easy or widespread. We see only a few women, fairly secretly man-
aging to carve out spaces for small matrices of matriarchy because of some
characters' wealth (Hattie, Bronwyn, and Laura), and also because of secret
but secure ties to the hoped-for ancient matriarchies (whether they are the
figurines in Europe or the actual secluded garden in the American dessert).
Even such secret and relatively small successes stand out as fictional miracles.

Alice Walker's Literary Goddess

A literary version of a goddess prehistory by Pulitzer Prize–winning author
Alice Walker highlights women's suffering at the hands of patriarchy in Africa.
Her novel *Possessing the Secret of Joy* demonstrates harmful effects of female

Fig. 10. Figurative carving of a naked woman displaying exaggerated vulva; one of eighty-five surviving corbels on the Church of Saint Mary and Saint David, Kilpeck, England, dated to twelfth century (many other such figurines exist in Ireland, Great Britain, France, and Spain); such carvings are often interpreted (like gargoyles) as intended to ward off evil spirits or death; others consider them survivals of pagan mother-goddess traditions.

genital mutilation (FGM), which Walker has worked to condemn and abolish.[5] Main character Tashi suffers from *choosing*, as an adult, after escaping as a child, to undergo FGM performed by M'Lissa, her village's *tsunga*—woman in charge of "cutting." M'Lissa tells Tashi of a moment from her childhood in her African village: she snuck to a tree where she had seen her mother venerate an object wrapped and hidden there. M'Lissa unwrapped the object that she had seen her mother kiss and found "a small smiling figure with one hand on her genitals, every part of which appeared intact" (Walker 1992, 213).

Although the text suggests there are African figurines of this type, the closest real-world carving to what Walker describes are Sheela na Gig sculptures, common especially in Britain and Ireland, often found on Romanesque (Norman) churches, castles, and other buildings, mostly dating to the Middle Ages, sometimes interpreted as "survivals" of pagan goddess idols or fertility symbols since they are overtly erotic. Others consider them iconography meant to ward off evil.[6] Sheela na Gigs (fig. 10) do indeed show women touching their intact and often unrealistically large genitals, usually apparently smiling quite widely, also often with extra-large eyes. Many consider these sculptures "grotesque" and "sometimes even comical . . . usually associated with 'hags' or 'old women,'" sometimes also showing details like facial scarring (which Tashi also has).[7] People debate whether they are "pagan idols of lust" or more akin to gargoyles. Walker seems to have sided with the pagan idol of lust interpretation, and M'Lissa learns one "secret of joy"—orgasm—from copying this idol. Although as a girl she returns to play with the figure often, she is afraid of the feelings it evokes and ultimately learns "not to feel," suffering greatly from her own FGM. Her mother, performing the female circumcision, which is "torture" for her (Walker 1992, 214), tries "to get away with cutting lightly," leaving the clitoris, "but the other women saw," and "what my mother started, the witchdoctor finished" and "showed no mercy," leaving her with brutal scars, truly mutilated (214–15).

M'Lissa says she "never cried after that" deepest of punishments to her womanhood and learned "that there is no God known to man who cares about children or about women. And that the God of woman is autonomy" (Walker 1992, 216). Her difficult lessons and lost innocence lead her to become the main mutilator of women's genitalia in her country, considered a national treasure by the government, but someone Tashi hates and decides to kill. Tashi cares for her in her old age and accuses her for the suffering she's caused, and M'Lissa explains that her true self was killed in the initiation hut: "I would have died. So I walked away, limped away, and just left her there [her younger, weeping self]. . . . She is still crying. She's been crying since I left. No wonder I haven't been able to. She has been crying all our tears" (218). Walker draws a moving, powerful portrait of a cycle of violence and cruelty in the name of patriarchal tradition.

Walker (1992, 274–75) evokes sympathy for M'Lissa, as another victim of this cruel and dysfunctional ritual tradition, but we nonetheless see Tashi as our main hero, making us see M'Lissa through her eyes as Tashi hates, cares for, and then kills M'Lissa, who seems to want Tashi to do it:

> I killed [M'Lissa] all right. I placed a pillow over her face and lay cross it for an hour. Her sad stories about her life caused me to lose my taste for slashing her. She had told me it was traditional for a well-appreciated *tsunga* to be murdered by someone she circumcised, then burned. I carried out what was expected of me. It is curious, is it not, that the traditional tribal society dealt so cleverly with its appreciation of the *tsunga* and its hatred of her. But of course the *tsunga* was to the traditional elders merely a witch they could control, an extension of their own dominating power.

Tashi perceives, before her execution for this state crime of killing a revered purveyor of tradition, the "curious" and pervasive patriarchal power behind the whole world of FGM that has so devastated her life and those of many other women. The text also affirms a different memory of M'Lissa, of the happier matriarchal time before: "Before the people became a tribe . . . considered an evil time, because although everyone knew they had a mother, because she had given birth to them, a father was not to be had in the same way . . . [And so] the house always belonged, in those days to the woman . . . But somehow this was seen as evil" (212). In other words, Walker's characters have preserved an oral history of matriarchal and goddess-centered prehistory. The novel fully embraces the goddess myth.

At another point in the novel, Tashi specifically remembers a myth explaining the origins of FGM that she heard the men in her village tell when she was little. But this memory comes only after years of therapy and help from friends, including from her stepson Pierre, who is a Jungian-trained psychologist.[8] Tashi, "much to [her] surprise," remembers a conversation overheard while she brought village elders (men) a tray of food:

> God wanted to have intercourse with the woman. . . . And the woman fought him. Her clitoris was a termite hill, rising up and barring his way. . . . When the clitoris rose . . . God thought it looked masculine. Since it was "masculine" for a clitoris [to] rise, God could be excused for cutting it down. Which he did. Then, . . . God fucked the hole that was left. (Walker 1992, 228–29)

Another circumcised woman listening to Tashi becomes angry and says she never knew this story but was merely told women's vulvas were dirty and that this ritual would clean them.

Tashi then remembers even more explicitly how the men told the myth, first conceiving of Man as "God's cock," which "scratches the furrow" to "drop the seed" (Walker 1992, 230). The men, referred to throughout the related myth as Number One, Number Two, Number Three, and Number Four, confirm their superiority and right to harm and subjugate women throughout, laughing, equating themselves with God and confirming each other's thoughts. Tashi remembers hearing them continue the story: "The *tsunga's* stitch helps the cock to know his crop . . . which after all belongs to God," showing mythic entitlement for men to dominate what "belongs" to him (231). They also say woman is "queen," a gift given by God, whom they must thus treat well, including "feeding her so that she will stay plump"—presumably meaning pregnant and thus docile, as well as tied to children. The men worry that "if left to herself the Queen would fly. . . . And then where would we be?" In other words, they fear women's independence, offering justification for why their "merciful" god "clips her wings" (231). This "clipping" refers to FGM, specifically clipping part or all of the clitoris and possibly also other parts of the genitals, such as the labia minora, labia majora, and nearby tissue; FGM can include as well infibulation (narrowing of vaginal opening) or any other harming of female genitalia. The World Health Organization provides more specifics and states definitively: "FGM has no health benefits, and it harms girls and women in many ways. It involves removing and damaging healthy and normal female genital tissue, and interferes with the natural functions of girls' and women's bodies."[9] The damage of FGM can include long-term, severe physical and mental trauma such as Tashi experiences throughout Walker's book.

The men in this remembered scene boast that the clipping makes women inert and static, forcing them to stay put to care for children and especially men (231). But the woman in that story nevertheless does rise up, "As a man would!" But "blind . . . she did not see . . . God's axe," which "struck the blow that made her Queen!" (232). This patriarchal god manipulates and punishes the woman for trying to rise up and potentially to fly—figuratively relating to independence or metaphorically relating to sexual flight, or orgasm. Yet even with clipped wings woman remains, to god and man, "beautiful enough for him to fuck." This misogynistic god is a sexual predator: "God liked it fighting! (Laughter) . . . God liked it tight! . . . God liked to remember what He had done, and how it felt before it got loose. . . . God is wise. . . . That is why He created the *tsunga*" (232). These patriarchs, laughing, slapping their lips over the food Tashi serves them as a little girl, do not even perceive her as important enough of a being to take into consideration during this scene.

Words such as these that the men laugh over, about "a sharpened stone and bag of thorns!" of "fighting," striking blows, and otherwise treating strong women harshly, could traumatize a young girl, who might realize (and has obviously retained this memory as a repressed trauma) that this is in store for her. These old men congratulate themselves, joke about their cruelty, and do not even notice Tashi, who "could have been a fly or an ant" (Walker 1992, 233). They joke that all men would prefer brutal sex like them: "Because He liked it tight! . . . God likes to feel big. . . . What man does not? (Laughter)" (233), but the novel does offer other kinds of men, like those caring for Tashi (her husband and stepson), who are kinder and gentler toward women. They do not share the old men's view that every "beautiful" woman's body "has been given us to be our sustenance forever. (Laughter, and the noisy eating of food)" (233).

Though young Tashi does "not particularly notice them, either," at the time, these representatives of old, punishing patriarchy endure in her subconscious memory and throughout much of our culture:

> They've always been there underneath the baobab tree, graybearded, old. . . .
> Gazing at them now from the safety of the prison chapel [after her arrest for
> murder] . . . I can see they are shells, empty of life. It is they who are being
> stuffed with food, while nothing but oppressive verbal diarrhea comes out. The
> child, taught to respect these elders above all others, could not have recognized

this. The old men discussing her and all the females of the villages did not care that she heard them. They knew she would not be able to figure out what they were talking about. They were discussing her, determining her life, and at the time she did not, could not, know. And yet, there in her unconscious had remained the termite hill, and herself trapped deep inside it, heavy, wingless and inert, the Queen of the dark tower. (Walker 1992, 233–34)

The "dark tower" comes up during many years of therapy, though Tashi doesn't understand it until this breakthrough memory. With her insight spurred here through the help of her friends, including some caring men, Tashi understands the patriarchal hegemony that she now perceives as ruining her life. She "kicks a stone" figuratively at these old men, planning an act—killing M'Lissa—to effect change in the form of resistance. Thus, memory of the myth, accepting the former or potential matriarchal and goddess-centered happy time, and full recognition of the oppressive patriarchy as a dysfunctional society are keys to any lasting "secret of joy" from the title. Ultimately the secret of joy might be read as female resistance to male domination over our bodies, our health, and our potential as humans, our ability to "fly."

In the myth the clitoris is a termite hill that blocks the way of the men, who believe they must cut it down through FGM. But the clitoris and women's ability to fly might also be freedom and joy in life, which men continue to cut down via painful intercourse and other forms of pain that FGM causes, along with social oppression. Her friends help Tashi to interpret the myth thus: "Religion is an elaborate excuse for what man has done to women and to the earth." But Tashi also remembers, "there were other religions . . . thinking of the little figure blissfully loving herself" (Walker 1992, 229). "Your little smiling goddess was destroyed," her friend explains, because man wants to feel big (229ff). Walker's myth for the source of FGM echoes the goddess myth depicting an earlier time when women were honored and life was better. This woman-forward world was then violently overthrown by patriarchy, using the "elaborate excuse" of religion (including myth, tradition, and ritual) for terrible actions to women and the earth. The goddess myth emerges within the fictional world, as in our own, during a time of crisis for women—suffering a ritual such as FGM conceived by men—to offer structural and functional means of healing or achieving balance.[10]

But who is the hero in this myth, and what does the mythic structure ultimately lead us to and reflect? Is it a way out of the imbalance, or merely a different look at the same repressive cultural constructs? After all, Tashi suffers greatly until she is executed, a fate she accepts, saying how tired she is and that

death is "easier": "it would kill me to get any older. What I have already experienced is more than enough. Besides, she says soberly, maybe death is easier
than life, as pregnancy is easier than birth" (Walker 1992, 249). Giving birth
was particularly hard for Tashi because of complications from FGM. Her story
is one of dominance and suffering at the hands of the patriarchy, applicable to
all women in the book and many in our world. Pierre, the Jungian stepson, further researches and explains the meaning of the termite mound myth of FGM
origin, which Tashi perceives as a "gift" of enlightenment: "as he continues to
untangle the threads of mystery that keep me enmeshed. *Chère* Madame, he
says, do you realize that the greatest curse in some African countries is not
'son of a bitch' but 'son of an uncircumcised mother'"? (275). He explains that
"these early uncircumcised women . . . [may have been] slaves. Slaves of other
indigenous Africans and slaves of invading Arabs . . . Originally bushwomen or
women from the African rainforest. We know that these people, small, gentle,
completely at one with their environment, like, if you will forgive my frank-
ness, elongated genitals," made that way from pulling so much on them, for
pleasure (275). Pierre says such genitalia became known "among European
anthropologists, as 'the Hottentot apron.' . . . these women with their generous labia and fat clitorises were considered monstrous" (276). Pierre's analysis
offers arguments some feminist scholars and social scientists have speculated
regarding treatments and theories of darker-skinned or subaltern women.

Walker explicitly connects the supposed goddesses, and related cultures,
of prehistory, for whom the "Hottentot Venus" was named, a real woman
who became a spectacle in nineteenth-century Europe.[11] Pierre continues,
"But what is less noted about these people, these women, is that in their own
ancient societies they owned their bodies, including their vulvas, and touched
them as much as they like. In short, *Chère* Madame Johnson, early African
woman, the mother of womankind, was notoriously free!" (Walker 1992, 276).
This reported land of free and happy women gives Tashi great comfort, paralleling the hopes of goddess culture. Fictional characters thus confirm a contested view of history and receive comfort similar to what some proponents
of goddess culture say they experience in their beliefs and practices of the
myth. Tashi writes, "Dying now does not frighten me. The execution is to take
place where this government has executed so many others, the soccer field. I
will refuse the blindfold so that I can see far in all directions. I will concentrate
on the beauty of one blue hill in the distance, and for me, that moment will be
eternity" (276–77). Tashi accepts dying for this vision Pierre has offered, of a
shining potential beauty in the distance (past or future), of embodying womanhood. Her hope reflects hopes of goddess culture as well, that women can

remember, reclaim, and find inspiration in the past, imagined as a time when women were revered and had control of their lives and bodies, as means of inspiring women and potentially all society today.

Late in the novel, in a scene from prison, Tashi interacts with her care-taker and spiritual daughter, Mbati, to whom she entrusts the carved figurine playing with her genitals: "the little sacred figure of Nyanda—I have named her, choosing a word that floated up while I held her in my hands—carefully wrapped in my most beautiful scarf" (Walker 1992, 270). She leaves this figure she thinks of as goddesslike with Mbati to give to her daughter. Mbati says the figure "looks like you" (170). Tashi answers: "No. . . . I could never have that look of confidence. Of pride. Of peace. Neither of us can have it, because self-possession will always be impossible for us to claim. But perhaps your daugh-ter" (271). This hopeful message anticipates the novel's final scene, which offers a message of resistance from the surviving women of Tashi's country. Many women gather silently along the route Tashi walks to her execution because they

> have been warned they must not sing. Rockjawed men with machine guns stand facing them. But women will be women. Each woman standing beside the path holds a red-beribboned, closely swaddled baby in her arms, and as I pass, the bottom wrappings fall. The women then place the babies on their shoulder or on their heads, where they kick their naked legs, smile with pleasure, screech with terror, or occasionally wave. It is a protest and celebration the men threat-ening them do not even recognize. (1992, 278)

These proud and hopeful mothers hold their intact infant daughters up—naked genitalia on display—to show Tashi as she walks to her execution that they will not have these girls mutilated. Other friends unfurl a banner read-ing, "*RESISTANCE* IS THE SECRET OF JOY!" (279). Walker thus reflects the reality that women are punished in our patriarchy, while also embracing and projecting some mythic hope that women might realize a better future by resisting. To achieve their consciousness of resistance, the women in this story need a savior, embodied in Tashi, who spans cultures—living in the United States as Evelyn and becoming educated about much of the world and his-tory (including the goddess myth). She learns and shares ancient history and myths of her African homeland, including a prehistoric, much happier, if not outright utopian time of women and goddesses.

In the real world, though FGM is condemned by many inside and outside of Africa and other parts of the world, the practice continues to be a reality for many women and girls, as do all forms of violence toward women. The sad story of Tashi from a generation ago is still the story of many real women in our world. The message of resistance is powerfully resonant, a kind of hope-punk: optimism in the face of oppression.[12] This novel helps raise awareness of FGM, its impact on women's lives, and its foundation in myth and ritual. Walker's myth of an earlier, happier time is appealing and fictionally reflects women fighting oppression to work toward change. Perhaps the novel helps raise awareness and inspire some real-world change, in the sense of reducing FGM in the world today. With a few references to a potential woman-forward, goddess-rich past, the novel rests in hope, that women can organize, build communities, resist, and persist.

Conclusion

These works by Silko and Walker shine as beautifully written and are nota-ble for being fairly realistic compared to many others I discuss. The works show how much women suffer under patriarchy but also how we can carve out spaces, like matrices within hidden or overlooked cracks, of (potentially cryptic) matriarchy and goddess- or woman-forward consciousness within the patriarchy. Though Tashi and Hattie and other women characters suffer greatly, they also end in places of hope rather than despair. BIPOC women writers Silko and Walker project hopeful, inspiring messages within fictional but still recognizably troubled worlds full of problems and prejudices. From a feminist perspective, these writers shift the gaze from a typically male one, beyond spaces where women exist only in terms by which white men per-ceive and judge them. While these women characters are judged and treated harshly, especially by men, they also find ways of projecting and enacting other possible lives and messages beyond those dictated by the men in charge in their worlds. We return to other more recent writers who shift gaze, reclaim some agency for women, and offer hope similarly in chapter 6, but first we visit some of the most popular genres dominated by men, in the film and television industries, where goddesses and powerful women are perceived through a more classically male lens as troubling, threatening, and disruptive.

Chapter 4

The Bad Goddess in Film and Television

Numerous films, television shows, music, comics, and other popular culture today also embrace a goddess perspective, but in film and television what prevails mainly are vilified, "bad goddess" worlds and perspectives. Considering that most television shows and films are written, produced, and directed by men, it is not surprising that it is harder to find positive portrayals there of goddesses or women-centered cultures. Patterns of goddesses and women's cultures that our culture appropriates and reimagines today tend to fit one of two extremes—wonderful or awful—reflecting the writer's or creator's perspective or bias. Our dualistic ways of conceiving of goddesses and matriarchy form clear patterns, and films and television by men portray goddess worlds in predominantly negative ways.

Film Depictions of Goddesses and Matriarchy

Thor: Ragnarok and Hela

The Marvel Comics universe superhero film *Thor: Ragnarok* (2017), based very loosely on Norse mythology, introduces the goddess Hela, Odin's first-born child, whom he introduces to Thor and Loki as "the Goddess of Death. Hela. My firstborn. Your sister" (*Thor* 2017). The script directions say, "That hits Thor hard. Loki can't believe what he's hearing." Thus this "goddess" with "violent appetites" that even Odin cannot "control" enters the scene, literally chaotically, upon her father's death, after he lovingly bids his sons farewell: "A piercing scream cuts the air as a figure is hurtled out of the portal, crashing out of this dimensional rift is Hela." Hela arrives hellishly, immediately antagonistic and demanding obedience. The film's Wikipedia page describes her: "Hela was the leader of Asgard's armies, conquering the Nine Realms with Odin, but Odin imprisoned her and wrote her out of history after he feared that she had become too ambitious and powerful. Odin then dies and Hela appears, destroying Thor's hammer Mjolnir. She pursues Thor and Loki as they attempt to flee."

Most of the film follows Thor and Loki's united efforts to defeat their evil sister, played by multiple-award-winner Cate Blanchett since "Marvel has been on the hunt for a 'bad-ass female'" (Kit 2015).[1] Enter the Goddess of Death, a vehicle for a fine actress to play an evil, powerful woman: "a genocidal monster slaughtering countless people in her pursuit of limitless power" (Mendelson 2017). Fans want more women on the screen to show a fuller range of possible characters and story arcs for women, beyond love interests or mothers, claiming that feminine representation is generally "underwhelming" in the MCU and in film in general: "If you do a Google search for lists of the best movie villains, those that feature women at all overwhelmingly cite characters that showed up onscreen 20-plus years ago—Nurse Ratched, the Wicked Witch of the West, Annie Wilkes" (Wardlow 2017). A 2018 search found many other women who have appeared as villains on-screen besides those three, but the call for a fuller range of women characters on-screen resonates with many.[2]

Hela deepens the MCU's range of women with a major actress playing a goddess on film in a way that fits a pattern of goddesses, or very powerful women characters generally, as forces of chaos, darkness, and violence, often perceived as even worse, less expected or more unnatural, than their villainous male counterparts. An early scene emphasizes Hela's extreme strength as she destroys hero Thor's hammer and bests both him and Loki in battle. But she uses her power for evil, the opposite of good, heroic god characters like Thor and Odin. Loki, the previous bad guy in these films, pales against Hela, seeming good-ish, allying with his brother against her. Blanchett says of her character's motivation: "She's been banished for a very long time and . . . [is] little bit cross. . . . There's a side of Death, which can be gentle and kind, and there's a side of Death, which can be brutal and savage depending on whose death it is. [She has] a lot of unresolved issues with Asgard [and] the more havoc she wreaks the stronger she becomes" (Cook 2017). This angry, brutal, powerful goddess from the dark side feeds on havoc or chaos "to symbolically castrate Thor then rain fire down on an entire kingdom" (Zinski 2017). Castrating, reveling in anger, feeding off chaos, demanding obedience are Hollywood goddess qualities—a far cry from the peaceful, loving mother goddess of goddess culture.

Although much of the rest of the film is "self-mocking" and "in on-the-joke witty," with "a morbid sense of humor" (Mendelson 2017), Hela shares in little of the laughter; she is deadly serious and angry, as in a scene near their final battle, where Thor shows humor but not Hela. He comments wittily on her "redecorating" of Asgard, their home, "I love what you've done with the place," while she responds seriously, "It seems our father's solution to every problem was to cover it up" (*Thor* 2017). When Thor tells her that their father told them both they were worthy, she replies: "You see, you never knew him, not at his best [nostalgic sigh]. Odin and I drowned entire civilizations in blood and tears. Where do you think all this gold came from? And then one day he decided to become a benevolent king. To foster peace, to protect life [with teeth]. To have you." Hela's anger shines through this exchange; she has no wish to reconcile with her brother. Thor acknowledges her extreme anger: "I understand why you're angry. And you are my sister, and technically have a claim to the throne. And believe me, I would love for someone else to rule. But it can't be you. You're just, the worst," to which she replies unrelentingly, "Okay, get up. You're in my seat." The two then agree briefly on one of their father's other sayings, which Thor starts: "a wise king never seeks out war," and Hela finishes, "But must always be ready for it." But this shared memory doesn't bring the siblings together; instead they charge each other in battle. Hela rages at her father having turned "good" and begetting a "good" son, Thor, who sees her in equally bad terms, "You're just, the worst," and the audience likely agrees with the hero protagonist.

The film portrays Hela as dark, literally: dark hair, dark makeup, dark clothes, horned (like Satan), interested in death and destruction, and almost all-powerful, a fearsome goddess indeed. Even her humor is dark and mean-spirited, as when she rips out one of Thor's eyes during a fight: "Now you remind me of Dad" (Odin wears an eye patch). Thor's clever humor and spirit keep viewers on his side, but our hero's powers are not enough to defeat Hela on his own. He must gather forces to collectively fight her. Hela also gathers forces but in a violent and threatening way, without Thor's wit and likeability. He finds inspiration conversing with a vision of Odin, then deals a mighty blow with his lightning power. Audiences cheer, as the stage directions show: "Thor and Hela are ENGULFED in a bolt of lightning!! KA-BOOM! Hela is BLASTED OUT of the lightning and sent CRASHING into the streets of Asgard. Her costume is tattered, the black extensions of her power hanging off her body in some places. She appears to be unconscious!" Though Thor becomes "a living storm," even his "biggest lightning blast in the history of lightning . . . did nothing," so strong is Hela. Thor realizes he and his band of helpers need Ragnarok—a chaotic final battle they had thought they needed to prevent: "Asgard's not a place, it's a people. This was never about stopping Ragnarok. It was about causing Ragnarok" (*Thor* 2017). Thor and Loki, former enemies now working together, help survivors escape and resurrect the demon Surtur to destroy Asgard. A Valkyrie (woman warrior) helps them apparently kill Hela, but fans anticipate a return of the popular Hela, an incredibly strong and powerful but also evil cinematic goddess.

In actual Norse mythology, the being Hel (the more common spelling in texts) rules over the underworld (Crossley-Holland 1980, 33–34). While she is sometimes perceived as a goddess (and giantess), she is traditionally portrayed as less powerful and less negative than the MCU version of the character. She is still dangerous and of a disreputable family, with the trickster Loki as her father, according to thirteenth-century Icelandic folklore scholar Snorri Sturluson: "generally presented as being rather greedy, harsh, and cruel, or at least indifferent to the concerns of both the living and the dead. However, her personality is little-developed" (Crossley-Holland 1980, 33), as she features prominently in only one story, "The Death of Baldur" (McCoy n.d.). Many scholars consider her "more of a late literary personification of the grave than a goddess who was actually worshiped or appeased in her own right," but this question has not been answered (McCoy n.d.). Other scholarly speculation about her includes that of folklorist Jacob Grimm, who "theorized that Hel (whom he refers to here as Halja, the theorized Proto-Germanic form of the term) is essentially," according to the "Hel (being)" Wikipedia page, an "image of a greedy, unrestoring, female deity ... [with] affinity to the Indian Bhavani ... likewise called Kali or Mahakali, the great black goddess. In the underworld she is supposed to sit in judgment on souls ... exceedingly like Halja ... one of the oldest and commonest conceptions of our heathenism." Hela is fearsome and powerful in traditional lore, but Hollywood exaggerates what little is known of her into a more powerfully malevolent being than how she appears when such goddesses originated and figured in myths. Just as with most ancient goddesses, our culture appropriates this one, for a renowned actress to shine as a female villain. Audiences enjoy hating her character, who is made much worse than the actual goddess of another culture and time.

In a pattern typical of films, television series, and comic books, Odin and Thor are also different in the films from their original mythic versions. Odin in particular is more benevolent, according to his page on the MCU Wiki: "Odin ... protector of the Nine Realms, father of Hela and Thor, the adoptive father of Loki, and husband of Frigga. During the ancient times, he was worshiped as the god of wisdom by the inhabitants of Earth. Once the greatest

warrior in all the Nine Realms, over the centuries he learned how to appreciate peace, eventually banishing his own daughter to Hel when she attempted
to subjugate the entire universe" and so on, helping his son Thor to become
the good hero of the films and comics. Odin parallels the Judeo-Christian
God, while Thor parallels Christ in his goodness, son of a father-god who
defeats evil in forms of a serpent and an evil trickster, champions humans,
and even gives up his life for them.[3] Many superheroes are Christ-like, making their fathers parallel to the Judeo-Christian God (Smith 2017).[4] One indicator of Odin's Judeo-Christian godliness is his portrayal by one of the most
revered actors of our day, Sir Anthony Hopkins, whose looks evoke God—a
thoughtful old man with a beard—at least as God is typically portrayed in
much art and film. The way Odin was actually perceived by the Norse who
worshiped him differs, according to oldest recorded sources of Norse myth,
the thirteenth-century Edda. Odin of old was probably inspired by Germanic
war gods as "terrible, arrogant and capricious, he inspired victory and determined defeat; . . . he required propitiation with human and animal sacrifice"
(Crossley-Holland 1980, xxvi).

Filmmakers appropriate ancient godly characters from another culture
and change details to make Odin feel more familiar and thus admirable by
many in our culture. To contrast the absolute good of Odin and Thor, who
were traditionally more ambiguous and complex, Loki and Hel, also more
ambiguous and complicated in older sources, become in these films extreme
forces of darkness or evil. The evil goddess Hela is worse than Loki here, who
teams up in this film (uniquely) with his do-gooder brother against their even
worse sister—*that* is how bad Hela is.

Many fans appreciate another strong female character in the film, the
Valkyrie, perhaps based on Germanic Brynhildr (Brunhild) of legend, a
character from Sturluson's Edda and featured in Wagner's Ring cycle (Kemp
2017). Played by Tessa Thompson, this powerful Valkyrie character appeals
more than Hela. Although not a goddess, Val does have supernatural powers,
including great strength, cunning, and abilities in battle. She is also an adaptor
who has found space for herself in a new world, and she shows humor that we
enjoy. More positive than Hela, Val nonetheless doesn't embody the romanticized goddess of the goddess myth. She is in fact all too human and contemporary seeming, hard-drinking, capable with technology, neither all-powerful
nor all-knowing. While this makes for a great contemporary, complex female
film character, it provides us a flawed superhero more than a goddess. This
film's women characters are appropriations relevant to our culture and not
very reflective of actual past characters. Neither is drawn to fulfill the goddess

myth but both show how we accept the premise of goddesses and related cultures from the distant past and how we freely reimagine such beings in ways inspired by and meaningful today. Film and television versions of goddesses and goddess cultures tend to be more negatively drawn, as troubled and problematic forces linked with chaos, compared to goddesses we see in modern novels by women.

Hellboy II and The 13th Warrior

A less intense, less developed goddess, more of a humorous moment than an actual character, appears in the film *Hellboy II: The Golden Army* (2008, based on another comic book series). This nod to goddess culture as a force of darkness comes near the beginning of the film, when a twelve-foot statue that looks like a huge Venus of Willendorf is in the background in an auction scene where things go awry. In a battle not connected to her, Hellboy runs behind the giant figurine, who looms visually in a number of scenes before and during the fight, and pushes her buttocks to knock her over, deciding to use her as a weapon. This effort to knock her over requires Hellboy's supernatural strength because she is so large. As he pushes her, Hellboy offers, "Sorry, lady!" The giant stone statue's slow fall is shot from below her front side, so that her giant breasts and belly tip toward the camera slowly, accentuating them. She finally crashes down and rolls so threateningly that Liz Sherman, a firestarter character who works alongside hero Hellboy, screams, "Run!" and the heroes do so. The giant goddess does squash some of the hideous, bug-like, flying creatures the heroes are fighting, but ultimately it is the fire power of Liz Sherman that finishes them off. Although this goddess is not a primary focus nor even a character, she *is notable* just for her size—larger than the giant hero Hellboy and reminiscent of the Venus of Willendorf on a poster displayed in Greenwich Village in the 1980s (White 2003). Her exaggerated feminine features, breasts, belly, and thighs become, however unwittingly, a force of destruction and chaos, though in favor of the hero's team. This scene can be read as a whimsical, fun moment, one of many in the film, of helpful but also destructive goddess power, with threateningly huge breasts and belly as part of a deadly stone body associated symbolically with power, violence, and chaos.

In the film *The 13th Warrior* (1999), from the Michael Crichton novel *Eaters of the Dead*, loosely based on *Beowulf*, we see prehistoric goddess cultures as deadly and negative.[5] A tribe of Stone Age savages survives and harasses "Norsemen" by attacking them and eating their flesh.[6] The Stone Age tribe, called the Wendols, represent the original (tenth- to eleventh-century Old

English) epic's monster, Grendel. In a Wendol home, the Norsemen find gruesome, bloody scenes of human corpses and body parts being prepared for consumption. After vomiting at the site of corpses, the main character, Ahmed Ibn Fahdlan (Antonio Banderas), notes, "They have been ... gnawed upon." A Norseman explains, "It is said ... they eat the dead." Ahmed wonders, "What kind of a man ... could do *that*?" to which another Norseman replies, "It's not a man, it's the Wendols." Another character approaches them with a little figurine held on the end of his sword, saying, "They are here"; another man spits on the figurine; Ahmed asks, "What is it?" Another replies, "It's the mother of the Wendol," and another swats the figurine away with his sword, uttering a curse. Ahmed then picks up the figurine and gives viewers a good look at it. It is remarkably like the Venus of Willendorf (even a fairly accurate size): a rounded female body with large breasts, belly, thighs. Later, after a brutal battle scene, Ahmed approaches a corpse of a Wendol and rips from his neck a similar figurine necklace. These prehistoric people, bloodthirsty, cannibalistic "monsters," pose a grave threat to the Norsemen heroes, whose strategy is to "Kill the mother. ... Kill their leader and they will break" (*The 13th Warrior* 1999). Thus, we perceive these monsters as matriarchal, goddess-worshiping savages.

Mother Wendol awaits the final showdown in a cave where Buliwyf (Beowulf) must penetrate among fierce savages to kill her, the dark leader of chaotic goddess power. Deep in the cave, Buliwyf encounters disgusting sights, such as the decomposing heads and bodies of his Norsemen brothers, until he reaches the lair of the matriarch. We see this representative of the goddess crouching before a fire with blood-stained skin, dark-ringed eyes, and long dreadlocks decorated with sea shells, as she crouches before a fire. She dips an animal claw into dark liquid in a gourd, staring intently, while a large snake slithers over her chest and under her arms. She holds her poisoned claw high while Buliwyf approaches with his sword held high in front of him. Once she stands up, we see a few brief scenes where she looks like the "snake goddess" of Crete with a high headdress, a cinched-in waist, and actual snakes as part of her décor. She makes growling noises as she breathes and cat-like noises when they start fighting a fierce but short-lived battle. She manages to scratch Buliwyf's shoulder with her poisoned claw just before he decapitates her. Although Buliwyf kills the matriarchal figure of this mother goddess culture to save his people, she fatally poisons Buliwyf, who dies thereafter among his Norsemen.[7]

This film's portrayal of Paleolithic culture is inaccurate, primarily in suggesting they ate human flesh, which no evidence indicates, but also in suggesting they might have lived deep in caves. So-called cavemen didn't live in caves because caves are too humid and dark. They lived in stone shelters, fully open to the air and sun, while caves were likely ritual spaces, which may be what the film meant in showing the mother preparing for battle there. But the key problematic contention of the film is that prehistoric people were "monstrous," literally representing the monster from Beowulf, Grendel. These savage killers are a far cry from goddess culture utopias. The film nonetheless accepts as true a prehistory of matriarchy and goddess worship, though recasting that past as chaotically bad. Some prehistorians believe that most Upper Paleolithic people may have lived fairly peaceful lives.[8] Regardless of scientific knowledge or speculation about actual prehistoric ancestors, Hollywood appropriates an imagined past to portray contemporary perspectives.

Wicker Man (1973 and 2006)

Another film portrayal of imagined goddess culture as a troubling force is *Wicker Man*, with two versions, one directed by Robin Hardy starring Christopher Lee (1973), and one directed by Neil LaBute starring Nicolas Cage (2006). Both depict a policeman who visits an isolated island in search of a missing woman and finds island inhabitants practicing a form of paganism that stretches back to pre-Christian times and that includes human sacrifice. Although the 1973 British version has received much greater critical praise and characterizes the policeman as a Christian man appalled by the island people's Celtic pagan practices, it is the American version, with a cult following who find it absurdly funny, that more fully explores the mother goddess theme. In both cases, though, paganism and goddess worship are portrayed as existing in our modern world as primarily negative and deadly practices from a contemporary perspective. In both, pagan rituals require sacrificing humans, and each male main character, whose morals, laws, and character are undervalued by these cultures, embody typical heroism in our culture. And each becomes a literal burning man.

In the American remake, policeman Edward Malus (Nicolas Cage) investigates his ex-fiancée's daughter Rowan's disappearance on an island where pagans are led by Sister Summersisle (played by Ellen Burstyn), who explains their culture to Malus after he tells her he suspects the girl he seeks was murdered: "We don't murder here," to which Malus replies skeptically, "Uh, huh. Yeah. Well, even if a victim *complies*, it's still murder." Malus asks angrily to whom they sacrifice and hears: "To the Great Mother Goddess who rules this island, with me as her earthly representative. . . . I'm the spiritual *heart* of this colony." Malus continues, "You honestly encourage this sort of worship?" Summersisle takes his arm and says, "My Celtic ancestors, all the way back, rebelled against the suppression of the feminine. So in the late seventeenth century, they fled to the New World. Unfortunately, they settled near Salem. So when they saw that the persecution continued, even here, ah, well, that started a long and painful migration westward." Her ancestors migrated west to settle the island, she continues, and "vowed *never* to enter into that other world again." Malus is incredulous: "How's that possible? You can't just—" but she interrupts him with her explanation, delivered among chuckles, "Oh, those pioneers needed little urging to isolate. They were looking for a simpler way of life." Even those who leave, like the woman Malus knew, eventually return, preferring their culture, she claims.

On this matriarchal island that embodies an imagined version of goddess culture, Malus worries that men are reduced to "second-class citizens." But Mother Summersisle assures him, "We love our men [she smiles]. We're just not subservient to them. The men are a very important part of our little colony [she chuckles]. Breeding, you know." Horrified, Malus invokes the god of patriarchy: "God! Quite a little racket you've got going for yourself here. Breeding? Sounds like *inbreeding* to me." Summersisle is unphased by his valorizing of love: "We procreate because that's the desire of the Goddess. To assure ourselves of worthy offspring. The strongest, the finest, the most sturdy of our kind," and Malus angrily responds, "I see. Female, right? And what if someone just happens to have a boy? What do you do then?" Summersisle says, "That depends" and turns away. This exchange underlines some goddess myth perspectives: the worship of mother goddess and matriarchy are linked; mother goddess followers claim love and compassion as key, hence Summersisle's emphasizing she is "spiritual *heart* of this colony"; goddess worshippers live in pastoral, agricultural, beautiful communities, where beekeeping and other agricultural activity form the film's backdrop; women were historically persecuted by Christians, first in Europe, where a "suppression of the feminine" drove them out, and then in the New World, where women "witches" were persecuted in Salem; and goddess worshippers are "not subservient" to men, who are valued as breeders for them. This goddess culture, however, is presented as a horror-scape from Malus's perspective.

Malus worries they've killed someone he'd come to perceive as his daughter (Rowan), but in fact both the girl and his former fiancée are still alive and part of the goddess culture on the island. His "father love" compels him to search for Rowan, presumably meant to contrast the colder, calculated emotions of the vilified mother goddess cult's distorted "mother love." He feels that "something bad is about to happen" but persists in trying to best Sister Summersisle and "save" Rowan. He tries to rally the men in the village to help him and challenges some of the women, but no one pays much attention to him— the men are passive, the women laugh at him. He frantically runs around the pastoral landscape searching for Rowan and finds the ferryman's corpse while masked girls observe. The "sisters," as all the women on the island call each other, plot against him, he thinks. At one point, Malus brutally punches one of the strongest-looking women in the face in anger and knocks another unconscious. His frantic energy seems crazy, while the women seem cultishly calm.

The ritual climax of the film shows residents wearing white clothes and masks engaging in incantations, with odd hairstyles, and words about needing to "balance the forces of dark and light." Malus again punches a woman, then runs away with a girl bound up in a white dress with a flower wreath in her hair—Rowan, who leads him to a clearing where everyone is waiting. Sister Summersisle declares: "You have been chosen to die a martyr's death. You will sit beside the gods and goddesses for all of eternity." Malus angrily threatens to shoot her and tries to escape, but they tell him: "It is a great honor, one that you cannot refuse. It is ordained. There is no way out." He screams "Stay back! You bitches! You bitches! This is murder! Murder! You'll all be guilty! And you're doing it for nothing! Killing me won't bring back your goddamn honey!" alluding to their beekeeping. But his sacrifice proceeds according to plan as the women chant, "The drone must die!" Malus is caged into a wicker shape of a man and burned alive, screaming. The women continue to chant, smile, and even film the great fire, and Rowan, who is possibly or at least figuratively Malus's daughter, participates as well. His masculine anger—at "bitches"—succumbs to a calm-but-deadly matriarchy.

The film ends by showing island women seeking new male victims in a bar in Seattle. We hear bees buzzing in this final scene, echoing Malus's final screams, and a new man walks unwittingly into the honey trap. Malus's patriarchal protests appear hysterical and powerless on Summersisle. The name Malus could mean "bad phallus," combining the Latin *mal* for evil and a shortening of the *-allus* part of *phallus*. Non-goddess-worshiping men seem to be so conceived from this matriarchal perspective. Malus's ineffectual protests and anger might signal how the audience is meant to respond to the women on the island. Although Cage overplays his role and acts extremely emotionally, which cult followers of the film laugh at, his murder is troubling. These predatory women may have a lovely, pastoral community, especially from an insider perspective, but from the outside, or from patriarchy's perspective, it appears horrific. These goddess-worshipers understand the modern world and presumably feel their matriarchy is superior, and perhaps that their history of suffering violence from European Christian cultures merits their abuse of some male members of that external mainstream society. But the film manipulates viewers into perceiving this goddess culture as weird, brutal, unjust, and terrifying.

The original 1973 film is typically classified as a horror genre film. In that script too there is some explanation of the pagan origins of the ritual:

> In pagan times, however, these dances were not simply picturesque jigs. They were frenzied rites ending in a sacrifice by which the dancers hoped desperately to win over the goddess of the fields. In good times, they offered produce to the gods and slaughtered animals, but in bad years, when the harvest had been poor, the sacrifice was a human being. In some cultures, it would be the king himself. In others, the most beloved virgin. Very often he or she would be kept hidden for months preceding the ceremony, just as the Sun is hidden from the Earth in winter. [Various methods are detailed] . . . The priest thus represented the goddess reborn and guaranteed another successful harvest next year.

This film also shows the policeman sacrificed because the locals believe this might help their failing crops (apples here). While Malus dies screaming things like "bitches" and "murder," Sergeant Howie, the sacrificed outsider policeman in the 1973 version, dies protesting that he believes in Jesus Christ and the eternal rest he brings. His testimonials are interspersed dialogically with the ritual words of the "heathens," though the final word of the film is "cuckoo," probably suggesting paganism is cuckoo.

The *Wicker Man* films raise a specter of goddess-worshiping cultures that share some aspects of contemporary ideas of goddess culture as matriarchal and agricultural and as involving unusual pagan survivals, though these become horrific human sacrifices in these films. But the films also incorporate modern clothes and other details, like cars and phones. Both show brutish cruelties toward men. These films try to answer questions like "If versions of pagan cultures still exist in our world, what would they be like?" and "How would these surviving pagan cultures clash with contemporary cultures today?" The fictional answers these films offer seem bizarre and frightening—hence their classification as horror films, and the upstanding, patriarchal (police)men's outrage, especially extreme in Malus's case. But many real-world neo-pagan or New Age goddess believers and practitioners today do not perceive such bizarre and dark aspects to the religion or related subcultures. Many in our culture are also neither believers nor practitioners of specific goddess faiths or practices but conceive of past goddesses in positive ways and imagine related, possibly matriarchal cultures having been or potentially being superior to our own, especially for women. They would likely find these films preposterous or at least misguided.

But ultimately all these films are reflections and creations of our culture, including our stereotypes, worldviews, biases, hopes, and anxieties. Our world, full of films, television shows, books, and other media, shows that we have adopted some faith in goddess-centered prehistory and possibly matriarchies, even when particular versions of that myth vary dramatically. Scientists believe it unlikely that matriarchal cultures existed long term or as utopias, attesting that we cannot know specifics of ancient rituals, ceremonies, myths, or beliefs, so modern pagan or New Age practices and beliefs are also primarily reflections of our world.[9] These films' myths are thus as invented and imaginary as any other contemporary version of goddesses and their cultures or myths. There is more appropriative imagination than actual continuation or accurate recreation of the distant past in all our current goddess myths.

In the major blockbuster films that we've considered, with their big stars and budgets, prehistoric mother goddesses and matriarchs assumed to have really existed are exaggerated as villainous, chaotic, deadly forces of feminine power that disrupt the social order of today's mainstream culture. Goddesses and their worlds constitute a mythic level of chaos, the opposite of cosmos. These films at least partly reflect our own culture's patriarchal worldview that powerful women are a scary and threatening force better avoided, or that at least should be mocked, rather than embraced or perceived in any positive way.[10] None of these films leaves us longing for goddess predominance or actual matriarchy in our world. Some of the novels we examine (in chapter 5) offer contrasting messages that alternatively romanticize goddess culture and matriarchies. But before we turn to such popular genre fiction, let us consider television shows that incorporate goddesses.

Television Depictions of Goddesses

Buffy the Vampire Slayer and Angel

Much beloved, critically acclaimed, fun, and serious television series *Buffy the Vampire Slayer* (1997–2003) features Buffy Summers as a spunky, resilient high school student with special powers to slay vampires and other monstrous beings. This series and its spin-off, *Angel* (1999–2004) were created by Joss Whedon. The "Buffyverse" conceives of our contemporary world as a battleground between the forces of good and evil, the latter manifesting in many supernatural creatures the heroes must fight. Certain girls are born with latent power that, around puberty, is activated to task them with fighting the many demons, monsters, and other manifestations of evil that become literal plagues in the contemporary world. In the mythology of the series, only one vampire slayer at a time is activated, then is teamed with a male "watcher" and controlled by a council of men. But many other girls around the world carry the as-yet-unactivated power, we learn late in the series. By the final season of her series, Buffy manages, with help of her "Scoobies" team, to activate all slayers worldwide, partly to empower more girls and partly to help with a giant final showdown with primal forces of evil.

Sarah Michelle Gellar plays the clever, agile, funny, appealing chosen one of her generation and fights evil with help from a band of do-gooder friends (the Scoobies)—especially the witch Willow, her watcher Giles (an adult), wise-cracking buddy Xander, prom queen Cordelia, and vengeance demon Anya. Buffy slays not only vampires but all manner of demons and monsters attracted to her small California town, which sits on a "Hellmouth." Angel (played by David Boreanaz) is Buffy's "good vampire" boyfriend, cursed to goodness by Roma people (whom he'd tormented as his evil self Angelus). After a few seasons on *Buffy* Angel gets a spin-off series, moves to Los Angeles, and with his super-vampire strength (portrayed as superhero strength with a few quirks), leads an agency to fight monsters similar to those in Buffy's world. Many of the foes in both series are presented as extremely powerful forces, sometimes originating in the distant past. In fact, some are presented as gods or the equivalent, dating to the primordial period, giving the story a mythic tinge. The most godlike prehistoric powerful beings in the series tend to be women who cause and represent chaos, wielded violently.

In *Buffy* season 5, Glorificus, or Glory, one of three gods from a hell dimension, is exiled to earth by her companions, doomed to imprisonment in the mortal body of a doctor named Ben, who sometimes emerges, while other times Glory takes control and manifests in our world. Glory the god is also known as the Beast and the Abomination, though her "true name" is never given, and in one episode the Scoobies speculate that it's possible she "predates the written word . . . pre-dates language itself" (season 5, episode 8). In her earthly embodiment, Glory will die when Ben does unless she can open a portal using what she calls her "key," a means to return to her hell dimension. The main villain in season 5, Glory is one of the toughest of Buffy's many foes.

From the first we see Glory as evil and powerful, seeking the key, a mystical energy nexus that some monks, aware of her, have hidden as a human being, who they place in Buffy's life as her little sister, Dawn. They give Buffy and all other characters implanted memories, about which Dawn knows nothing (Croft 2015). The key, Dawn's blood, will unlock an evil dimension that would allow Glory to return home and would also allow demons to come to earth. Glory regularly tortures humans, eating their energy or souls, and seems stronger than Buffy in physical fights. The monks who know about her and who created Dawn call Glory an "abomination." Glory ends up being so strong and evil—though her human counterpart Ben is good-natured, making her somewhat dualistic—that Buffy ultimately sacrifices her own life to stop this god(dess). One critic explains that Glory "functions in a Jungian sense as 'the Terrible Mother,' determined to sacrifice [the whole world] for her own self-ishness" (Croft 2015). Buffy dies because of Glory in this season, after receiving a vision from an ancient prehistoric slayer—the "First Slayer"—who tells her, "Death is your gift." Buffy has a fairly peaceful death, falling into an abyss, to save her sister and the world (season 5, episode 22). Buffy's watcher, Giles, kills Glory's human host Ben to ensure the goddess's complete demise. The next season Buffy's friends use magic to resurrect her, but her return causes her enormous suffering. She tells Spike, an evil, government-controlled vampire who becomes her boyfriend and seems to be the only one who understands:

> I was happy. Wherever I was, I was happy, at peace. I knew that everyone I cared about was all right. I knew it. And I was warm. And I was loved. And I was finished. Complete . . . . I think I was in heaven. And now I'm not [near tears]. I was torn out of there. Pulled out, by my friends. Everything here is hard and bright and violent. . . . This is Hell. Just getting through the next moment, and the one after that, knowing what I've lost. [Pause] They can never know. Never. (season 6, episode 3)

Buffy doesn't want to hurt her friends with the knowledge that she finds this world to be hell, but the viewer sees her life as full of suffering, frequently and throughout the series (Magoulick 2006). The result of Buffy's interaction with a feminine god from prehistory is death and removal from heaven into "hell," reflecting various levels of chaos caused by the actions of the goddess Glory. Glory is not a good goddess but a force of darkness and chaos for our hero Buffy.

Angel also features powerful godlike women from prehistory, first the seemingly good goddess Jasmine (season 4, 2003), who takes most of the good, main character Cordelia's life when Jasmine is born. The team sees that Cordelia's supernatural pregnancy is threatening her, so they plan to kill the baby. But Jasmine (played by Gina Torres) bursts "from Cordelia's womb in a flash of blue-green light," in which "the godly woman materializes and . . . appreciates the world around her and thanks Cordelia for giving her life. Guiltily, Angel (played by David Boreanaz) offers the woman his sword to punish him for his earlier intentions of killing her" ("Shiny Happy People (*Angel*)" Wikipedia page). All the characters then exhibit "strangely peaceful behavior" and are happy to worship Jasmine, who apparently offers them inspiration, comfort, and hope. The characters seem driven to please and worship her. She appears to want to bring about a utopian, peaceful world with no suffering, as the beautiful, loving mother goddess of everyone's dreams.

In Jasmine's first episode, "Shiny Happy People," everyone seems immediately brainwashed into loving her: they fall upon their knees when they behold her—eventually even those who watch her over the television fall under her spell. She tells Angel and his team: "For so long you've all been drowning in the fighting and the pain. I'd like to help." A TV reporter interviews her: "We want to know everything about you. Start at the beginning," and she replies, "In the beginning, before the time of man, great beings walked the earth. Untold power emanated from all quarters—the seeds of what would come to be known as good and evil. Yet there was a balance. But the shadow stretched." We thus see her origins in mythically ancient times, an earlier primordial period. In the next episode, "Magic Bullet," she gathers more followers, to whom she speaks kindly, saying things like, "My love is all around you. . . . Everything is becoming connected. . . . No one will ever have to feel lonely again." Her followers blissfully accept her promise of utopia.

But we also see un-brainwashed people perceiving a darker side to Jasmine, the goddess figure. At the end of "Shiny Happy People," one main woman team member, Fred, who bloodies herself trying to please the goddess, perceives her, uniquely, it seems, as a decaying corpse covered in insects, rather than the beautiful goddess. Jasmine then tells the others that Fred must be killed, which offers viewers the first hint, beyond our main characters' unusual demeanor, that this goddess is not *all*-loving. The Devourer, as she is also known, has a darker side—devouring humans to fuel her power. Her true, non–magically enhanced appearance includes the hideous, decaying, maggot-filled face that Fred first sees. In the "Magic Bullet" episode (season 4, episode 19), when asked what happened to people just brought into her room, Jasmine peacefully admits, "I ate them." Janet Brennan Croft (2015) summarizes her nature: "She claimed to be bringing utopia to earth, but used mind control to overcome the free will of her followers and secretly fed on the bodies of human beings. She had previously done the same in another dimension as a trial run." Angel and his team, whom Fred manages to slowly infect (or disinfect?) so that they too see the true, darker side of this goddess, then assume that the Devourer must be stopped. They believe that if left unchecked, Jasmine could destroy, rather than save, the world—slowly consuming more and more people.

Angel's son and Jasmine's father, Connor, perceives her true nature but still decides to stay allied with her, threatening Angel and the team trying to stop her, "We're gonna tear you apart" (season 4, episode 20). Though it took her years to manipulate the lives of many of the characters to get herself born into this world, and though she has formidable goddess powers, Jasmine is ultimately defeated by Angel and his team. But whether this goddess's demise is good or bad is debated in the show. For instance, in the episode "Peace Out" (season 4, episode 21) Connor tells the main characters fighting Jasmine: "All your talk about saving the world. Well, now somebody's gone and done it. Made everything right, and good [angrily]. And you can't stand it because you're all so full of yourselves [whispers in Wesley's ear]. Don't you get it? You're all alone now. All of you. You're the ones left out in the cold. You, don't, belong." Another character replies, "If belonging means following some bogus god and killing in her name, then you're damn right we don't." Jasmine promises peace and love but is controlling and demands human sacrifices and "a temple . . . something massive and awe-inspiring, yet warm and nurturing, celebrating the gentle pleasures of a peaceful, precious coexistence where violent behav—" Her speech is interrupted by violence, as she screams for her followers to kill Angel, who defeats her instead.

During the battle, Jasmine asks Angel why he "chose" this "chaos," as she perceives his world without her control. They meet on a bridge in the battle-torn city, with people wandering and screaming, crying or suffering, and Angel tells her, "Jasmine, it's over, you've lost," which she denies, "I've lost? Do you have any idea what you did?" Their dialogue continues:

ANGEL: What I had to do.

JASMINE: No. No, Angel. There are no absolutes, no right and wrong. Haven't you learned anything working for the Powers? There are only choices. I offered paradise. You chose this!

ANGEL: Because I could, because that's what you took away from us, choice.

JASMINE: And look what free will has gotten you.

ANGEL: Hey, I didn't say we were right. I said it's our right. It's what makes us human. . . . I'll die before I let you hurt anyone else. (season 4, episode 20)

The concept of free will is often connected to gods and the meaning of human life in philosophy, and Angel keeps reminding Jasmine of the high cost of her utopia—many human lives. Jasmine points out Angel's own moral ambiguity, in having killed many humans as a vampire, but he seems to think her sins are greater: "Rain of fire, blotting out the sun, enslaving mankind, and yeah, oh, yeah, hey, you eat people! . . . Thousands of people are dead because of what you've done." Jasmine responds, "And how many will die because of you? I could've stopped it, Angel. All of it. War, disease, poverty. How many precious, beautiful lives would've been saved in a handful of years? Yes, I murdered thousands to save billions. This world is doomed to drown in its own blood now" (season 4, episode 21). Her argument makes some sense, if indeed her actions would have saved billions, but heroic Angel stands firm: "The price was too high, Jasmine. Our fate has to be our own, or we're nothing."

The debate between this goddess and the male vampire hero interestingly sums up dichotomies these analyses reveal—power-hungry, chaotic destroyer versus beloved mother of utopia. The episode ends with Connor sarcastically proclaiming the result of Angel's team's actions: the "end [of] world peace . . . Congratulations!" (season 4, episode 21). A magical being whose birth from two vampires Jasmine manipulated, Connor is torn between his father (Angel) and his daughter (Jasmine), though ultimately he kills Jasmine when she's about to kill Angel. Connor's and Jasmine's questions about these acts continue after this episode, whose double-entendre title "Peace Out" raises questions of Jasmine's potential goodness. Then, the next season, Angel and his team join a literally evil law firm they've been fighting for years. This moral compromise suggests their characters are not necessarily the heroes working for the good of all mankind—a theme the show explores in the following, final season.

The goddess Jasmine remains a complex and ambiguous character, clearly portrayed as more a force for chaos than good by the main characters and in terms of the series' universe. The fourth season of *Angel* has been pretty widely criticized by fans as its worst, and Charisma Carpenter (Cordelia) was written out of the series because of her real-life pregnancy, which Whedon found annoying. Though long hailed by many as a feminist, Whedon's feminism has more recently been questioned (White 2017).[11] Croft (2015) notes that both goddesses, Glory and Jasmine, serve as a midseries "turning point, with our heroes defeating god-like beings, followed by conflicts with a seemingly more mundane evil (The Three, Wolfram and Hart), and then building to a final conflict with a primal evil (The First, The Black Thorn)." She also sees differences between the two powerful characters: "Glory is only interested in returning home at any cost, but Jasmine wants to keep the world intact yet under her control to feed her appetite for human flesh." Whatever their motivations, both goddesses' desires threaten humanity and the show's heroes.

Season 5 (2004), *Angel*'s final season, introduces another goddesslike figure from prehistory, apparently from an underworld this time, to take over the life and body of the last remaining good woman in the cast, Fred (played by Amy Acker). Illyria, who takes over Fred's body, is a powerful woman demon and another destructive force who threatens the world. She presents as a less ambiguous goddess than Jasmine, one who is initially without a good side and only interested in power and control, as when she proclaims: "My army will rise. This world will be mine once again," and, "When the world met me, it shuddered, groaned. It knelt at my feet" (season 5, episode 16, and season 5, episode 19). But after her resurrection in Fred's body, Illyria soon realizes that her power base and temple are destroyed: "It's gone. [She falls to her knees, runs her hands through the sand.] My world is gone," leaving her "unsure of my place. . . . I must learn to walk in this world" (season 5, episode 16). The team of do-gooder men fight powerful Illyria as they fought Jasmine, finding their lives disrupted by her. But this goddess character is defeated not by the men but by the modern world (where her base has evaporated), so that she is left unable to act with significant goddess-level power. Lonely without worshippers, she remains with the men, some of whom loved Fred, and whose body, somewhat altered, she still inhabits.

Illyria seems to want to live in Fred's world, though for a while the men continue trying to kill her, hoping to bring back Fred. Ultimately, they only manage to weaken Illyria somewhat before letting her help them. She becomes something of a misfit goddess, as well as an intriguingly ambiguous character at this point, offering commentary like "It always begins the same. A ruler turns a blind eye to the dealings of battles from which he cannot gain, and a deaf ear to the counsel of those closest to him. As his strength increases, so does the separation between he and his follow—[she's interrupted by one of the men shushing her]" (season 5, episode 21). She has goddess knowledge, but she is diminished by the men—being shushed while offering insight that proves to be correct. The series thus seems to be playing with an almost-feminist awareness of the power dynamics between men and women, even women as powerful and insightful as goddesses. Nonetheless, this goddess is mocked, and all the women on the team are destroyed by goddesses who use their bodies. Though Illyria adapts to our world, the series ends rather abruptly before developing the character much.

None of these examples from the "Buffyverse" is exactly a Venus-type goddess. The closest is the "good Jasmine," who offers love, peace, and a utopia for the price of some sacrifices and worship. But Jasmine's uglier devourer side cannot be tolerated as an acceptable darker side of her goodness in the series. These super-powerful goddesslike women from prehistory are to greater or lesser extents forces of darkness that bring about chaos. Even those that can be read more complexly as morally ambiguous or confused demonstrate destructive violence. They reflect duality but focus too much on the dark side, subsuming or destroying the women in the series, even the main hero, Buffy. Both series can also be read as projecting messages of strong women as threatening, dangerous, and living ultimately unhappy, even tortured lives (Magoulick 2006).[12] Whedon's work has won praise over the years as feminist, thoughtful, fun, and empowering for women. Yet he has also been criticized and his messages can be analyzed as less clearly feminist, including as details of his misdeeds toward his wife and women who worked for him have emerged. His goddesses, like his series, have their fun, witty, and interesting moments, but they ultimately project a more chaotic influence in the Buffy-verse than the good goddesses that goddess culture imagines.

True Blood

The HBO series *True Blood* (2008–2014), based on a series of novels by Charlaine Harris known as the Southern Vampire Mysteries (first published in 2001), also features a few prominent goddess-type characters. The series develops a world where all manner of supernatural beings from stories of many cultures and times periods are real and living among us in our contemporary world: vampires, witches, faeries, shapeshifters, werewolves, and more. The first season traces protagonist Sookie Stackhouse's (played by Anna Paquin) relationship with an apparently good vampire, Bill Compton (Stephen Moyer), his more ambiguous vampire friend Eric (Alexander Skarsgård), and other supernatural beings in her community, where she works as a waitress. In season 2, a two-thousand-year-old vampire "sheriff" named Godric (Allan Hyde) seeks the meaning of life and builds a church-like community that seems to want to help vampires and humans. Meanwhile, the main antagonist of that season, Maryann Forrester (Michelle Forbes), comes to their town, Bon Temps, as a mysterious, powerful, supernatural female character who worships Dionysus and is attracted to Sookie's best friend, Tara (Rutina Wesley). Maryann is generally interpreted as a Maenad—thus connecting her to mythic women; she has supernatural powers, is connected to a Greek mythic past, and appears immortal, likened by another character, Daphne, to Gaia and Isis. She possesses power to transform into a clawed, bull-like monster and mainly seems interested in manipulating humans, many of whom she can mentally control to do her will, during which time her eyes turn completely black (hinting at evil). She uses her powers to generate ecstatic, frenzied, drunken worship of Dionysus in orgies she orchestrates (*True Blood* Wiki). Maryann is at times nurturing, showing positive goddesslike qualities. But she is also frequently sadistic and murders some people. She attacks the hero, Sookie Stackhouse, and plans to sacrifice shapeshifter character Sam Merlotte (Sam Trammell), since she believes she needs to sacrifice a supernatural creature to bring Dionysus back to earth. The mayhem she causes increases throughout the season, but the good characters Sam and vampire Bill manage to trick Maryann and use their powers to kill her, saving the town from frenzy or chaos. Maryann, with supernatural powers connected to prehistory, and some motherly qualities, has goddess tinges and is notable for her mean-spirited enjoyment of creating chaos, such as violent orgies and murders.

A more clearly goddesslike antagonist in the *True Blood* series is season 5's Lilith (played by Jessica Clark). Also known as the Progenitor, Lilith is worshiped by some religious vampires, the Sanguinistas, as one of the oldest beings on earth, second only to God, and the original vampire (made by God). Humans were made to sustain her, according to the Sanguinistas' holy book (*True Blood* Wiki). She is based on the figure of Lilith from Hebrew mythology, generally considered a kind of feminine demon (stemming from earlier Sumerian myths), and often interpreted as a coequal first human created in chapter 1 of Genesis.[13] In *True Blood* Lilith is a force of chaos who tries to turn humans and vampires (who often cooperate in the series) into enemies, so that vampires see humans only as food. Lilith uses her powers to seduce each vampire into believing that she has specially chosen him or her as her "first"—to lead the other vampires. She thus turns them all against each other. She corrupts Bill, making him commit various bad acts, like killing two-thousand-year-old Guardian of the Vampire Authority Salome Agrippa, and even making him turn against his friends Sookie and Eric. When Eric sees Bill turning on him, he warns Bill about Lilith: "She's a mad god, Bill. She's nothing but destruction. Don't do it." When Bill won't listen, Sookie steps in and says, "Bill, this isn't you" (season 5, episode 12). Eventually Bill's friends bring him back to his better nature, but the goddess Lilith and her blood cause havoc and destroy many lives before Bill's redemption.

True Blood is about a main woman character with supernatural qualities. We eventually learn along with her that Sookie is part faerie and has some powers she uses for what the audience considers the greater good. She helps her friends and is goodhearted but is also often tortured in various plotlines before things are resolved. The series ends by giving her a happy ending, with a literal and extended family. Though part supernatural (with powers) and a force for good, Sookie is not a goddess in that universe. The actual goddesses in the series (or the closest to them) are presented as dark forces of chaos. Even if Sookie is considered enough like a goddess to count as a good one, the series could be seen as presenting at best an ambivalent portrayal of goddesses. Sookie is not all-powerful, and she is very much a flawed creature of this world, just trying to do her best, with some humor and joy but also much suffering.

A Hip Young Goddess in *The Magicians*

A trilogy of novels by Lev Grossman and also a SyFy television series, *The Magicians* (2015–2020) imagines college students at Brakebills University for Magical Pedagogy, where selected young people are trained as magicians. Quentin Coldwater (Jason Ralph) passes rigorous admissions tests, but his best friend Julia Wicker (Stella Maeve) is not admitted, which we later learn is because of a timeline altered to try to fix a destructive time loop. The rejected/dejected Julia is a key character who feels a need for magic and so seeks alternative avenues to develop her magical potential with a group of "hedge witches" (unofficial, noninstitutional magic practitioners) run by an expelled Brakebills student. Quentin's friends at Brakebills also become key characters: Alice, Penny, Eliot, Kady, Margo, and a few others, including some teachers. Some of these students try to summon Quentin's girlfriend, Alice's, dead brother, who had attended Brakebills years earlier. But instead they accidentally summon the Beast, whom Quentin is warned about in dreams he doesn't heed. The Beast stems from a magical universe with portals to this world, named Fillory, similar to C. S. Lewis's Narnia, an alternate, magically accessible land. Quentin's love of Fillory novels helps him and his friends navigate there to eventually solve the mystery and plague of the Beast, who attacks Brakebills and threatens everyone's access to magic. Most of seasons 1 and 2 (thirteen episodes each) revolve around the story arc of stopping the Beast and dealing with the aftermath of his destructiveness. His defeat is achieved only at great personal cost to the band of students and the world at large. At the end of season 1, Alice gives her life and Quentin is deeply wounded, and by the end of season 2, the source of all magic in all worlds, a wellspring located in Fillory, is polluted as a result of these battles.

Both the novel and series embrace the idea that doing magic is hard work, as Eliot explains early in the first novel: "'The reasons why most people can't do magic? Well.' Eliot held up a long, thin finger. 'One, it's very hard, and they're not smart enough. Two, it's very hard, and they're not obsessive and miserable enough to do all the work you have to do to do it right'" (Grossman 2009, 44). These characters are often miserable and bear a lot of worldly weight. The part of the show that involves a goddess character surrounds Julia's quest to acquire magical skills outside of Brakebills. As her self-trained hedge-witch powers grow, Julia gathers a group of other outsider magicians interested in "religious magic," including Kady, who was in Quentin's class before being expelled from Brakebills. These outsider magicians seek to summon a "god," which turns out to be the goddess Persephone, who they hope will give them power to rewrite the past, including reviving dead characters and erasing bad acts. Julia proceeds in this quest in spite of prophetically troubling dreams that she ignores. Julia and her hedge-witch friends' ceremony goes terribly wrong when they actually summon Reynard the Fox, conceived of in this universe as a troubled god, son of Persephone, who kills many and rapes and impregnates Julia, leaving her deeply traumatized.

In the season 1 finale, Julia foils the other students' plans to kill the Beast in Fillory in order to kill Reynard, but she fails. Alice (Olivia Dudley) then sacrifices her life to transform herself into a powerful but evil being to kill the Beast; many lives and magic itself are casualties. Julia spends most of season 2 trying to terminate her pregnancy and defeat Reynard, which takes a while. She loses her shade (soul) in the process, leaving her amoral and detached. Alice still exists, but she is now a demon-like, evil being. Thus, the two lead women characters lose their souls and goodness, becoming troubled, powerful beings early in the series. They are tormented in a common pattern of punishing powerful women in popular culture (Magoulick 2006). Grossman even describes the way the television series develops Julia (compared to his books) as "more of a chaos agent" (Britt 2017).

As the women's stories continue and their beings evolve, they continue to change significantly in the television series compared to the books. Shadeless Julia returns Alice's shade rather than her own during a quest where she also encounters the real Persephone, also known in this series as Our Lady of the Underworld: Persephone and Hades "used to come and go like clockwork every fall and spring, but a while back, they just disappeared. . . . Ms. Persephone. She hasn't come here for a really long time and no one knows where she is" (season 2, episode 11). Everyone misses "Our Lady" and wants her back. Julia, still angry about the catastrophic results of their ritual to summon her, interprets her absence as intentional and mean-spirited, calling her a "self-centered bitch," and saying, "we were stupid to love you" (season 2, episode 11). This episode portrays the goddess as narcissistic and uncaring, as her bitter and evil son Reynard says of her: "It is all about her. Power, attention, grinding men and gods into the fucking dirt! And then she leaves!" (season 2, episode 11). But we also learn that Reynard's hatred and destructiveness are a result of loving her and feeling abandoned—probably also true of others in the underworld and generally.

Once Julia figures out how to kill Reynard (requiring another sacrificed life), Persephone finally appears to plead for Reynard's life. Julia argues, "You ignored us," and "Did you know what he was doing? Of course you did. He raped me," and "Why would I trust you? Come the fuck on, lady" (season 2, episode 11). But then she complies and lets Reynard live, and in thanks, Persephone gives Julia her shade and, we later find out, a gift of the spark of her own goddesshood. We learn in the season 2 finale that "the old gods" have "turned off the flow of magic" after the death of the Fillory gods (thanks to Quentin and Julia), so now no one except Julia has any magic left, and most of season 3 follows a quest to gather seven magical keys that the team believes will help restore magic to all realms.

There are two rape victims in the series, Julia and the Beast—who was originally a young boy in the household of the Fillory series writer, who molested the young boy for years, triggering his beastliness. Julia makes the deal with this Beast to get an enchanted knife to kill Reynard, though that plan fails, and everyone (including the audience) is then angry at Julia. We thus perceive both victims of rape as villains by the end of season 1, a troubling plot twist.[14] We are often manipulated to dislike or disapprove of powerful women characters, and this ugly twist gets worse: "Julia and Martin [the Beast] are both obsessed with getting revenge on their rapists. . . . Their trauma becomes the only thing that matters to them, and they'll destroy worlds to get their vengeance," and though Julia will get a "redemption arc, . . . no one should need a redemption arc after going through a sexual assault" (Weidenfeld 2016). Julia's treatment is troubling on several levels. Though many viewers enjoy the show overall, there are significant plot problems and some troubling messages, such as the women's power coming from semen: "Julia was raped and Alice drinks a mason jar of semen [of a Fillory god, so that] . . . semen . . . give[s] you powers" (Murray 2016).[15] From a feminist perspective, the show lacks women characters who can function in a healthy way independent of male influence. Though the women are also tortured in various ways, the same can be said for most of the men characters, so the show projects a brutal view of life for magicians (and maybe young people) generally, not just women.

Julia is troubled by the "seed" of her magic in season 3 (coming from her rapist), though it's now the only magic left, and it is powerful "white magic" that she is able to grow, as Persephone explains: "I planted a seed for you to grow. . . . It doesn't matter where it comes from. It matters what you do with it." But Julia remains angry: "I don't *want* it. I don't *accept* it, I don't want a *molecule* of his power." Persephone responds, "Do you think the chosen want to be chosen? It's not his anymore. It's yours" (season 2, episode 5).[16] Julia's conflicted feelings about the source of her magic makes the "good magic" somewhat tainted and poses questions (as in her dialogue) of the goddess's goodness. But the goddess also describes Julia as "chosen," and later that season, in a direct confrontation with the now powerless Reynard, who taunts her, Julia answers, "You feel that? Your tiny spark has grown bigger in me than it could have ever in you" (season 3, episode 12). Thus, Julia eventually realizes that her power, seeded though it may be from an evil god, can be used for good.

Julia evolves into a good goddess, but she is not romanticized; there are issues with her character, and she remains of this troubled world.[17] As her good goddess nature grows, the messenger goddess Iris visits Julia and tells her she must leave earth to train: "You fulfilled the task Our Lady Underground gave you—to grow the spark, and now you are the flame . . . [You are] A full-on goddess, correct," to which Julia gasps, "Holy shit!" (season 3, episode 13). Julia's hip response to assuming ancient power makes her feel contemporary in her goddesshood, though not particularly wise or articulate. She quickly protests her goddess-in-training duties, insisting that she should help her friends with their quest, which Julia learns is connected to the god Prometheus's power, and that the questers could let loose the Monster, a fearful creature. Iris wants Julia to learn "building and shaping worlds," but Julia can't "let go" of her human friends, who, except Alice, ignore the danger of the Monster. When all hope seems lost for the questers, Julia disobediently leaves goddess training to help, then screams when doing so makes her lose her powers, "I'm not con, connected to anything anymore" (season 3, episode 13), meaning her goddesshood is diminished. Sadly, the magic she unleashes is lost anyway. The Monster (known also as Nameless) survives in Eliot (Hale Appleman) and the powerful library (or the Order of the Library of the Neitherlands, a magical library with librarians who control much magic in this universe) takes all the magic released, so Julia again seems to make a large mistake, despite her trajectory toward good-goddesshood.

Everyone again dislikes Julia and hates Alice at this point because they don't understand that Alice tried to help keep the Monster out of Eliot. Both powerful women are diminished and magic-less. Thus, we perceive the two main women characters as punished and despised for actually being smarter and trying to do good. In season 4, the questers try to save Eliot, possessed by the godlike Monster, and to break the library's stranglehold on magic. Season 4 also introduces another goddess, "the Sister" of the Monster, who is even more fearful and chaotically destructive than her horrible brother. The Sister requires an adequate body for her reincarnation and ultimately only Julia works as host. Her very goddesshood (nascent in her again) makes Julia suitable for the Sister—a much more powerful goddess, who is evil. Julia tries to call on Persephone to help her resist the Sister, but Persephone fails (apparently dying). The twin monster gods, Nameless and his Sister, slaughter many librarians and are preparing to kill most magicians. The heroes manage to send the two bad gods (who cannot be killed) into the Seam, though the main character Quentin dies doing so. The key image viewers receive is of Stella Maeve, physically identical to Julia, as an extremely powerful and destructive goddesslike being, responsible for her best friend/our hero's death, though there is the caveat that it's not *really* her, and Julia survives (as herself) for the final season.

The message of the series in terms of the goddess characters up to this point is mixed at best. The young, emergent, goddess/not goddess Julia sometimes acts for good and sometimes makes huge mistakes and causes great harm and chaos. Fans at a major sci-fi convention in 2018 attested to "hating" her.[18] Yet even when without a soul, Julia makes some good choices and acts to help others. But many remember her selfish and harmful choices more, though perhaps most would applaud the character's fifth, final season, where she becomes a mother with a more healing arc. In a universe that posits the reality of magic, connected to gods, monsters, and some humans, goddess power is regularly questioned or presented as inadequate or even troublingly bad. Absent Persephone is dissed by her loyal servants and petitioners for much of the plot, then her power proves inadequate, and in season 5 her absence so distresses Hades that he loses control of his realm, triggering a return of the Beast in the series finale. When given power to attain her own goddess status, Julia is sickened by the perversity of the source of that power, and though she flirts with being a good goddess herself for a time, many of her actions (even some efforts to help her friends) have chaotic and destructive results. In season 4, her regained, nascent power makes her a useful conduit for a terrible, evil goddess. Embodying goddesshood makes Julia selfless at times but also shows a lack of real power and sometimes agency on her part, even as a goddess, in not perceiving the greater threats of the Beast, the Library, the Monster, and the Sister, all of which we viewers understand as deeply threatening or problematic.

Often lacking full agency and wisdom and making choices viewers dislike, Julia seems sad and angry through most of the series. Her goddesshood seems to offer little ability to perceive long-term effects of actions or to offer or receive comfort. Other goddesses in the series also seem to care minimally about humanity. Though all main characters are tortured and live troubled lives in the series, the most powerful women, especially Julia, are the most tormented and disliked, at least by some fans. Season 5 Julia is pregnant, probably because Maeve was pregnant when filming, and motherly Julia is gentler, seeming less of a threat without goddess power, and comfortably (from patriarchal perspective) domesticated. Julia's magical pregnancy advances quickly, and since the father is a traveler (Penny 23), Julia can at times tap into the fetus's power to travel (thus achieving some magic), but she also suffers psychotic episodes from it, and the baby's birth threatens Julia's life. She and the baby are fine ultimately, and the baby's power will be used to help Julia and Penny seek their scattered friends, so Julia's story ends with a hopeful magical quest. But this once-goddess, awful and good in turns, settles into a goddess culture ideal of motherhood, lending her overall character arc a taste of more romanticized goddesses we consider in chapter 5. She suffers much, loses many powers and almost her life, but seems happy, still with some power and potential, as a mother.

Goddesses in *The Magicians* are a bit different from the other series and films we've examined in their mixed, more complex aspects. Some goddesses are good (at least in terms of intentions, though not necessarily powerful enough to enact those intentions), some are ambiguous, many demonstrate little concern with humanity, and one (in Julia's body) is downright evil. Many of the most powerful beings in the series who use magic for evil, selfish, controlling, or chaotic-seeming purposes are women: Alice (at times), Librarian Zelda (at times), the Faery Queen (at times), Marina, Margo (at times), the Moon in season 5, and the Sister/Julia. There are also good sides to many of the women characters with significant power. The power of women in the series overall, even goddess power, is unpredictable and variable, making this series less completely dualistic (in terms of vilifying goddesses) of those we've reviewed, but the show still includes some typical extremes and clichés of television goddesses as dark forces of chaos. The show balances men and women characters and a few non-Western ones in ways critics appreciate, "as a sex-positive, queer, and often feminist exploration of all things magical" that offers "an understanding that life is not fair, things rarely go as you plan, and the wheel always turns. In an unpredictable world where keys open invisible doors and gods can die, you can only control one thing: how much fun you have as the ship sinks" (Fleenor 2019). The show is far from perfect but at times is fun, hopeful, and thoughtful. *The Magicians* includes momentary dips into the kind of intersectional, hopepunky rhetoric we see in chapter 6. But often, this show echoes the "bad goddess" pattern as well.

Conclusion

Many popular culture portrayals of goddesses in films and television shows today incorporate goddesslike characters as powerful female forces *not* in the vein of all-loving mother goddesses of a goddess culture myth—she who is connected to peaceful, egalitarian, and ecologically superior communities ruled by women. Rather, these pop culture goddesses tend to be negative forces that pose threats to our world. Since male-run industries like those of film and television have utterly imagined or appropriated these goddesses, it is not surprising that they are violent, threatening, disruptive, and deadly.[19] Our culture, steeped in the patriarchal male gaze, regularly perceives powerful women and goddesses as villainous forces connected to deadly, dark power. The metaphorical message is easy to read through a feminist lens: powerful women are a threat that should be feared, avoided, belittled, coopted, diminished, mocked, controlled, or destroyed. More romanticized portrayals of goddesses abound in speculative fiction works written by women (chapter 5), which embrace the goddess myth's positive perspective.

Chapter 5

The Good Goddess in Popular Fiction

Many writers of popular genre fiction, specifically speculative fiction or fantasy, are women who embrace ideas of goddess culture ideas and matriarchal prehistory in more positively spun myths. Many such women writers have for more than fifty years been portraying romanticized goddesses and matriarchy as part of a lost, lamented past, the polar opposite of the kind of darkness and chaos presented in film and television goddesses (chapter 4). These women writers tend to embrace the goddess myth via imaginative and sometimes anachronistic or biased past worlds they create where the goddess was still worshiped or remembered, though some novels bring her into modern times. Such fictional goddesses and goddess-based cultures are idealized as a kind of utopia that many goddess culture believers espouse, though sometimes the goddesses, related religions, and related communities of women are also depicted as oppressed and/or endangered, usually by our more familiar patriarchal institutions and overall cultural attitudes of more recent history.

Jean Auel's Earth's Children Series

Best-selling author Jean Auel romanticizes life in a time some presume was goddess-centered, the Upper Paleolithic era, in Europe. Her six books from the Earth's Children series, thirty-one years in the making, embrace a mother-goddess-centered, sometimes matriarchal prehistory. Auel has been praised for her research into prehistory, even being named an officer of the Ordre des Arts et des Lettres by the French minister of culture and communication in 2008. In preparing to write her books, she studied survivalist skills, Stone Age culture (things like making fire, tanning leather, knapping stone), traveled to sites of prehistoric ruins and relics, and met experts who helped her research. Some of her work draws from the premises of early Victorian archaeologists and their followers like Marija Gimbutas, which as seen have been reconsidered and questioned. Still, her series of six epic books, set in Europe about 30,000BP, have sold more than forty-five million copies worldwide and have been translated into eighteen languages. *The Clan of the Cave Bear* (the first novel in the series) was made into a motion picture directed by Michael Chapman in 1986, starring Daryl Hannah as main character Ayla.[1]

Ayla, heroine of all six novels, is incredibly resourceful, capable of amazing feats of endurance, strength, and intelligence. A Cro-Magnon human (*Homo sapiens sapiens* or modern human), she is orphaned as a young girl and raised by Neanderthals in Ice Age Europe. The series follows her life first among the Neanderthals (*The Clan of the Cave Bears*, 1980, likely set in what is now Russia or Ukraine), then among other Cro-Magnons, and eventually in what is now Dordogne, France. Ayla comes of age, developing skills as a hunter, surviving as an outsider with "the clan" (Neanderthals), then living entirely alone for years in the Ice Age. She adeptly domesticates animals and in various ways innovatively adapts to and thrives in her environment. When she meets and lives with other Cro-Magnons, she adapts further, especially to the culture of her mate, Jondalar. Much of the series (beginning toward the end of book 2, *The Valley of the Horses*, 1982) portrays her romance and long-term relationship with Jondalar—skilled lover and flintknapper. The couple travels across much of what is now Europe with their animals (horses and a wolf), showcasing the Upper Paleolithic life Auel researched. Readers follow the couple's journey and then life in proto-France. Throughout her travels and even among her original clan of Neanderthals, Ayla is kind, thoughtful, intelligent, creative, and loving, consistently drawn to spiritual insights, because of which qualities she trains and excels as a shaman.

Ayla learns various religious traditions, including the concept of a great goddess, from other Cro-Magnons when she leaves the clan of patriarchal Neanderthals and finds her people, as well as during her and Jondalar's travels (in *The Plains of Passage*, 1990). She finds that most of her fellow Cro-Magnons honor the goddess and are matriarchal, just as the goddess myth imagines of this time. Most of the other humans she meets also have comfortable and peaceful lives, usually happily welcoming the attractive and skilled pair of travelers. The last two books in the series, *The Shelters of Stone* (2002) and *The Land of Painted Caves* (2011), portray Jondalar's community in which Ayla becomes family, all living in a kind of idealized goddess culture. Ayla immerses herself especially in their goddess-focused religion after settling in this land of the Zelandonii, the name of Jondalar's people in Auel's world. The -*doni* part of this name is also the word for "mother" and "goddess"; thus their name means "people of the Mother Goddess." Ayla is recognized by the head priestess of her new home as spiritually powerful, able to tame animals (new to the Zelandonii); she is a great healer, compassionate, kind, and wise beyond her years. Thus, the woman called "the First"—chief religious leader of the whole region—takes Ayla as her main acolyte, to train as a Zelandoni, that is, shaman or priestess.

We learn along with Ayla about the Great Mother and perceive this culture's resonance with contemporary goddess culture. For instance, in the final novel, we discover the Zelandonii "didn't have a concept of private property; the notion that land could be owned did not occur to anyone. The earth was the embodiment of the Great Mother, given to Her children for all to use, but the inhabitants of a region thought of their territory as their home. Other people were free to travel anywhere, through any region, even distant ones, as long as they used consideration and generally accepted courtesies" (Auel 2011, 342–43). Auel projects a sense of humans' respecting and honoring the earth throughout her series, and we see here how the series gets its overall title of "Earth's Children." These early modern humans living close to nature are courteous, cooperative, and generally presented as happy and loving. They are also peaceful: "We all know how to kill animals that the Great Mother has given us so that we can live, but the Mother does not condone killing people" (440). There are some characters who stand as antagonists to our heroes, helping advance some plot points, but for the most part, we see a peaceful and happy world—just as the goddess myth suggests. Auel also incorporates the modern notion that women are natural mothers and inherently more loving, as in this scene when Ayla reassures a young woman worried about being a good mother: "'You will be,' Ayla said . . . 'especially once you are home with your mother. She will help you. And even if you didn't have a mother, you would fall in love with your baby just like most mothers do. It's the way the Great Mother made women, at least most women, and many men, too. You are a loving person. Amelana. You will be a fine mother'" (386). The series fictionalizes ancient humans in a way that fulfills most ideals of the goddess myth and embraces a main role for women as mothers. Women are leaders as well as mostly peaceful, loving, egalitarian, ecological, and kind.

We find other aspects of the goddess myth incorporated in a lengthy mythic poem that Auel (2002, 759) includes numerous times in the last two novels in the series and that opens:

Out of the darkness, the chaos of time,
The whirlwind gave birth to the Mother sublime.
She woke to Herself knowing life had great worth,
The dark empty void grieved the Great Mother Earth.

The poetic myth continues for seven pages, telling the story of how the Great Mother takes a lover, is lonely, and bears a son whom she almost loses to chaos. This son might be the sun, "bright glowing heat" who gives us warmth only half the day. She fights chaos to restore at least a half-day's worth of his light to our world—thus the other half of the day is cold and dark—night. The mother, feeling the loss of her son, then births all non-human creatures of earth from "her cavernous room . . . her womb," before deciding to create another:

A child who'd remember Who made the creation
A child who'd respect. And learn to protect
First Woman was born full grown and alive. (764)

This "First Woman" (proto-human) has gifts of perception, learning, discernment, and knowledge to live, but she is lonely. So the Mother finally creates "First Man" as her companion. She gives them the earth as their home:

The water, the land, and all Her creation.
To use them with care was their obligation.
It was their home to use, But not to abuse . . .
She taught them to love and to care when they mated.
Before She was through, Her children loved too.
Earth's Children were blessed. The Mother could rest. (764–65)

This myth reflects goddess culture heavily but also echoes the Judeo-Christian myth of Genesis, although replacing women in the key roles of creator-god and first human made in God's image. This first human has godlike knowledge: perception, learning, discerning, and knowledge. As in Genesis, chapter 2, the first human (though a man in Genesis) is lonely, so God makes a mate. Both myths give the human care and dominion over the rest of the earth, though the "obligation" to "use them with care" is more in line with the goddess myth than Genesis. The myth also emphasizes dualities and near the end highlights the "Gift of Pleasure and sharing" (sex and family life) that the goddess imparts to humans—a gift Auel explicitly celebrates throughout most of the novels with fairly graphic sex scenes. Though there is rape depicted in the series, for the most part Cro-Magnons mate faithfully and respect each other's bodies.

Auel positively celebrates goddess culture as peaceful, coexisting with nature, living in a balanced cosmos, emotionally loving, sexually free, creative, with mainly harmonious family dynamics, and other positive traits from matriarchal side of the dualities listed in tables 2 and 3. The books also feature actual, so-called Venus figurines, as her characters travel across great distances and see the figurines used in imaginative and mostly goddess-related contexts, such as matriarchal cultures approaching utopian status, who incorporate them in rituals. Auel's romanticized portrait of goddess culture among prehistoric humans strikes some reviewers, especially of the last few novels, as maybe a little *too* peaceful and blissful, to the point of being boring: "There is not much of a plot" in *The Land of Painted Caves* (Hand 2011).[2] Like Gimbutas and anyone who claims to know what prehistoric people believed, Auel engages in heavy speculation, some of which, like humans and Neanderthals interbreeding, has been proven true, but some details of when and where are still unclear.[3] Auel also anachronistically projects idealized, modern sensibilities onto this distant past, for instance having scenes of things akin to contemporary festivals, vacations (with hot springs), and artists (in a modern sense).

Fans appreciate the love-positive message of the series, Ayla's extraordinarily resilient and innovative spirit, and the "arresting, often strikingly vivid panorama" the novels paint of this Paleolithic past (Hand 2011). Hand (2011) describes as well the "vast leaps in the development of early modern human culture and society, often (if improbably) introduced or encouraged by Ayla herself . . . a hit parade of human cultural evolution: Hallucinogenic herbs! Discovery of paternity! Dawn of art appreciation!" Many critics have noted how remarkable Ayla's character is, taming animals, creating/discovering tools/technology, braiding her hair, using soap, birth control, and so much more.[4] She is good at everything, from cooking, to hunting, to tracking, to healing, to empathizing (a kind of proto-therapist), to sex, to mothering, to training animals, and more.[5] Yet for all the cultural developments "encouraged by Ayla herself," this amazing central character "doesn't really change during the course of her event-filled life; she remains plucky, inquisitive, inventive, brave, loyal and sometimes impulsive" (Hand 2011). One example of this stability is that an insight she achieved as a young teen just before she left the clan (in the first book), that men have a role in procreation, is the same insight she revisits at the climax of the final book (more on this below). Ayla's stability and that of her culture seem problematic, or at least unbelievable and somewhat tiresome, to some critics.

Readers debate whether Ayla (and Auel) should be called feminist. In response to Bernard Gallagher's disappointment in what he calls the "failed feminism" of *The Clan of the Cave Bear*, Clyde Wilcox (1994, 69) analyzes roles of women throughout these novels and concludes that Auel "may not portray a prehistoric feminist utopia, but taken in context they have a strongly feminist message. She depicts a pre-history that is perhaps even more egalitarian than our present society, in which men and women must share evenly the burdens and opportunities in order for both to survive." This modern, idealized ethos of men and women cooperating is appealing and what we'd expect of goddess fiction. These modern, popular works of speculative fiction written for contemporary consumption clearly draw from and support the goddess myth. But some writers question not only Auel's feminism in the novels but also her commitment to racial equality. Ayla survives the brutally patriarchal culture of the clan, where she is regularly raped and mistreated, by one Neanderthal in particular. Among what the clan calls "the Others" (Cro-Magnons), Ayla builds a better life in a matriarchal culture. Thus, Auel also incorporates some of the kind of dualities (of matriarchy versus patriarchy, with matriarchy as better) typical of the goddess myth. Ayla is a leader, but her sexuality, motherhood, and empathy, stereotypical feminine traits, are keys to her successes.

Young Ayla of *The Clan of the Cave Bear* is a particularly endearing, empowered hero, as goddess culture would hope for one following its tenets. The dramatic tension and basic storytelling of this debut novel is also generally considered superior to the later novels, in which Auel's copious descriptions of the Mother's "Gift of Pleasures," sex scenes, seem to many a descent into a romance novel trope; some perceive it as paleo-pornography. There are plenty of gratuitous, lengthy sex scenes, though many readers enjoy the romance story as a satisfying, positive, even empowering one:

> The main character, blonde Homo sapien Ayla, is adopted by a pack of Nean-
> derthals (called Flat-Heads by humans) and must learn to survive first among
> the group and then on her own. Talk about female empowerment! Ayla follows
> the classic romance novel heroine pattern: she's buxom, blonde, had a tough
> childhood, is great with animals, a natural healer, and is in possession of a Mag-
> ical Vajayjay. She also has a pet lion. Unfortunately for the plot (great for Ayla,
> bad for readers), in book two (*Valley of Horses*) she discovers cunnilingus in the
> form of Jondalar. (Dickson 2002)

Though Ayla's discovery of sexual pleasures is fun, some find it reductive. Women's fiction, perhaps especially romance novels, is often belittled in our culture at large. But the positive messages supportive of love and good sex that such novels can offer is appreciated by many readers. Romance novels have a huge fanbase and market and appeal to many around the globe, but are also taken less seriously and studied less by critics than most other genre fiction, like detective fiction, science fiction, and fantasy. Yet for more than thirty years critics have considered how romance novels "'examine, dissect, subvert, discuss, revel in and reject patriarchal constructions of masculinity,' said Sarah Frantz Lyons," helping women find a place in the world and imagine happy endings (Pearse 2015). Romance novels can show women's perseverance and empowerment (though usually in domestic spaces) and explore women's sexuality in positive ways, but the whole genre and often its main characters, including Ayla at times, rest in emotional and domestic spheres of sexuality, motherhood, and often psychological dependence. Still, Ayla appeals as an admirable, smart, spunky, happy woman.

Reducing the series to "paleo porn" and mocking the romance aspect are problematic for a few reasons, including one reader's belief that the real point of the books is Ayla's perseverance, even in the face of great adversity and pain: "The books are brimming with scenes of 'Pleasures,' but it's all noble and grown-up and terribly dull. Because, after all, the true pleasures of *The Clan of the Cave Bear* are not in the sex we all think we remember, but in Ayla's adolescent suffering and perseverance which makes her sexual awakening feel like such a revelation" (Oler 2014). Oler (2014) also likens Ayla to an early version of Katniss Everdeen (in the Hunger Games series), as "speculative fiction about a young girl's survival and resilience in an elaborately imagined authoritarian society, [as she] becomes a skilled hunter, a gritty survivor, and a protective mother," all before she is thirteen. Romance, paleo porn, coming of age, feminist goddess culture utopia, or literary dystopia—Ayla's story is debated, as it was created, in terms of social concepts relevant to our society. This is not surprising, since the books are written in and for our world, including to fictionalize modern ideas of prehistoric goddess culture. Like all speculative fiction, these books revolve around the social concerns, issues, and paradigms of the world and times from which they emerge, more than any imagined alternate world, be it past, present, future, otherworldly, or fantastical.

Heroic Ayla endures and eventually thrives, reflecting the kind of admirable spirit but also stability that many admire today and idealistically attribute to goddess culture, which is believed to have endured in peaceful, near-utopian times for many thousands of years. Adult Ayla is arguably less compelling than the youth of *The Clan of the Cave Bear* (1980),[6] who challenges the patriarchal gender restrictions of the clan, for instance teaching herself to hunt, though hunting is strictly forbidden for women. But Ayla is overall adept and intelligent enough to survive her punishment to be allowed to break tradition as a woman hunter. She also breaks the rules of the ritual of the elder male shamans at the first novel's climax, swallowing some of their secret hallucinogenic brew—partly because she must chew it and doesn't have as large a mouth as the typical Neanderthal women who perform this task. But her adoptive father Creb, who perceives she's having a vision, loves her enough, because of who she is, to let her share in this forbidden experience, which gives her apparent insight into the future. Young Ayla pushes boundaries and is extremely intelligent and resilient, enduring much abuse, including rape, banishment, and having to abandon her beloved half-Neanderthal son. Her intelligence, kindness, and forward-thinking vision—she literally sees into the twentieth century (a slight fantasy element)—connect her to us endearingly as a worthy and lovable woman of goddess culture.

But these feminist hopes that young Ayla raises deflate as the series continues and she settles into her mate's world and patterns, including that of matriarchy, ironically. Even though she is a revered medicine woman and shaman, rather than continuing to find and shape herself, she focuses more on fitting in, molding herself to Jondalar's culture's expectations, basically settling down. In addition to her less exciting narrative, in the final book, *The Land of Painted Caves* (2011), Ayla seems *too* modern, with a too-comfortable life and modern sensibilities.[7] For instance, the midsummer, modern festival-like gatherings, mint tea, easy travel, and even the nuclear family life pattern the Mother inspires all feel too familiar. While Auel is celebrated for her research on the distant past and Ice Age cultures, she is not a prehistorian, and her books speak to us via modern sensibilities, including the goddess myth, which also is problematic as an imagined, "tedious" matriarchy.[8] Celebrating humanity, our fictional potential, and women's ability to thrive and enjoy life sexually, spiritually, emotionally (mainly via a strong nuclear family here) satisfies some readers, but via a modern ethos that reflects contemporary cultural patterns and worldviews.

Romanticized, modern-value-based presentations or appropriations of the past serve and reflect our culture, but ultimately not in the way we probably think. Consider what becomes most important to Ayla as she gains insight through her largely happy life and via the human culture of her day: to be a sensual woman, a compassionate healer and counselor, a loyal and loving mate, and most importantly, a loving mother. Her emotional, sexual, and home life, along with a nurturing profession, are keys to her success, especially after the first novel. Portraying the past as superior, ecologically, socially, with shared resources, medicine, egalitarianism, and so on, may seem like a positive image to build future hopes on. And Ayla feels like a worthy feminist heroine at times. But even with her modern insights and feelings, Ayla experiences a climactic near-death experience (after some shocks, like seeing Jondalar with another woman) during a ritual in the final novel that provides her ultimate insight to help shape the future of her tribe, which could mean us. This "big reveal" lesson reflects origins of the goddess myth: that men have an active role in conceiving babies. Ayla suspects and articulates this same insight (men's role in making babies) clearly in *The Clan of the Cave Bear*, and scientists now believe humans would never *not* have understood the reproductive process in terms of both sexes being necessary.

Ayla's repetitive or static revelatory insight leads her, in the series' final pages, to share what she interprets as the Mother's call for monogamy and for *men* to be more equal in their society, including having a more active role in family life, such as caring for *their* children. Ayla, Jondalar, and their daughter live happily ever after, we assume, and Ayla's insight makes their whole society better, a message presumably meant to resonate for us. Her insight to create a better domestic life for humans by giving men responsibilities in familial life is not dissimilar to some goals of the feminist revolution of the 1970s (e.g., men sharing responsibilities of home life), which is when Auel started working on this series. It is not a bad insight, working toward stronger families and happier people with men and women as equals. But neither is this message earth-shatteringly original or particularly forward-thinking, from today's feminist perspectives. Ayla's and Auel's climax rests in building a happy shared home life, reflective of hoped-for cultural patterns of mainstream society today. Though the series' message is positive and love-forward, it is also primarily reflective of upper-class, white, mainstream, cis-heteronormative culture today. The whiteness of Auel's message and characters feels especially ironic now that we know now that the early humans in the time the books are set would have had black skin. Blonde Ayla and blue-eyed Jonadalar's stories might not have shot so quickly to, nor stayed so long at, the top of best-seller lists had the characters been accurately darker skinned.

Marion Zimmer Bradley's Avalon Series

Another phenomenally successful writer who romanticizes goddess culture and matriarchy positively, in line with the second wave of feminism, is Marion Zimmer Bradley, whose first and most famous novel in the Avalon series, *The Mists of Avalon* (1983), became an international best seller, reimagining the legend of King Arthur from the perspective of the women in his life, especially Arthur's half-sister Morgaine (in other versions of the Arthur myth named Morgan le Fay).[9] Another eight books, written partly by Diana Paxson (at times with Bradley, who is listed as author on all the books), tell various additional stories in this Avalon universe, including some set in England at earlier time periods with different characters, and some developing connections to ancient Rome and the lost Island of Atlantis. This fictional Avalon universe features many strong women characters who helped shape history connected to any aspect of broader Avalon mythology. Many characters in the universe embrace the goddess myth as fact, and the books trace various cultures, times, and places where goddess culture is presented as thriving, remembered, or diminishing. Goddess culture is always perceived in this fictional universe as a positive force that makes cultures and individuals better, and patriarchy is generally presented dualistically as a negative counterpart—a force for darkness and doom. The series embraces the goddess myth in a romanticized way.

In one novel from the series, *Ravens of Avalon* (written with Diana Paxson), we see some of the goddess philosophy of the series, reflective of the neo-pagan community. A student training to be a priestess of a Druidic religious house is quizzed by a teacher about whether there are many gods, only two, or one. The student answers (referring to another teacher), "Lhiannon teaches us that all of those are true. . . . All the goddesses, all that we see as womanly and divine, we call the Goddess. But when we pray, She wears one face or another—Maiden or Mother or Wisewoman, or Brigantia or Cathubodva" (Paxson 2007, 49). This fairly complex view of the goddess allows one to embrace various "versions" or aspects of goddesses into a single being—a concept popular with many neo-pagans. They may particularly worship, evoke, or feel inspired by a specific goddess and related traditions, but she is considered reflective of and perhaps an embodiment of the Great Goddess or goddess culture. Throughout Bradley's and Paxson's novels, women are strong, heroic characters devoted to the goddess in all her incarnations. And this goddess represents a unifying though complex force. Any difficulties these women encounter—such as Morgan le Fay being considered the villain in the Arthurian legend—are understood in this novelistic realm as history's being recast to make women the villains, whether those women are human or divine.

Bradley's *The Mists of Avalon* is the most popular novel in the series, the first published, and an international best seller. The novel is still in print in many languages and was also made into a TV miniseries (2001 by TNT, adapted by Gavin Scott, directed by Uli Edel, and starring Julianna Margulies and Anjelica Huston in lead roles). The *Washington Post* calls it "a magisterial retelling of the Arthurian legend from the perspective of the women in the story" and calls Bradley "a titan of genre fiction who extended a hand up to many, many other authors through her role as an editor" (Rosenberg 2014). The novel has four parts whose titles suggest the perspective of portraying goddess culture and its decline: "Mistress of Magic," "The High Queen," "The King Stag," and "The Prisoner in the Oak." The book traces matriarchy's descent from the time when the goddess and women ruled ("Mistress of Magic" and "The High Queen") to the gradual rise of the king, patriarchy, and Christianity's subsequent punishment and disempowering of old pagan ways (assumed here to be goddess-centered). The main protagonist is Arthur's half-sister, Morgaine, often portrayed as a villain, but here a priestess of the main seat of goddess culture—Avalon.

Bradley's version of Arthurian myth animates the protagonist Morgaine as a goodhearted, powerful, misunderstood hero who witnesses and plays an unwitting role in the tragic demise of both her king-brother (whom she loves) and of ancient goddess culture in pagan Britain, as it is being usurped by Christianity. Morgaine carries the ancient title Priestess of Avalon, descending from a long line of powerful women who practice ancient magical arts connected to worship of the Mother Goddess, which is deeply connected to nature. Avalon is a powerful natural site and source of much pagan magic in the series. Trained as a priestess of the Mother Goddess, Morgaine is groomed to succeed her Aunt Viviane as Lady of Avalon. While masked as part of a pagan ritual, Morgaine participates in a fertility rite—the Great Marriage—where she sleeps with the future high king. She and her half-brother Arthur (also masked during the rite) are both horrified the next morning when they realize they've had sex. Morgaine feels angry and deceived and is also pregnant with the child of legend who will kill his father and uncle. Another of Morgaine's aunts (not the one who presided over the ritual) maneuvers successfully to raise the son and enculturates him to hate Christianity and the court that embraces it—Arthur's Camelot.

Arthur straddles the line between honoring the old traditions (including the goddess) and embracing Christianity. Arthur's Christian wife Gwenhwyfar is portrayed here as a Christian fanatic who causes trouble and strained relations, believing her childless state is due to Arthur's stubborn pagan tolerance. Gwenhwyfar betrays to Arthur a confidence from kindly Morgaine about the child she had with Arthur (whom he hadn't known about), causing Arthur to banish Morgaine to faraway Wales. She is perceived as a queen there because the locals respect the old ways and know of her lineage, powers, and title. Morgaine and her Welsh lover become champions of the goddess traditions, are considered the local king and queen, and eventually fight Arthur for the greater kingdom—to save traditional pagan ways. The coup fails, Morgaine leaves Wales, and her son goes to Camelot, not revealing his true identity or lineage, gaining the name Mordred ("Evil Counsel") and rising to the rank of knight. Mordred tries to usurp his father's throne when most of the knights are away on the quest for the grail, and Arthur is mortally wounded in the battle. Morgaine arrives as Arthur is dying to guide him through "the mists of Avalon" for his eternal rest on the sacred island connected to the goddess and the old ways; she also vows to tell Camelot's story. After her 1999 death, Bradley's ashes were scattered at Glastonbury Tor in Somerset, England, which some consider a possible actual site of Avalon.

Morgaine's magical powers include "second sight," which the goddess gifts her, and transfiguration. The older, tribal Britains who remember the traditions revere her, and she is an extremely charismatic and sympathetic character. Readers perceive her as a victim doomed to witness the goddess's demise. Morgaine doesn't hate Christianity itself so much as the teachings and actions of certain Christians who torment her people. The end of the novel rests on her hope that the goddess will survive to some extent into our own day, through the worship of the Virgin Mary, other women saints, and cryptic rituals, which pave the way for paganism to arise again in our time. Early on in the novel, we see the kind of power the goddess had back then, even as her mysteries are forgotten. Lancelet is portrayed here as Morgaine's cousin, love interest, and one who remembers some of the goddess culture from his youth. Morgaine and he talk after having sex that she finds frustrating: Morgaine "turned away, hiding her burning face in the grass. Power from the earth seemed to flow up through her, filling her with the strength of the very goddess herself: 'You are a child of the Goddess,' she said at last. 'Do you know nothing of her Mysteries?' 'Very little, though my father once told me how I was begotten—a child of the Great Marriage between the king and the land'" (Bradley 1983, 152). Morgaine connects to goddess power here via the earth, pressing her face to the earth and feeling power flow into her. We also hear that the goddess is worshiped in "Mysteries," rituals that also convey power. Most of the main characters descend from goddess culture.

Later, in a scene after she has made love with Lancelet again, though he feels guilty for it (and she again is frustrated), she remembers her early life in the House of Maidens, when she was surrounded by so many who would have understood, and laments life choices that have brought her to this place of relative solitude, "*what have I been doing all these long years, away from my Goddess?*" (Bradley 1983, 326). Here Morgaine's despair represents an echo of modern pagans, who reinvent rituals and communities that try to recreate this imagined past and, they believe, give them a taste of the kind of experiences past women like Morgaine might have enjoyed—living connected to their goddess(es). Morgaine's longing for her previous supportive community of mostly women speaks to a modern pagan longing as well. A main pleasure of and impetus for modern pagan and New Age spiritual practices that worship the goddess are the communities they develop of like-minded people sharing moving rituals and beliefs.

Toward the end of the very long saga (about nine hundred pages) of a very long life, Morgaine returns to her beloved Isle of the Goddess, wondering about all the destruction, of the Round Table and also Avalon. She perceives, "It seemed that the world was shifting," which indeed many pagans perceive as having happened when Christianity and patriarchy replaced goddess culture (Bradley 1983, 804). Morgaine also "wondered if the Goddess had deserted them," because her power is diminished and the magical isle seems so changed (803). Again, part of the goddess myth, and something many in our culture believe, is that Christianity defeated paganism, punishing many women during that change (for instance burning many "witches") and shifting the world into a pattern that makes all our lives much harder. Women have long suffered under the patriarchy, including during Christianity. But we have little to no evidence that women's lives were significantly any better before that, though it is possible some might have been at particular places and moments. In the novel, Morgaine feels the shift of power from women and goddess culture to men and Christianity very powerfully and sadly. The shift is presented as a tragic demise of a superior, more loving and peaceful culture to a more violent and troubled one, from her perspective, and for most women, she also perceives. She realizes in her lonely later years that "she could look only within" for the goddess and any comfort (803).

But the novel rests on a hopeful rather than a sad note, as Morgaine receives a prophetic insight in a dream, via Lancelet: "Take this cup, you who have served the Goddess. For all the Gods are one God, and we are all One, who serve the One" (Bradley 1983, 871). Morgaine's vision confirms the unitary nature of the god(dess), inspiring her to reconcile with Christian nuns who built their church on an old pagan well on her sacred island. Water they give Morgaine from it to drink helps her remember: "It was like Viviane's voice in her ears: *The priestesses drink only the water of the Sacred Well*" (874). This insight—that some of the old traditions may be continuing, albeit obscurely—cheers Morgaine, and finally she comes to perceive the goddess as surviving cryptically, even among Christians; her insight is specifically inspired by Saint Brigid: "*But Brigid is not a Christian saint, she thought. . . . That is the Goddess as she is worshipped in Ireland. And I know it, and even if they think otherwise, these women know the power of the Immortal. Exile her as they may, she will prevail. The Goddess will never withdraw herself from mankind*" (877). Bradley delivers a message of hope for neo-pagans (and others), that the goddess (in various guises) exists among and within us, even if we don't realize it. We may perceive her in various glimmers in our world, for instance in women saints, in certain holy places, and even in some cryptic rituals.

Morgaine's ultimate insights reflect beliefs of goddess culture, that she may be accessed through rituals we might remember, have visions of, or recover through new ritual quests. Goddess culture is accessible even in our contemporary world, as Morgaine affirms: "The Goddess is within us, yes, but now I know that you are in the world too, now and always, just as you are in Avalon and in the hearts of all men and women. . . . *It is in Avalon, but it is here. It is everywhere. And those who have need of a sign in this world will see it always*" (Bradley 1983, 878). Avalon, representing a time when women had power (literal and figurative) and could access that power through the Great Goddess (in many guises), lives on "*everywhere.*" She can be perceived by "*those who have need,*" meaning any of us, neo-pagan or not. This imagined world creates a fictional longed-for space that many in our culture seek to recapture or recreate—or, we could argue, simply create and appropriate—in the lap of the loving goddess. Such communities can be strong, long-lasting, and powerful for participants, who, as this book openly suggests, by believing in any ancient heritage of goddess power (like Morgaine experiences) can access, remember, and experience goddess culture and insights—an appealing and comforting myth.

This re-visioning of the one of the most popular stories of ancient times, typically told from a masculine perspective with a focus on Arthur, one of the first great, revered rulers of Western civilization, is here appropriated to document goddess culture and its decline, but not ultimate defeat. This modern myth of imagined goddess culture hero Morgaine has inspired many women readers today. One woman who identifies as a witch, meaning a practitioner of neo-pagans spirituality, published on her blog an interview explaining her fulfilling personal journey:

At eighteen, I read Marion Zimmer Bradley's, *The Mists of Avalon*. In this fictional world, I found the goddess-centered spirituality that felt like home, but I assumed those ways were dead and trapped in a distant past. That book awakened a deep spiritual longing within me and I fantasized about becoming a priestess of the great goddess like those in the book. I found out years later that the author was a modern pagan priestess, drawing on her own experiences. (Michelle 2017)

There are other fans who find similar inspiration in the Avalon series to shape their lives around the kinds of beliefs and culture this novel fictionalizes. Many other readers simply enjoy the work as feminist fantasy without necessarily believing the novel's claims about goddess culture literally. Readers appreciate the Arthurian legend from a woman-centered perspective and the idea that women may have had power, can be recast as villains for the wrong reasons, or are underappreciated or ignored by history. The book has, according to numerous testaments, changed the consciousness of many women to more feminist perspectives.

Both Marion Zimmer Bradley and Diana Paxson had or have deep ties to neo-pagan and alternative religious communities. Bradley was involved in things like Darkmoon Circle, her Aquarian Order of the Restoration, and other local pagan groups in the Bay Area of California, where she lived, during the sixties, seventies, and eighties. In 1981 in Berkeley she, Paxson, and another woman incorporated the Center for Non-Traditional Religion, which later morphed into the Fellowship of the Spiral Path, an organization that continues at the time of this writing.[10] Many neo-pagan groups embrace the Avalon series and the neo-pagan, goddess-centered beliefs reflected therein. As one scholar puts it, referring to Bradley, "Clearly, she is a kindred spirit to NeoPagans" (Fry 1993, 77). Paxson and Bradley helped found the Society for Creative Anachronism and were long devoted to alternative lifestyles. Bradley in particular was long revered and held tremendous influence as an editor and publisher in science-fiction/fantasy communities, feminist spiritual communities, including neo-pagans, and among the general public. Carrol L. Fry (1993, 78) writes that Bradley's works use gender-centered myths "as a vehicle for feminist themes" and that "one could do no better than use Marian Zimmer Bradley's novels as an introduction to . . . the Earth Mother concept . . . and feminist spirituality."[11] Later in her life, Bradley claimed a return to Christianity: "I just go regularly to the Episcopalian church. . . . That pagan thing . . . I feel that I've gotten past it" (Oliver 1999). As positive and appealing as these novels and the apparent real-life commitment to goddess culture as a positive force for the world *seem* to be for her and many readers, there is sadly a darker side to Bradley's life and work.

Her daughter, Moira Greyland, came forward in 2014, fifteen years after Bradley's death from a heart attack, to allege sexual assault and severe physical and emotional abuse from ages three to twelve, by both her mother and father.[12] These allegations shocked and horrified many in the sci-fi/fantasy and pagan communities.[13] Many writers, publishers, and editors promised after learning the news to donate profits from anything connected to or inspired by Bradley's work to charities focused on victims and prevention of sexual abuse. Many neo-pagans and others express support for Greyland and other victims. Paxson (n.d.) added a "Marion Zimmer Bradley" page to her official website that stated, "I was shocked and appalled to read Moira Greyland's posts about her mother. . . . Child abuse is one of the most terrible of crimes, because the perpetrators are those who should be the victims' protectors." She also writes to clear up confusion about the two authors having lived together: the families were very close, spending holidays and Sunday teas together, and Bradley's son was at the time of her post living with Paxson. However, the families did *not* live together, Paxson attests; they maintained separate households, and Paxson knew nothing of the abuse. Greyland confirms these claims in a quote on Paxson's site.

Greyland also published poems and a book about her experience.[14] The horror of her life at home, contrasting her mother's success and influence, are painful to contemplate. Bradley not only perpetrated much abuse but publicly defended her husband (Greyland's father), Walter H. Breen, who was accused of child sexual abuse multiple times. Bradley facilitated his crimes for many years and Greyland (2015) explains more abuse she suffered: "both parents wanted me to be gay and were horrified at my being female. My mother molested me from ages 3–12. The first time I remember my father doing anything especially violent to me I was five. Yes he raped me." She says both parents hated that she was a girl, suggesting deep-seated sexism. They also believed "everyone is naturally gay" (both had same-sex relationships while married) and tried to make Greyland gay, probably leading to her anti-gay beliefs (Greyland 2015).[15] Bradley's work, especially *Mists*, remains beloved by many fans. Yet many also express shock and horror over this news and the different light it casts on all her work.

Greyland explains in an email to *The Guardian* that she waited fifteen years to speak out in hopes of preserving her mother's good influence on the lives of many: "I thought that my mother's fans would be angry with me for saying anything against someone who had championed women's rights and made so many of them feel differently about themselves and their lives. I didn't want to hurt anyone she had helped, so I just kept my mouth shut" (Flood 2014).

She says she wanted to protect her mother's reputation and work because she "regarded her life as being more important than mine" (Flood 2014). This information of Bradley's cruel abuse has caused many to reconsider *Mists*, especially one scene:

> [This] throw[s] passages . . . into a new and disturbing light. Take one passage about a Beltane ritual. Bradley writes that "The little blue-painted girl who had borne the fertilizing blood was drawn down into the arms of a sinewy old hunter, and Morgaine saw her briefly struggle and cry out, go down under his body, her legs opening to the irresistible force of nature in them." Without the context of Bradley's personal history, it is possible to read this sentence as a description of an ancient religious practice that is unsettling both in its depiction of an altered state and behavior that contemporary readers would not find acceptable. In the context of her testimony, and an article she wrote about sensual relationships between older and much younger women in literature, we lose the reassurance that the author shares our moral and ethical presumptions. (Rosenberg 2014)

Greyland (2015) notes Bradley's own words have helped many accept her troubling "moral and ethical presumptions," since during trials for her husband, Bradley "had testified, blandly," with disregard for molested children,

> and didn't bother denying tying me to a chair and attacking me with a pair of pliers, claiming she was going to pull out my teeth. With her cold admissions, nobody could put much of ANYTHING past her. In any event, since the truth came out, the pedophilic themes in her books became very obvious to people who had previously chalked them up to history or the license granted to an author of fiction.

Many former appreciators now reread/rethink Bradley's work, perceiving it differently from how they had before this news, finding "pedophilia threaded through her other work" (Jernigan 2017).

The title of a piece by Jessica Jernigan (2017) expresses the typical upset: "The Book That Made Me a Feminist Was Written by an Abuser: 'The Mists of Avalon' Changed My Life—How Do I Reconcile That with What I Now Know about Its Author?" Jernigan read *Mists* multiple times as a teenager, and felt it awakened her feminist consciousness, so that she "arrived [at] . . . a women's college in 1989 . . . ready to smash the patriarchy." But Jernigan says the only scene she finds in *Mists* that suggests abuse is that quoted by

Rosenberg, of the blue-painted girl raped in a ritual. Jernigan invokes infamous recent cases of sexual assault and misconduct in Hollywood, like that perpetrated by Harvey Weinstein, wondering if we can still appreciate artistic works associated with known abusers or rapists: "When someone says they've been assaulted, abused, harassed, I believe them. But I believe them, in part, because of lessons I absorbed from *The Mists of Avalon*." Jernigan's titular quandary is real, and she settles on a compromise in her own life of not recommending the book to others, or reading it again herself, while still keeping in her heart the character "Morgaine—what she has meant to me, what she has become in my personal mythology—while I reject Bradley." Keeping the fictional character in mind, even if only personally, while rejecting the author of that character is a compromise that points to issues of art more generally. Many have argued in recent years over the value of art created by terrible or objectionable people. Can we watch Woody Allen, marvel over art by Picasso, listen to Wagner, and so on, without remembering the terrible actions or philosophies of the artists? Does the art mean something different with the artists' crimes in mind? Is the message about the beauty of goddess culture, the power of feminists in this novel, and the actual good it may have brought about in people's lives diminished by Bradley's terrible character and awful real-life actions? Perhaps not fully, as the fiction itself still contains many positive images and powerful women characters; it doesn't overtly promote a culture of rape, violence against children, or molestation as a primary aim. But it may not be *as* feminist and uplifting as many have thought for many years. At the very least, it problematizes that conclusion. Greyland writes: "The matriarchy she created was not just and good; it was oppressive and terrifying and left her children feeling like caged animals, wishing for escape or death and much too frightened to cry" (Greyland 2018). Like all goddess myths today, the myth Bradley created is an imperfect product of our culture and times. Both Bradley's and her myth's feminism are questionable.

Classical Goddess Literary Moments

Other women writers have incorporated goddesses into their fiction in ways that match some of the gendered assumptions of goddess culture, including Eudora Welty in the short story "Circe" (1955) and Margaret Atwood in "Circe/Mud Poems" (1974) and her novella *The Penelopiad* (2005). Judith Yarnall (1994, 184) finds that both these women writers incorporate similar characteristics in their versions of Circe: "insofar as woman creates, whether as artist or mother, she is goddess; and insofar as she opens her heart to love or grief, she is mortal woman. Both Welty and Atwood touch and explore the seam between these roles." Atwood's Circe "is connected with sacred natural forces, with the moon—to which she has built temples—and with the earth—to which she keeps her head pressed, hoping to collect 'the few muted syllables left over'" (187). Yarnall sees Atwood as diminishing Circe's status as well, "priestess rather than a goddess," identified with the island's landscape (187–88). Via the twenty-four Circe poems, Atwood "explore[s] the condition of such a woman on the periphery of patriarchy and in relationship to a male equal . . . to discover the limits of power conceived as the will to dominate rather than as the capacity to love" (193). Yarnall concludes that both writers portray Circe "in an attitude of yearning," which I would argue most such backward-looking goddess myths tend toward (193). Bradley more openly evokes a similar yearning, writing it into the plot of the Avalon series, but Auel's book could also be conceived as valorizing a lost past. Such yearning applies to much speculative fiction about goddess culture in imaginings of a previous "real" goddess culture. These fictions nostalgic for and creating goddess myths differ from Madeline Miller's (2018) complex fictional version of Circe (chapter 6).

Atwood's novella *The Penelopiad* (2005) embraces goddess culture, though it is focused on a human protagonist rather than a goddess. Atwood gives voice to Odysseus's lauded wife, Penelope, admired mainly because she remains faithful in spite of the many years her husband is away at war, then lost traveling. In spite of social pressure, Penelope cleverly weaves ways to evade the suitors who would take his place and fortune. What haunts Atwood's version of this steady, smart wife is the hanging-to-death of the twelve maidens (an event referenced in Homer's *Odyssey*), at least one of whom was like a daughter to Atwood's Penelope. Upon his return, Odysseus blames the slaves for sleeping with the suitors, though Penelope had asked them to do so as part of her plot to keep the suitors at bay (in Atwood). When the men hang the maids anyway, Penelope is devastated. The girls speak, chorus-like, from the afterworld: "think, dear educated minds, of the significance of the hanging! Above the earth, up in the air, connected to the moon-governed sea by an umbilical boat-linked rope—oh, there are too many clues for you to miss it!" (130). What Atwood's chorus evokes here are connections to the Goddess myth—that women are connected to the moon and the earth, and that there is a watery birthing aspect to the girls' deaths via "umbilical . . . rope." She even ties the number of women involved to the thirteen lunar months, often a focus in goddess culture, considering, "The thirteenth was our High Priest-ess, the incarnation of Artemis herself. She was none other than—yes! Queen Penelope!" (131). Penelope is named a priestess of goddess culture; the hang-ing of the twelve maidens thus reflects patriarchal overthrow of matriarchy.

Atwood (2005, 131) builds this connection overtly: "possibly our rape and subsequent hanging represent the overthrow of a matrilineal moon-cult by an incoming group of usurping patriarchal father-god-worshipping barbarians. The chief of them, notably Odysseus, would then claim kingship by marry-ing the High Priestess of our cult, namely Penelope. No, Sir, we deny that this theory is merely unfounded feminist claptrap." A re-reading of these events of Homer as a coded, embedded, cryptic myth of the goddess culture ver-sion of prehistory is smoothly woven into the novella, via casting the maidens as a chorus, able to overtly address skeptical readers and insist the clues are obvious and not "unfounded": "such overthrows most certainly took place all around the Mediterranean Sea, as excavations at prehistoric sites have dem-onstrated over and over" (131). Atwood also evokes, "those ... double-bladed ritual labrys axes associated with the Great Mother cult" and the "Year King," which other writers have speculated as related to goddess culture.[16] Atwood deepens a goddess culture interpretation, describing how Odysseus and all patriarchy usurped the previous culture, in this case of Odysseus proving to be himself: "For the rebelling Year King to use Her own bow to shoot an arrow through Her own ritual life-and-death axes, in order to demonstrate his power over Her—what a desecration! ... Would you like to see some vase painting, some carved Goddess cult objects? No? Never mind ... Consider us pure symbol. We're no more real than money" (133). The chorus of hanged girls paint themselves and the symbols of their story as reflecting matriarchy violently murdered or overthrown by no less than one of the great heroes of patriarchy. They suggest goddess believers would have made better ritual use of the usurped symbols like the axes: "In the pre-patriarchal scheme of things ... [the ritual] would have been better conducted" (132). Superior though this previous women's world may have been, as also suggested by romanticizers of the past like Bradley, Walker, Auel, it is gone, dead as these symbolic maid-ens. But Atwood's Penelope, lonely in the afterworld (where the girls seem to blame and ignore her) chaffs at being the "edifying legend. A stick to beat other women" into submissive, loyal, womanly duty, as she is typically read: "the quintessential faithful wife" (2, xiii).

Atwood gives these women characters from ancient myth—with relatively minor roles therein—vivid and moving contemporary fictional voice. We hear a main character and a knowing chorus singing the goddess myth, and the message echoes most other versions of it. The women lament that the superior, woman-dominated, goddess-honoring past was overthrown, that we must all suffer under the bloody, punitive patriarchy. Penelope, the twelve maidens, and, we can assume, all women suffer greatly in the aftermath. Atwood's maidens suffer for virtually all eternity, as the story is told from their afterlives in the underworld. Penelope survives in her world, although being a faithful wife doesn't make her husband a good one who stays home with her. Mostly, the story is about her torment over not saving those girls, then being alone. The fate of *those girls*, all past girls, we can extrapolate, hangs over us all.

Conclusion

These fictionalized, reimagined and appropriated distant pasts from Paleolithic, classical, and early medieval periods portray woman as having better lives or remembering ancestors who did in times when goddesses and women were honored. Yet they don't project much hope. Just as Morgaine feels lonely and Penelope can never quite get the girls' attention in the afterlife, so too are we disconnected from any such pasts. These popular fictional creations of the goddess myth by women romanticize the past in ways that are arguably *not* any more feminist than vilified versions of the bad goddess (chapter 4). Both exaggerated poles are fantasies that reduce women to one extreme or the other. The bad goddess views from chapter 4 allow us to hate powerful women as purveyors of chaos and destruction. These good goddess myths may feel satisfying or hopeful, as worlds of revered and powerful women, but they too embrace unrealistic, extreme exaggerations. These good goddess myths are set so long ago that they are comforting fantasies more than world-changing inspirations. None of these works offers specific models for women or cultures that actually challenge traditional roles, but if these fictions do change women's consciousness, that is a relatively small-scale effect. And given Bradley's troubled, abusive life, one could argue her embrace of goddess culture did not improve her. Plus, there are many other vehicles for imagining and enacting change, including much other speculative fiction (chapter 6). Jernigan (2017) affirms a similar insight, noting that as she turned away from Bradley , she found much other great literature and inspiration, including in the sci-fi/fantasy world, that helps women look forward hopefully in terms of gender roles and feminism. She affirms: "I believe Moira Greyland. Her life matters more than any fiction" and suggests other titles and writers for today, some of which I examine in following chapters. Fiction can matter very much, but real lives matter too.

Our fictions can influence worldviews, shape paths, and inspire activism, values, politics, and personal relations. Contemporary goddess myths offer particular interpretations or appropriations of imagined (often distant) past times that are filtered and shaped through a variety of lenses appropriate to the times, concerns, worldviews, and experiences of their creators. Good goddesses in women's speculative fiction may shift the gaze of feminist theory from that of white men to that of women, which seems progressive. But romanticized versions do not offer much more for feminists to cheer about than those portrayals in film and television on the opposite end of the spectrum of vilified versions of goddesses. Romanticizing goddesses as loving, good, and peaceful (but dormant or gone) and vilifying them as a dark and destructive forces of chaos both cast women in unrealistic, essentialized extremes. Focusing on women and considering their perspectives can feel satisfying, but when that focus ends up resting in a place of motherhood (Ayla), yearning for a lost past (Morgaine), or inability to act as motherly as hoped, or to feel fulfilled (Penelope), the message is troublingly imperfect.

Goddess enthusiasts would likely decry as biased my observations of current versions of the myth falling into oppositional binary patterns. But numerous other versions of the myth in our culture reflect and adopt these patterns similarly, making it hard to ignore. This commonly recurring pattern in appropriations—either romanticized by best-selling women authors such as Atwood, Auel, and Bradley or vilified in television and film, dominated by men—both present polarized, dualistic, reductive representations of women that form fairly consistent mythic patterns, women as nurturing, emotional, motherly, sexual, but also lamenting or suffering beings, or contrarily powerful women as violently destructive forces of chaos. These extremes leave little to no space for real women living in our world. Neither essentialized role provides inspiration or speaks to us in any but sad and distant, echoey voices. Some recent works break these patterns to offer more thoughtful and relevant glimmers of hope.

Chapter 6

Mixed Messages in Modern Myths

Many contemporary goddess myths fit the extremes presented in chapters 4 and 5, with film and television tending to vilify the goddess as a dark and chaotic force, and popular speculative fiction romanticizing her as loving, good, and peaceful. There are as well some fictional goddesses in recent years who exist more complexly toward the middle of the spectrum of goddess myths—mixing dark and light, troubling and promising qualities. These less completely dualistic, more ambiguous or blended goddess beings reflect today's world and seem more aligned with intersectional feminism, incorporating multicultural and feminist characters that seem to also offer more actionable hope, as hopepunk theorizes. They largely escape the male gaze, as well as easier, more generalized and traditional binary patterns and conclusions, to offer characters with definitive, though not easily attained, agency. We believe them truly heroic, potential models for rethinking our own culture and old patterns.

A Minor Goddess with Grand Humanity in Madeline Miller's *Circe*

Madeline Miller's 2018 novel *Circe* offers a first-person narrative of a classical Greek goddess, typically portrayed in ancient works as a powerful witch with a prickly, sometimes problematic nature: the "Sea witch of Aiaia" who turns Odysseus's men into pigs, creates monsters, and helps murderers. Circe is introduced in Homer's *Odyssey* (written circa 800 BCE) as "a great and cunning goddess": "Thence we sailed sadly on . . . and came to the Aeaean island, where Circe lives a great and cunning goddess who is own sister to the magician Aeetes—for they are both children of the sun by Perse, who is daughter to Oceanus" (Homer 1897, book 10). Homer describes Circe's stone house "in the middle of the forest" and writes several lines about animals she tames: "wild mountain wolves and lions prowling all round it—poor bewitched creatures whom she had tamed by her enchantments and drugged into subjection. They did not attack my men, but wagged their great tails, fawned upon them, and rubbed their noses lovingly against them." Homer's description of the men as "poor bewitched creatures . . . drugged into subjection" suggests he disapproves of Circe's witchcraft. He also describes her as "singing most beautifully" and weaving "a web so fine, so soft, and of such dazzling colours as no one but a goddess could weave." Some of these qualities, of loving animals and weaving beautifully, seem positive, but Homer may have included such details as proof of her goddess powers, which she also uses to turn most of Odysseus's men into pigs, clearly not positive toward the hero.

When Homer's Circe meets Odysseus himself, he overpowers her, with Hermes' help, using the herb moly that counters her spells. She recognizes who he must be and immediately offers sex: "At this, I [Odysseus] drew my sharp sword and rushed at her, as if I meant to kill her, but with a cry she slipped beneath the blade to clasp my knees, and weeping spoke to me with winged words: . . . 'Come, sheathe your sword, and let us two go to my bed, so we may learn to trust one another by twining in love'" (Homer 1632–33, book 10). This Circe, easily conquered and humbled, swears not to harm the hero, turns his men back into themselves, feeds and clothes them all richly, and offers them respite on her island:

Ulysses, noble son of Laertes, tell your men to leave off crying; I know how much you have all of you suffered at sea, and how ill you have fared among cruel savages on the mainland, but that is over now, so stay here, and eat and drink till you are once more as strong and hearty as you were when you left Ithaca; for at present you are weakened both in body and mind; you keep all the time thinking of the hardships—you have suffered during your travels, so that you have no more cheerfulness left in you. (Homer 1897, Book 10)

Odysseus (called by his Latin name Ulysses in this translation) does indeed stay and seems to like it there: "Thus did she speak and we assented. We stayed with Circe for a whole twelvemonth feasting upon an untold quantity both of meat and wine" (book 10). So attractive is Circe's hospitality that Odysseus' men have to urge him to continue their journey after twelve months. Before he leaves, Circe offers advice for him to "go to the house of Hades and of dread Proserpine to consult the ghost of the blind Theban prophet Teiresias

whose reason is still unshaken. To him alone has Proserpine left his understanding even in death, but the other ghosts flit about aimlessly" (book 10).
Homer's Circe is thus on balance a good witch and goddess, who after a first
hostile act transforms into a good host and advisor to the hero, even helping
their ship sail successfully as they leave her island: "Circe, that great and cunning goddess, sent us a fair wind that blew dead aft and stayed steadily with
us keeping our sails all the time well filled; so we did whatever wanted doing
to the ship's gear and let her go as the wind and helmsman headed her" (book
11). Especially in contrast to Calypso, another island goddess that Odysseus
lives with and who refuses to let Odysseus leave her for seven years, Circe
appears more reasonable. Her description by Homer as a "great and cunning
goddess" seems at first a bit terrifying, but ultimately more positive. Yarnall
(1994, 24) concurs, arguing that Circe "embodies the power of the feminine
in its primordial, highly ambivalent form. Because Odysseus does not shrink
from this power, but rather opens himself to it, Circe becomes beneficent and
Odysseus becomes more whole. In effect, she gives him her blessing." The primordial feminine embraces the patriarchal hero.

In centuries after Homer's *Odyssey*, many others revised this view of Circe,
making her emblematic of various human foibles. For instance, Socrates sees
the episode of her transforming men into pigs as representing overcoming
self-control regarding gluttony (Xenophon, *Memorabilia of Socrates*, book I,
3.7, referenced in Yarnall 1994). Others assume it is a lesson about carnal lust,
while others cast Circe as a prostitute.[1] Yarnall (1994, 195) analyzes numerous such examples and concludes that transformed versions of Circe result
from biases, including "a profound distrust of the body and a fear of the loss
of rational control that is an integral part of sexual experience," which is "projected on to Woman." Post-Homer, "for a very long time . . . the basic pattern
of seductive Woman impeding starry-eyed Man in his pursuit of distant glory
obtained" (197). Atwood's novella *The Penelopiad* was published after this analysis, but Yarnall (1994, 199) considers Atwood's "Circe/Mud Poems" (1980), a
poem cycle about Circe, and believes that Atwood, like James Joyce, "really"
exposes "the dualism, of the whole folly of projecting on to Woman the burden
and delight of the carnality that we all bear." She finds in Atwood "a wistful
imagining of what life and relationship would be like if men and women cast
aside the securities of power hierarchies and together faced the mystery of
their existence. . . . What if? she asks" (199). Yarnall almost seems to anticipate Miller's *Circe* when she hopes that "Circe would suffer a death as gentle
and natural as the one that Homer's Tiresias predicts for Odysseus, and the

archetypal core of her power would be freed for us to use in creating new myths to dream onward" (199). Subsequent new myths try to fulfill such hopes.

Atwood's novella *The Penelopiad* features Odysseus's wife Penelope during the years after the Trojan War, as she waits for her husband's return and must fend off the suitors vying for her hand and her husband's land. She regularly hears stories of his adventures:

> Odysseus was the guest of a goddess on an enchanted isle, said some; she'd turned his men into pigs—not a hard job in my view—but had turned them back into men because she'd fallen in love with him and was feeding him unheard-of delicacies prepared by her own immortal hands, and the two of them made love deliriously every night; no, said others, it was just an expensive whorehouse, and he was sponging off the Madam. (Atwood 2005, 67)

Throughout, Atwood offers more plausible accounts of Odysseus's journey, as here, suggesting he is really waylaid by prostitutes, worldly temptations, and traps, like jealous fathers or bars, rather than actual monsters, gods, and witches. This Circe had "fallen in love with" Odysseus and feeds him "unheard-of delicacies" with which presumably no woman could compete. Penelope is thus taunted with visions of her husband's unfaithfulness with a superior being. Since Penelope is our narrator, we are bound to perceive Circe negatively, a temptress with an unfair advantage of "immortal hands" and godly abilities, or an "expensive . . . Madam." Whether worldly or magical, Atwood's Circe offends Penelope, at least in stories Penelope hears of her.

Madeline Miller includes all the same events from Homer but transforms Circe into a narrative voice and a sympathetic character, not a sex worker but a goddess who also becomes a witch. While Atwood imposes a contemporary perspective on the Homeric story, imagining grittier, less-enchanted possible explanations of Odysseus's voyage and Circe's nature, Miller assumes the characters and mythology from Homer are real. But she also humanizes the gods and heroes, especially Circe, to paint a moving story of a sympathetic goddess. One reviewer suggests humorously, "The archaeological evidence is sketchy, but the first pussy hat was probably knitted by Circe. Among nasty women, the witch of Aeaea has held a place of prominence since Homer first sang of her wiles" (Charles 2018). While Circe may traditionally be conceived as a proto "nasty woman," Miller paints her from a contemporary feminist perspective. An NPR reviewer also appreciates Circe's strengths as a woman, seeing Circe's braids, specifically mentioned in Homer, as evidence of her agency rather than her exotic beauty: "This Circe braids her hair because she has work to do" (Quinn 2018).[2] Miller (2018, 206) herself nods directly to Homer's view of women, having Circe say: "Later, years later, I would hear a song made of our meeting... I was not surprised by the portrait of myself: the proud witch undone before the hero's sword, kneeling and begging for mercy. Humbling women seems to me a chief pastime of poets. As if there can be no story unless we crawl and weep." Miller's Circe meets Odysseus as more of an equal, neither bowing, crawling, nor weeping. She has a mind sharp enough to match Odysseus, perceives his flaws as well as his strengths, and doesn't bow before his greatness. Miller makes Circe her own goddess and woman, a powerful voice worth attending to.

This Circe is ignored, mistreated, lonely, and diminished during the first ten thousand years of her existence in her Titan father Helios's obsidian halls, amid other more powerful gods. Her siblings taunt her, her golden father "believed the world's natural order was to please him" (Miller 2018, 4), and later Athena tries to kill Circe's son. When she finally enacts witchy abilities, Circe is exiled: "she must be punished. She is exiled to a deserted island where she can do no more harm" (74). The gods, whom Miller draws largely as childishly selfish, capricious, and mean-spirited, fear what they cannot control, as when Circe realizes her father Helios's reaction to learning about his witch children's power: "I understood with an odd jolt. He is afraid" (68). But the island Aiaia, meant as a place of exile and punishment, instead gives Circe "a giddy spark" of hope: "I stepped into those woods and my life began" (81). Circe, an ignored, mocked, dismissed "lesser goddess," grows into her power on the island: "Had I truly feared such creatures? Had I really spent ten thousand years ducking like a mouse? I understood now Aeëtes' boldness, how he had stood before our father like a towering peak. When I did my magics, I felt that same span and heft. I tracked my father's burning chariot across the sky. Well? What do you have to say to me? You threw me to the crows, but it turns out I prefer them to you" (88–89). Circe transforms the solitude meant to be a mockingly cruel punishment of lonely existence into a space to bloom, growing confident and powerful.

The witch is known for transforming humans into more beastly creatures, living with tamed beasts, and for hosting Odysseus for a year during his voyage. In some versions she bears him children who establish important cities. Witches, sometimes just women living alone or independently, following the model of this original lone witch, have been persecuted for centuries.[3] The idea of a woman living on her own, not fulfilling expected roles as wife or mother, is an anomaly that is easily recast or scapegoated as an abomination to mainstream society. Independent and/or powerful women have regularly been feared, considered strange, threatening, or assumed to have "power"—which explains how they could live on their own, often deep in woods or immersed in nature, unlike the generally perceived "right" way to live. But Miller creates an independent woman who prefers solitude, who carves out of her space of exile a way to survive and thrive, who draws power from being unusual and alone in nature. Unlike most women feared, slandered, and persecuted as witches in history, this Circe really has significant power. She is born a goddess but learns to craft her sorcery power through "*pharmaka* . . . herbs with the power to work change upon the world" (Miller 2018, 67). Circe later assesses that this power emerges largely from her will, work, and determination: "Let me say what sorcery is not: it is not divine power, which comes with a thought and a blink. It must be made and worked, planned and searched out. . . . It can fail . . . if my attention falters, if my will is weak. . . . Witchcraft is nothing but such drudgery" (83–84). *Will*, whether divine or human, she later confirms, is key: "I have come to believe it is mostly will" (338). We start to realize that this goddess is different from most we have seen, not all-powerful, all-knowing, for good or ill, but one who works hard, including at fostering her observation skills. She wills and shapes her power.

Miller's (2018, 6) goddess-witch has hawk eyes: "my mother . . . named me Hawk, *Circe*, for my yellow eyes, and the thin sound of my crying." She uses these unusual eyes to *see* the nature of the gods. To Circe, most gods are "ugly"—childish, lazy, petty, selfish, spoiled, as the novel repeatedly portrays them, mostly in Circe's voice:

Gods hate all toil, it is their nature. (83)

Let me tell you a truth about Helios and all the rest. They do not care if you are good. They barely care if you are wicked. The only thing that makes them listen is power [her sister Pasiphaë tells Circe] (146)

Every moment mortals died . . . No matter how vivid they were in life . . . they came to dust and smoke. Meanwhile every petty and useless god would go on sucking down the bright air until the stars went dark. (159)

[Asking Odysseus about the Trojan War] "What was the fight over?"

"Let me see if I can remember the list." He ticked his fingers, "Vengeance. Lust. Hubris. Greed. Power. What have I forgotten? Ah yes, vanity, and pique."

"Sounds like a usual day among the gods," I said. (200)

Every moment of my peace was a lie, for it came only at the gods' pleasure. (230)

"Gods pretend to be parents," I said, "but they are children, clapping their hands and shouting for more." . . . Gods never give up a treasure. (328)

No god can be called steady. (355)

"You see?" I said, when I was finished with the tale. "Gods are ugly things." (375)

I thought once that gods are the opposite of death, but I see now they are more dead than anything, for they are unchanging, and can hold nothing in their hands. (386)

Having inherited some of her father's all-seeing, perceptive nature, Circe helps readers perceive gods as unadmirable, even despicable. These gods match modern scholarly assessments: "the Greeks conceived their gods as an expression of the disorder of the world in which they lived. The Olympian gods, like the natural forces of sea and sky, follow their own will even to the extreme of conflict with each other, and always with a sublime disregard for the human beings who may be affected by the results of their actions" (Knox 1997, 88). Though Circe is herself a goddess, she is unusual in evincing humility, kindness, compassion, and admiration of humans.

Young Circe is formatively influenced by witnessing a key episode in Greek mythology, Prometheus's punishment for "his foolish love for mortals" (Miller 2018, 17). His "hellish torments" are portrayed as a dramatic novelty and spectacle for most of the other gods, "faces dark with excitement. You cannot know how frightened gods are of pain. There is nothing more foreign to them, and so nothing they ache more deeply to see" (17). While the other gods enjoy the novelty of Prometheus's suffering, Circe sympathizes, staying after the others got bored, bringing him some nectar, and finally asking him, "what is a mortal like?" (22). He explains, "They are each different. The only thing they share is death," and when she further questions him about why he helped them, he tells her, "'Not every god need be the same'" (22). Circe is rebelliously bold here, since she knows her attention would anger her father and Zeus. This moment becomes a spark that shapes much of her life, causing "a strange feeling . . . a sort of humming in my chest" (22). Like Prometheus, she too sympathizes with and admires humans. Hermes later reveals to her that Circe's strange voice, "the thin sound of my crying," that she is often mocked for by other gods, is actually human: "You sound like a mortal" (93). Before her banishment to Aiaia, Circe falls in love with and later works her first transformation on a human, Glaucos, whom she finds "wondrous" and who makes her feel "warm" (38).

Glaucos proves unworthy of her love, for once she transforms him to a god, he decides he can do better than her and is cruel in his rejection. Her pain leads her to transform the nymph he chooses, Scylla, into a monster, which ends up being Circe's deepest regret. Ultimately, she uses some of the last of her godly power, combined with some witch power, to kill Scylla (meant partly mercifully), though it is no easy matter and takes her many years to figure out and accomplish. Throughout her life, Circe maintains patterns of perceiving the bad qualities of gods, admiring the potential of humans, wondering about mortality, and perceiving how humans may embody qualities she desires. Humans can certainly be bad in Miller's novel. Circe suffers a violent rape and promises of more by men who visit her island:

> The man threw me back against the wall. My head hit the uneven stone and the room sparked. I opened my mouth to cry out the spell, but he jammed him arm against my windpipe and the sound was choked off. . . . I fought him, but he was stronger . . . or maybe I was weaker. The sudden weight of him shocked me, the greasy push of his skin on mine. My mind was still scrambled, disbelieving. . . . A mortal would have fainted, but I was awake for every moment. (Miller 2018, 188)

Circe hears the other men hoping for their turn to rape her, then "my throat clicked. I felt a space open in me," and rather than putting them to sleep as she'd planned, she speaks a spell that transforms these metaphorical beasts into the pigs they are to her (188). So she doesn't admire all humans, and the novel hereby offers justification for her most famous act in Homer's original, an act historically perceived as hostile and capricious, a reason to fear and dislike witches.

When Miller's (2018, 239, 240, 242) Circe bears Odysseus's son, she suffers a very difficult pregnancy and childbirth involving "extremities of misery," a "tearing contraction," the need to cut herself open to deliver her son, and then an endlessly "screaming" and difficult baby. Circe worries deeply about her son Telegonus's fate, once she realizes Athena wants to kill him. Circe begs Athena to spare her child, whom Athena wants dead because she knows the prophecy that he will later kill his father Odysseus, Athena's favorite. Miller portrays the goddess Athena as merciless, angry, powerful, and arrogant, "a terrifying vision: the goddess of war, ready for battle . . . Athena was known for her wrath" (248, 249). But Circe defies Athena, asserting her own witch power to protect her son. It requires tremendous effort, three days each month, to cast spells to form a shield over the island and to make "the island itself" work to protect Telegonus: "the weight of those spells was dragging at my neck like a yoke" (254, 255). We see that her hard work saves her son, but he remains difficult. Circe tries to be a good, loving mother, and some might question how feminist it is to draw a powerful, ancient, goddess as finding fulfillment as a mother and eventually a wife. A *New York Times* review finds, "The novel's feminist slant . . . appeals," but also considers it disappointing that "Miller has determined, in her characterization of this most powerful witch, to bring her as close as possible to the human" (Messud 2018). This diminishes Circe, the reviewer thinks, because "Miller's sentimental leanings and her determination to make Circe into an ultimately likable, or at least forgivable, character. This narrative choice seems a taming, and hence a diminishment, of the character's transgressive divine excess."

Themes of mortal potential shape Circe's life, and at the novel's end she seems in the process of transforming herself into a mortal to live out her life in mundanely human terms with her lover, Odysseus' son Telemachus, and his mother, Penelope (who both come to the island). The novel ends: "All my life I have been moving forward, and now I am here. I have a mortal's voice, let me have the rest. I lift the brimming bowl to my lips and drink" (Miller 2018, 385). This liquid is a potion from a Titan's spilled blood that Circe "heard" humming magically to her via flowers she used also in earlier transformations. Remember her assertion that magic is mostly will (338). Circe comes to understand and practice her power gradually, through hard work, slower than her siblings, who mock her for her lack of cunning, assuming she is weak. Though sent to Aiaia as "a disgrace to our name," she "learned that I could bend the world to my will" (84). She teaches others, such as Penelope, who after much practice "smiled her inward smile. 'You were right. It is mostly will. Will and work'" (380). Circe grows throughout her long life toward a *will* to be human; thus, we can assume that when she drinks from the brimming bowl, her magical, godly elixir, along with her will, *will* embody her ultimate transformation, god to human. Although Messud finds this "taming . . . of the character's transgressive divine excess . . . a diminishment," it could also be read as making her more complex than the typical angry, destructive, chaotic goddesses, or the romanticized, perfect ones, patterns we have seen repeatedly throughout Western civilization (chapters 4 and 5). Miller reconceives traditionally perceived/portrayed, evil/tricky "transgressive divine excess" of goddesses.

Circe chooses to be human because she has perspective of how shallow and awful immortality makes most gods. As Prometheus pointed out in her youth, she, like him, can "be different." She trains herself and uses her power to choose and form a different way. Compared to most gods' violent, mean, selfish, despicable natures, Circe's unusual life demonstrates that even powerful, independent women, even a goddess or a witch, need not merely be conceived in stereotypical and extreme ways—such as evil, destructive, or "cunning" (Homer 1632–33 and 1897), nor need she be romanticized as motherly, loving, and perfect. This powerful woman shapes for herself an admirable, worthy life: righting her wrongs, owning her faults, claiming her joys, and emerging out of her pain, loneliness, exile, scorn, punishment, and solitude as something *new*. Many real-world powerful, isolated women throughout history have suffered, been tormented, borne blame, and sometimes trod new ground. Circe *persists* through troubles to forge a new path, in spite of millennia of hatred, mistreatment, abuse, and scorn. She takes responsibility for her mistakes, mistakes of power; she rejects easy rewards and fame; she tends her garden; and she builds a home and thrives in an unconventional life that she shapes. While her choices seem domestic at times, including marrying and bearing more children, she still seems more admirably full of agency and wisdom than many of the goddesses considered thus far. Readers *like* Circe's character, our goodhearted, wise, kind narrator.

There are plenty of goddesses who are violent in *Circe* (especially her sister Pasiphae and Odysseus's protector Athena), and no romanticized visions of the past or goddesses, but the goddess we relate to, cheer, and admire is an emergent, dynamic, hopeful one. There is also a sort of matriarchy on the island because many nymphs and minor goddesses are sent to live with Circe over the years, and later the bond between Circe and Penelope is strong. But this is no matriarchal paradise. Circe is annoyed by most of the women sent to her, and all the women suffer a little on the island and must work hard for their power. Circe voices the hard work and will required for women today to be independent and strong, and given all of what we know of history, it is a kind of magic that we are starting to experience as well, as women who can live independently, carve out our own spaces, embrace whatever power we can find to use our voices to reshape our world.

Socially Relevant Goddesses in Tomi Adeyemi's *Children and Blood and Bone*

Nigerian American Tomi Adeyemi writes best-selling contemporary speculative fiction incorporating goddesses, along with issues of race and oppression. Her series (reportedly in film production by Disney and Lucasfilm) begins with the novel *Children of Blood and Bone* (2018), featuring an adolescent girl whose life and world are troubled by an oppressive, prejudiced leader in the fictional land of Orisha.[4] Our hero, Zélie, is a maji, born with magical potential, and the novel opens with her learning impressive fighting skills that Mama Agba teaches oppressed girls.[5] Zélie needs to know how to fight because the Orishan ruler, King Saran, from a different, nonmagical race (the Kosidán) hates the maji and has committed violent raids—one of which killed Zélie's mother. He also outlaws magic, tries to destroy its source (three magical objects), and oppresses all magi. Zélie and her brother, along with the king's children (who all come together) embark on a quest to try to restore magic. Magic is linked to goddesses in this book, and our hero Zélie believes goddess magic could help all Orishans.

Magi in this fictional universe are recognizable by their dark brown skin tone and white hair, contrasting the lighter skin and darker hair of the Kosidán. Adeyemi creates heroic, "good" characters of color, hoping to redress unequal representation in sci-fi/fantasy and in the world: "I'm going to make something so good, and so black, that even racists are going to have to see it" (Lubbock 2018). Vann R. Newkirk (2018) discusses the book's way of confronting contemporary race issues: "In assigning Zélie the gift of drawing strength from remembrance of the dead, Adeyemi taps into a capacity that has become so important for black protest today . . . staging scenes that obviously parallel the spectacle of police brutality and black death in America . . . explor[ing] the ways in which violence—especially as it plays out (very graphically) in male control over female bodies—ricochets through history. Both women [characters] come to see more clearly how inequities of color, class, and gender converge." Adeyemi (2018, 526) explains in the author's note within the book that it was "written during a time where I kept turning on the news and seeing stories of unarmed black men, women and children being shot by the police. I felt afraid and angry and helpless, but this book was the one thing that made me feel like I could do something about it."

In the novel, the Orishan king makes race an issue, calling maji "maggots" and demanding their oppression and extermination, out of fear of their differences and potential power. The racism and sexism in the novel reflect real-world racism, sexism, and microaggressions.[6] The king's son, Inan, at first follows his father, hates Zélie, and believes killing her will destroy all magic, including that emerging in himself. Zélie's touch, during a tussle early in the capital, when our heroes acquire the magical scroll that sets off their quest, awakens some latent magical ability in Inan, which he suppresses, tries to hide, and is terrified to have—knowing his father considers all such people maggots to be squashed. But the white streak that stubbornly keeps appearing in his hair (a physical indicator of anyone with magic), his growing emotional connection to Zélie, and his undeniable magical abilities all make him torn between loyalty to his father and wanting to embrace different ideas, such as letting all races live together cooperatively in Orisha, a notion Zélie tries to inspire in him. Zélie is a fairly tortured hero, reminiscent of Katniss Everdeen from the Hunger Games novels.[7] She is coming of age in a brutally unjust world that killed her beloved mother, squashes her magic that causes euphoria and comfort when she experiences it, and promotes policies and attitudes that have left her and many others in her world vulnerable to horrendously racist oppression and suffering. Plus, Inan, one of the most powerful men in the kingdom, relentlessly pursues and tries to kill her, until they finally meet (about two-thirds through), and then their relationship turns romantic for part of the novel. But after feeling a love connection with him, Zélie is distressingly betrayed by him.

Maji have strongest connections to goddesses in this world. Goddesses are the source of their magical power and part of the religious structure that under the oppressive king exists only secretively, underground. The Sky Mother, the principal god revered especially by the maji, is the mother of all other gods and creator of humans: "In the beginning, our Sky Mother created the heavens and the earth, bringing life to the vast darkness" (Adeyemi 2018, 159). She has a male counterpart and is a good and loving goddess: "Sky Mother loved all her children, each created in her image," and each of her god and goddess children are given "a part of her soul, a magic they were meant to gift to the humans below" (159). The last of these goddesses, Oya, "didn't take from Sky Mother like her siblings. Instead, she asked Sky Mother to give," a story Zélie has heard growing up and then sees magically animated at a holy temple the children find during their quest (160). The power of Oya, whom Zélie feels particularly connected to, is profound, a "mastery over life" and "power over death" (160). But the myth continues to explain, "not all her children could handle such great power. She became selective, like her mother, sharing her ability with only those who showed patience and wisdom. Her siblings followed suit, and soon the maji population dwindled. In this new era, all maji were graced with coiled white hair, an homage to Sky Mother's image" (161). We learn in this myth that Sky Mother and her children are powerful and good, but that their "gifts" (magic) are given selectively and can be handled only by good people. That magic is powerful and somewhat dangerous. Thus, goddess magic or power is real in this world, but not always accessible or safe.

Zélie often feels afraid of her power. Oya is sometimes described as "wrathful" and is more connected to the night than the day: "the image of Sky Mother in my mind begins to fade. A goddess with skin like the night takes her place, clothed in waves of red, beautiful with her dark brown eyes" (Adeyemi 2018, 258). Zélie feels unworthy of her quest and finds it painful to use her magic, especially "blood magic"—a darker and more powerful form of magic that requires blood. But she gets help and comfort from the goddesses as well:

Oya shines in my mind like a torch against the dark. Unlike the chaos I glimpsed when I used blood magic, this vision holds an ethereal grace. She stands still, but it's like the entire world shifts in her presence. A triumphant smile spreads across her lips—

"Ugh!" My eyes fly open. The sunstone glows so brightly in my hand, I have to look away. Though the initial rush of its touch has passed, I can feel its power humming in my bones. It's like Sky Mother's spirit has spread through my body, stitching every wound left by the blood magic's destruction. (258)

Zélie's power does not corrupt her, thanks partly to the loving goddesses who comfort her. Orishan goddesses affect various characters and are perceived as loving and trustworthy, guiding Zélie in positive ways, more like what we'd expect from a religious framework that incorporates goddesses from the goddess myth perspective.

Zélie proves herself again and again to be goodhearted, strong, intelligent, and capable, worthy of her good goddesses' regard. Her quest is to take the three sacred objects to a sacred island that only appears on the centennial solstice, there to perform a ritual to reawaken magic for all with latent abilities. In the final climatic battle on the island, she doubts herself, not having felt any magic for days. But she continues to pray, "*Please, Sky Mother*, I pray again. *If you can fix this, fix it now*" (Adeyemi 2018, 495). Everything seems to go horribly wrong, and Zélie believes she has failed when one crucial object is destroyed. Then she realizes that she might forge "a new connection to Sky Mother and her gifts through our spirits," through "blood" and "bone," so she gives of her own blood, which causes "spiritual pathways [to] explode within me" (517). Her new ritual, combining some elements of the old, appears to work, "as the light invades every fiber of my being, the whole world shines," and she perceives: "We are all children of blood and bone. All instruments of vengeance and virtue" (519). This "truth" she perceives manifests in a feeling of her "mother's arms" embracing her. She feels this "spiritual embrace" coming from a blend of her own mother and the goddess Oya (519–21). Zélie appears to die in the ritual, and the goddess offers tremendous, heavenly comfort to this poor, tortured soul who held the weight of the world in her young hands: "Hot tears sting my eyes as I collapse into her spiritual embrace. Her warmth soaks into my being, making every crack whole. I feel all the tears I've cried, every prayer I've ever sent" (521). Zélie's ritual that blends new and old will forge new pathways in Orisha, we are led to believe in the novel's conclusion, but the new goddess, combining qualities of both her mother and the goddess Oya, promises to stay with her on earth, before sending our hero her back to the living world to forge more new pathways: "'It's not over, little Zél. It's only just begun'" (523). This brave young girl has a power-filled and goddess-connected coming of age that is painful, joyous, and promising. Her climatic struggle, then insight and comfort from the Goddess anticipates further adventures in sequels. Her great insight that "we are all children of blood and bone" may be literal, in that previously non-maji characters seem to have had their own magical awakenings via her new ritual.

The author's note explicitly connects her novel and the oppression her characters suffer to the Black Lives Matter movement: "I shed many tears before I wrote this book. Many tears as I revised it. . . . All the pain, fear, sorrow, and loss in this book is real. . . . If you cried for Zulaikha and Salim [children who are killed in the book], cry for innocent children like Jordan Edwards, Tamir Rice, and Aiyana Stanley-Jones. They were fifteen, twelve, and seven when they were shot and killed by police" (Adeyemi 2018, 526). Adeyemi invokes some specific real-world tragedies for us all to remember, "a long list of black lives taken too soon," noting, "This is just one of the many problems plaguing our world and there are so many days when these problems still feel bigger than us, but let this book be proof to you that we can always do *something* to fight back" (527). By directly tying her story to actual oppressions and violence, Adeyemi suggests the ultimate magic is the power of fiction, which she believes can change lives.

Adeyemi's goddesses are loving and powerful but also have a darker side, such as blood magic and connections to death. But they are real forces in her imagined world who help children fight tormentors and lead them on a path toward restoring justice. Adeyemi's fictional goddesses fit neither of the typical extremes we usually see with goddess culture myths. Some of them seem like mother goddesses in some classical ways—loving, powerful, just, kind, and helping to improve lives. But they also seem more complex and less romanticized. They are not all-powerful, or they would not be threatened by an oppressive human dictator's designs, and they are open to change—like Zélie's adapted ritual. They offer love and comfort but also fear and death at times (Zélie taps her power and kills many in fight scenes). They seem to allow for humanity's free will, letting us decide whether to embrace their "magic" of love, peace, and justice, or death and pain, to change either set of parameters, or to let either shine or fade. Adeyemi's fiction is an example of Afrofuturism and a revolutionary act: "at Afrofuturism's core is the recognition that reimagining oppressive pasts and envisioning far-off futures are closely linked revolutionary acts—meditations on the nature of power that can revive the creative potential of speculative fiction" (Newkirk 2018).

Adeyemi promises new power not only for Zélie but for other characters too, leading us to anticipate more exciting adventures in sequels. Adeyemi believes that some fiction, including speculative fiction of goddesses, might make us truly rethink our world and choices, while also imagining new potential pathways, mythic or real. Her work is more promising than much pro-goddess fiction—less romanticized than Auel and Bradley and less completely dark than much film and television. Bringing race into speculative fiction helps the genre move beyond second-wave feminist realms of matriarchal dreams or patriarchal fears to a newer feminism that reflects current realities, recognizes modern problems, but also includes glimmers of hope for change. The fantasy of magic that can help one overcome oppressive forces in human society shows the powerful potential of speculative fiction.

N. K. Jemisin's Emergent, Hopeful Goddesses

Another award-winning contemporary African American woman writer of speculative, Afrofuturist fiction considers similar topics—oppression and magical power to fight it—from an even more complex speculative perspective. N. K. Jemisin, 2020 MacArthur fellow, engages social issues like gender, race, social oppression (including slavery), and environmentalism via compelling main characters, BIPOC women who become goddesses. The Inheritance Trilogy brought Jemisin to critical notice in the sci-fi/fantasy world. The first novel therein, *The Hundred Thousand Kingdoms* (2010), features main character Yeine, nineteen years old and self-described as "short and flat and brown as forestwood, and my hair is a curled mess. . . . [I'm] sometimes mistaken for a boy" (Jemisin 2010, 7). Yeine embodies some godly nature and descends from her mother's Arameri ruling line, though her mother fled far north when she married. Yeine's grandfather (the Arameri ruler) calls her back to her mother's home, Sky, to compete as a potential heir, after her mother's mysterious murder. Though young, despised by many (considered barbaric and foolish), and used by others (or hoped to be used), Yeine demonstrates agency in navigating this complex, difficult, and new (to her) world and situation. She fights to maintain her identity, carves a space for herself, negotiates the wills of powerful gods and rivals, and asserts her will in her ascension to a goddess spirit or power that rises in her.

The Maelstrom is the original creator entity in this world that birthed the universe and the Three, main gods who seem gendered (two men and a woman) but also beyond most physical limitations. They can be corporeal or incorporeal, have tremendous power, and travel anywhere, but are not omnipotent nor omniscient. Itempas (a.k.a. Skyfather or Bright Itempas) is god of law, order, and light; Itempas is second child of the Maelstrom, who thousands of years before the series murdered his former sibling and lover, the Maelstrom's final, girl child, Enefa—goddess of twilight, dawn, balance, life, and death. Itempas also enslaved Nahadoth, the Nightlord, god of chaos and change, eldest and most dangerous god. The godlings, immortal children of the Three gods or other godlings, are also enslaved or imprisoned in Sky, their powers limited. The most notable godling is Enefa's firstborn trickster son, Sieh, god of childhood, mischief, innocence, and caprice, who appears as a child during most of the book, befriends Yeine, and longs for his lost mother. Itempas traps and enslaves all these godly beings in Sky, a city on a pedestal high above the city of other humans. Only those with Arameri blood dwell in Sky, some as rulers, most as servants; their blood is needed to operate the magical technology of the place. Itempas set up the city to require all enslaved gods and godlings (Enefada) to obey Arameri commands. The Enefada trapped and hid part of Enefa's soul long ago, hoping to revive her and bring her back, partly to free them, partly out of love.

Yeine, raised to be chieftain in her father's matriarchal land of Darr, realizes within a week that she is meant to be a sacrifice, one who will wield a magical stone that allows the next Arameri ruler to ascend. But the stone, which holds some of Enefa's soul, kills the one who wields it after a short burst of power. Yeine is despised and mocked by many (including her rival cousins) because of her mixed race and blunt Darre manners, but the gods, especially Nahadoth and Sieh, mostly help her, though it's not always clear what their motivations are. She discovers that she also carries part of Enefa's soul, hidden in her by the Enefadeh. At times Yeine feels Enefa seeming to take over her being.

A repeated phrase, "Once upon a time there was a little girl," (Jemisin 2010, 138 and elsewhere), clues us to Yeine's similarity to fairy-tale heroines. She is young and parentless as the tale opens, must travel a great distance from her home, is thrust into an unfamiliar world full of dangers and magical challenges, seeks to find the right path, and develops her own identity. She also has a dangerous, dark suitor in Nahadoth, who kisses her at their first meeting and becomes her lover. Yeine solves various mysteries, including her mother's death, the truth of the gods' war (a suppressed history), the political and social system in her new home, how to deal with the changes in her own nature, and then how to understand and survive the Succession Ceremony, related to Enefa's power. Yeine allies herself with the Enefadeh, though Nahadoth explains they want her life. The liaisons she makes and kindnesses she shows help her fateful choice, allowing Yeine to assert enough of her own soul to not be completely subsumed.

During the climactic ceremony, where Yeine is meant to use the stone to name the next ruler and thereafter die, readers are surprised that Viraine, whom we learn is really Itempas (hiding in human form), murders Yeine. The text clearly states in her voice, "And I died," but then her consciousness continues, floating above the scene to describe it, as the gods argue (Jemisin 2010, 363). Yeine watches and listens, finally perceiving via Enefa's soul remnant, that it is she, Yeine, whose soul will take her place as the Third God. Enefa speaks to Yeine in a disembodied way: "Your body must change" (374). She notes how "strong" Yeine is, "strong enough to take my place," though Enefa's "essence . . . necessary for this world to continue" will apparently be part of Yeine, who becomes a sort of hybrid goddess, still part-human (2010, 374). Yeine absorbs the stone into chest as her new goddess heart, assuming Enefa's power and essence into her being. She also affirms after her human death, "I remember who I am now. I have held on to myself, and I will not let that knowledge go. I carry the truth within myself, future and past, inseparable. I will see this through" (364). This young heroine, underestimated by many, takes an active role in forging her own goddesshood, and we are given evidence of her power and wisdom as she rises from the dead to assert her will. She retains her name, Yeine, as a new goddess based on Enefa, sharing some aspects but also original. Goddess Yeine ends the plague of stagnancy that she and others perceive in the world Itempas ruled, raises a tree to hold up Sky (replacing Itempas's structure), appoints a ruler she finds worthy, punishes Itempas and others who wronged her, and flies away across the universe with Nahadoth as lover and companion, ready to learn and grow: "I could not help grinning like a human girl. 'Take me away, then,' I said. 'Let's get started'" (395). Earlier she answered Nahadoth's query, "What would you want?" with "Something better" (296–97). Hopeful, fairy tale aspects of the novel are evoked throughout, but unlike most fairy tales, the main characters are gods, suggesting myth. This goddess may be nascent and borne of a relatively young and inexperienced girl, but she is nonetheless hopefully promising and original, little or nothing like either the romanticized good mother, nor the vilified force of chaos.

Jemisin's subsequent, multiple-award-winning *The Broken Earth* trilogy develops similar themes and at times a similar storyline, but with a significantly older character, one who demonstrates even more agency and consciousness of her choices, if perhaps less power (that we see, anyway). *The Fifth Season* (2015), *The Obelisk Gate* (2016), and *The Stone Sky* (2017), consecutive winners of Hugo awards for best novel, trace the transformation of a powerful woman to a being that could arguably be considered a goddess—an almost immortal being (able to be killed, like Enefa), with enormous magical power. Unlike Yeine, Essun is not named a goddess outright in the series, which also lacks many of that earlier novel's fairy-tale elements. In this imagined world, a single super-continent called the Stillness is plagued by geological cataclysms and severe "seasons" that can last millennia and threaten all life, including things like glacial winters. Orogenes are humans who inherit genetic traits that allow them to magically control and manipulate energies of their planet—in small and large ways. Their earth is a living consciousness whose core is magical energy, it can act, and it is angry at humanity, mainly for stealing its power and losing its moon millennia earlier. The earth retaliates with deadly seasons, but the one that opens the books is caused by Alabaster, an extremely powerful Orogene and former mentor, friend, and partner to Essun, the woman protagonist who also has enormous power and who wants to heal ancient rifts. The earth's anger at having its energy and life-force "stolen" for human comfort offers fairly obvious parallels to our world's abuse of planetary resources for comfort and profit, to the detriment of the planet itself, as well as all life. Parallels exist, even though our planet has no magical energy like this speculative world.

The Orogenes manipulate the earth's magic or energy in ways that can either help or be deadly, so they are generally feared, persecuted, called by the slur "rogga," and mostly controlled by an organization called the Fulcrum, whose Guardians recruit Orogenes as children, train and control them (often harshly), harness their power, and are themselves controlled by rods of the earth's magical core imbedded in their brains. Most ordinary people in the Stillness live in "comms," agrarian communities. Orogenes Alabaster and Essun each have Stone Eater companions—mysterious and powerful beings literally made of stone. After Alabaster (watched by his Stone Eater) cracks apart the single continent of the earth, a season begins that will devastate most life for thousands of years. His complex motivations are mainly meant to end a millennia-old battle over earth's powers. In a comm where she'd sought a quiet, peaceful life after years of training and working for the Fulcrum, then rebelling and hiding from them, Essun helps protect her comm's particular land area from immediate, deadly results of Alabaster's act (a rift she can feel happening). But Essun's husband, realizing his children are "roggas," murders their baby son (out of fear for his power) and leaves with their young daughter, whom he hopes to change (getting rid of her power). Essun is leaving when the comm turns against her (realizing she's an Orogene); to save herself she kills many of them, then sets out on her quest to seek her daughter.

Stone Eater Hoa narrates her story at various stages of her life (where she takes different names)—child Damaya, young woman Syenite, then middle-aged woman Essun.

Jemisin's world and the two main characters, Essun and her daughter, Nassun, break conventional stereotypes of such speculative fiction: "Her epic yarn of a divided and warring mother and daughter . . . unquestionably subverts or inverts the conventions of old-school fantasy in innumerable ways. . . . Neither of them, I can assure you, is a flaxen-haired princess type or a believer in universal harmony and peaceful coexistence" (O'Hehir 2017). Essun is a middle-aged, tall, large-hipped, "strong-looking, well-fleshed," woman with hair "in ropy fused locks" and "skin . . . unpleasantly ocher-brown by some standards and unpleasantly olive-pale by others" (Jemisin 2015, 10). Since Paleolithic humans were brown-skinned, Essun might be considered a more accurate embodiment of some ancient goddess figurines than older goddess fiction (like Auel). But she differs significantly from most goddesses portrayed in other fiction and film.

In addition to breaking ground by creating an unusual, ordinary-looking, middle-aged, brown heroine, Jemisin also tackles huge social issues in her work—like slavery and environmental abuse. Writer Naomi Novik (2015) celebrates Jemisin's ability to blend themes of oppression and systems of power into her fictional world-building:

> N.K. Jemisin's intricate and extraordinary world-building starts with oppression: Her universes begin by asking who is oppressing whom, what they are gaining, what they fear. Systems of power stalk her protagonists, often embodied as gods and primeval forces, so vast that resistance seems impossible even to contemplate. When escape comes in her novels, it is not a merely personal victory, or the restoration of a sketchy and soft-lit status quo. Her heroes achieve escape velocity, smashing through oppressive systems and leaving them behind like shed skins.

The power of such unusual characters is explained as involving DNA that allows some humans to tap into earth's magic, an ability that also makes them vulnerable to prejudices that are relevant in our world: "*They're afraid because we exist. . . . There's nothing we did to provoke their fear, other than exist. There's nothing we can do to earn their approval, except stop existing—so we can either die like they want, or laugh at their cowardice and go on with our lives*" (Jemisin 2017, 109). This painful realization resonates with many of the disenfranchised in our world, but the novel also offers hope.

Another critic appreciates the insights about discrimination relevant to our world offered in the novels of Jemisin and Adeyemi:

> These two African American female authors delve into the horrors of the slave trade by honestly and unflinchingly incorporating it into their science fiction/fantasy trilogies and inviting us all to reassess the legacy of slavery in a time where we perhaps need it most—a time where Donald Trump's rhetoric of "America First" (a 1930s Nazi-accommodationist, Anti-Semitic platform), "blame on both sides" in Charlottesville, depictions of Hispanic immigrants as rapists, drug dealers, and invading animals, and knee-taking African American NFL players as unpatriotic—opens up a platform for racism and White nationalism. Now more than ever, we need to realize that hate only begets hate, and the only real way forward is through radical love. . . . Jemisin and Adeyemi give us ways to imagine slavery and avenues to begin conversations about the racial wounds that are central to American identity. (Murphey 2018, 113)

These heroines of color survive familiar oppressions, often by hiding their power, then wielding it when needed. And their powers are immense—even in their worlds where such powers are known. Essun and her daughter are stronger than most Orogenes and are often underestimated. They survive their "broken earth" when others cannot because of that power, but they also suffer for it. Essun perceives more of the big picture, based on having lived through cycles of oppression, abuse, hope, family-building, family loss, and more.

Hoa is much older, more powerful and knowing, and he takes a childlike form at first, similar to Sieh. Though not named a god, he is powerful and also matches Sieh in longevity, his sometimes childlike nature, and his attachment to and love for the main character, in this case Essun. When his child-form joins her on the road, he states simply, "I like you," then never leaves her (Jemisin 2015, 82). Though child-sized, he is unusual, for instance, completely white (even his eyes), unworldly, powerful (easily killing a threatening predator), and old-seeming, prompting Essun to wonder: "'What in fire-under-Earth are you?'" (112). But Essun accepts him nevertheless, partly because he senses where her daughter is, helps her, and is loyal and undemanding. An ancient text (quoted as a chapter epigraph) explains his kind: "Sentient Non-Humans: They are an arcane thing, . . . an alchemical thing. Like orogeny, if orogeny could manipulate the infinitesimal structure of matter itself rather than mountains. They possess some kinship with humanity, which they choose to acknowledge in the statue-like shape we most often see, but it follows that they can take other shapes" (83). This sentient, human-like, but different, more-powerful-being is arguably godly. Hoa fought others of his kind to "claim" Essun earlier (when her name was Syenite) when she first tapped into an obelisk, revealing her power: "The moment of the obelisk's pulse was the moment in which her presence sang across the world: a promise, a demand, an invitation too enticing to resist. Many of us converged on her then, but I am the one who found her first. I fought off the others and trailed her, watched her, guarded her . . . Listen. Learn. This is how the world changed" (443). Essun feels special to ancient, powerful Stone Eaters, holding "promise" for changing the world, like Yeine.

At the climax of the trilogy, Essun does try to save her world by returning the moon to its orbit, using a mixture of her magical abilities and the ancient gate technology from many millennia before, when Hoa was a slave of exploitative humans. Hoa was one of a small group of "tuners" bred to tap the earth's magic and control a huge series of technological instruments (Obelisks) above the earth's atmosphere—together called the Obelisk Gate. The tuners planned to rebel not only against their absolute oppression—being used as tools, not treated as people—but also to stop the abuse of others with similar DNA, who are horrifically used as living batteries, attached to needles in giant sockets in the earth, to power everything that makes life comfortable in Syl Anagist: "*someone* must suffer, if the rest are to enjoy luxury" (Jemisin 2017, 334). After learning the fate of these tortured souls, whose DNA helps create Hoa and his kind, DNA carried on in Essun and other Orogenes, Hoa ponders rebellion: "There are stages to the process of being betrayed by your society. One is jolted from a place of complacency by the discovery of difference, by hypocrisy, by inexplicable or incongruous ill treatment. What follows is a time of confusion—unlearning what one thought to be the truth. Immersing oneself in the new truth. And then a decision must be made" (311). The tuners perceive the horrors of slavery as injustice, and readers perceive ways that this novel reflects our world's oppressions.

Hoa feels "betrayal" by his world and horror at realizing what he and the other tuners are, slaves: "We do not assert ourselves, we constructs. We tools" (Jemisin 2017, 316). But he also realizes that they cannot escape, since "all the world is Syl Anagist" (317). The tuners' realization or enlightenment foments their plan to fight the forces of power and abuse, to rebel against prejudices, by destroying the Obelisk Gate that they are meant to activate (for Syl Anagist to have even more of the earth's power). But no one realized the earth was alive and magical as well and had its own plan for revenge of abuses against it—to destroy virtually all life on its surface, to save itself (339). The angry, sentient earth wrestles with the tuners for control, and the tuners (via Hoa) are able to direct some energy away from earth—toward the moon, saving some people (340). The earth, Hoa thinks, "understood that we were tools of others, not actors of our own volition," and so, "made us part of it . . . like stone" (341). The tuners are spared, made as immortal as earth and stone, "part of it," meant partly as reprieve (alive), partly as punishment—to always feel the pain of the earth (Jemisin 2015, 341). These events also spur the earth to trigger devastating seasons, survived by some partly because Hoa and his kind help, as with the "stone lore" that offers instructions. Though they help humanity survive, Hoa feels thereafter "too ashamed of the monster I'd become." But Hoa retains some hope: "You survive. . . . I did my best. Helped where I could. And now, my love, we have a second chance. Time for you to end the world again" (Jemisin 2017, 342–43). Essun wants to return the moon to heal the earth, ending seasons, pain, and abuse, but she also knows that using the obelisks to do so will kill her, since each time she taps into the ancient technology, part of her turns to stone.

At the climax of the trilogy, Essun finds her daughter Nassun, who is also angry, mostly at her mother for not having raised her well (she thinks), at herself for killing her father (who'd tried to kill her), at the loss of her beloved guardian, and at the world. Nassun first wants to destroy *everything* (the moon and the earth) and then to turn everyone into Stone Eaters. Despair and anger fuel both women, as Essun reacts destructively from emotions too (at times), for instance killing many when threatened. But during the climax, as mother and daughter struggle to control the gate, the more experienced and understanding Essun lets Nassun win, though by then she has turned almost entirely to stone. Moved by her mother's sacrifice, Nassun decides to complete her mother's task, which she seems to do. Readers worry that Essun is dead (which she thinks she will be), paralleling Yeine's death, before she is reborn a goddess. Hoa manages Essun's metamorphosis into a Stone Eater, a being like him, immortal and powerful.

Hoa explains the process of creating a new Stone Eater as difficult and unpredictable, a "reordering of molecules," that can change the host (lost memories, lost sense of identity). But he is patient while she gestates in the earth, as he loves her nature, which he wants her to retain:

I have brought you here, reassembled the raw arcanic substance of your being, and reactivated the lattice that should have preserved the critical essence of who you were. You'll lose some memory. There is always loss, with change. But I have told you this story, primed what remains of you, to retain as much as possible of who you were. . . . So I wait. Time passes. A year, a decade, a week. The length of time does not matter. . . . I wait. I hope. . . . And then one day, deep in the fissure where I have put you, the geode splits and hisses open. You rise from its spent halves, the matter of you slowing and cooling to its natural state. Beautiful, I think. Locks of roped jasper. Skin of striated ocher marble that suggests laugh lines at eyes and mouth, and stratified layers to your clothing. (Jemisin 2017, 396–97).

This affirmation of a middle-aged brown woman celebrates her awakening as a virtually eternal being (who could live for many thousands of years) with great powers—like Hoa. Just as Essun herself is more mature, and her story slower and full of more suffering, so too her reawakening as a goddess is slower and more complex than Yeine's. Like Yeine, Essun seems to emerge with her selfhood intact, still brown-skinned, with "locks of roped jasper," still aged ("laugh lines at eyes and mouth"), now essentially a goddess. Hoa wants a partner, goddess to his god (terms I'm imposing), partly because he is lonely, but also because Essun's nature is worthy. Her gestation and transformation into a powerful and eternal, stone being, part of earth but with a distinct consciousness, is a freshly imagined concept of what our culture might appreciate as a goddess.

Essun is a well-developed character whom we follow over many years of abuse, some love and cherishing, and growing intelligence, experience, and skill, as witness to all manner of human prejudice and accomplishment. This mother fights for and mourns her children, though we also learn she never sought motherhood—first she was ordered to conceive, then her husband wanted children (Jemisin 2015, 51). She has been connected to and responsible for terrible, deadly events like killing entire villages. Our first views of her are of a "bitter, weary self . . . bewildered, shocked self" (1). She knows hate, including self-hatred: "These people killed Uche [her son]. Their hate, their fear, their unprovoked violence. They . . . oh, uncaring Earth. Look what you've done . . . You close your eyes, aching and shaking and thinking. *No. I killed Uche. By being his mother.* There are tears on your face . . . Stupid, stupid woman. Death was always here. Death is you" (59–60). When we see Yeine kill (after her rise to goddesshood), she seems barely affected by it—perhaps because she sees it as just, perhaps because she is young. But Essun regrets her violent power: "you despaired of ever repairing the harm you'd done" (Jemisin 2017, 398). Essun is an older woman and deeper character, capable, perceptive, introspective, emotionally complex. She grows up as chattel, hated and feared for her power, and is used and abused by the Fulcrum as a pawn in violent, larger schemes. But we also see her emotional growth and her increasing ability to control her powers, sometimes using them for good (also true of Yeine). She suffers from others' hatred and violence, even while recognizing herself as "stupid" and "Death" with a capital D. But when she "dies" and is reborn a stone goddess, we are hopeful, like Hoa, for an emergent, *good* being.

The child/student Damaya becomes the controlled, rising Orogene Syenite, then the renegade who names herself Essun and builds a quiet but happy-ish life (for a while). She also chooses or accepts her transformation into a stone being by activating the gate that she knows will change her, killing her old self. Difficult as it is for Essun to become a woman she wants to be, she nevertheless regularly persists in asserting her own agency, deepening her power, seeking wisdom and compassion, and becoming a character we like (as Hoa does). She is abused, hated, forced to live in ways she doesn't want to, and tormented by her own powerful acts (some of which she is ordered to perform, some of which she chooses). We trace her growing comfort with her power, watch her making choices, and finding ways *to act* (asserting her will) repeatedly, in ways we understand. She embodies a powerful woman survivor with agency. She is imperfect but resonant of hope.

In the final pages, Hoa wonders what this newest goddess version of Essun will be like, "hoping" for a companion to share his desire to try to make the world better: "Because that is how one survives eternity" (Jemisin 2017, 397). He asks the emergent Stone Eater Essun, "What do *you* want?" and her reply, "'I want the world to be better," makes him (and readers) want to leap for joy—though stone beings cannot leap (298). This freshly conceived goddess-like being born from a suffering, flawed human woman wants to use her powers for good, retaining enough of the best of her humanity, and recalls Yeine's wish for "something better." This book ends with her taking Hoa's hand to remake the world—again, similar to Yeine teaming up with Nahadoth to get started on their hopeful wish. Hoa agrees happily:

> "Then let's go make it better."
> You look amused. It's you. It's truly you. "Just like that?"
> "It might take some time."
> "I don't think I'm very patient." But you take my hand.
> Don't be patient. Don't ever be. This is the way a new world begins.
> "Neither am I," I say. "So let's get to it." (398)

The work that these two immortal and powerful beings are eager to engage, to make a better world, suggests a compelling and hopeful promise of speculative fiction as well—making better fictional goddesses.

Essun's looks seem to evoke goddess culture, embodying some prehistoric figurines: "strong-looking, well-fleshed," a mother with ample hips and breasts, and "ropy fused locks." A similar physical version of what we have long imagined and appropriated as a great mother goddess is transformed by Jemisin into a more balanced and complex kind of goddess. Essun's brown skin and ropy hair are incidental to her character—a middle-aged, powerful, underappreciated, abused, controlled woman who survives oppression, war, hardship, and personal tragedy, but also experiences joy and love, and projects hope. Essun moves beyond the usual clichés of loving mother and sexual, emotional, nurturing being, nor is this emergent goddess merely angry and chaotic. She embodies and mixes such qualities in a more human way, even while her powers are profound. Jemisin does not embrace the goddess myth in typical ways in either series. Her sentient earth, for one thing, though magically powerful, is *masculine*, angry, punishing, and referred to regularly in the series as "Evil Earth." It causes seasons and makes humans suffer—though at the end Hoa decides just to call it "The Earth—for the sake of good relations I will no longer call it Evil" (Jemisin 2017, 396). Even with this concluding concession, this conception of earth differs from most goddess myths, as this myth differs overall from typical patterns.

Both of Jemisin's unique, brown-skinned characters mix complexly good and bad impulses and actions and are called "mongrel" for their mixed race, recalling our world's prejudices—where darker skin or mixed race can be perceived by some as less desirable or less worthy, or can provoke fear, derision, and mistreatment. These mixed-nature, brown-skinned protagonists reflect and grow into more tempered, balanced, complex, hopeful natures as goddesses. Though Essun is treated as a slave by the powerful Fulcrum (especially in her youth) and hated by those considered more fully human in her world, much of this prejudice results from her orogenetic powers rather than her skin color—all Orogenes are under Fulcrum control, serve them, and are hated or feared by most non-Orogenes, regardless of race. Even before she meets Hoa, Syenite (younger version of Essun) seems rebellious. She and her mentor, Alabaster, resist Fulcrum efforts to kill them several times. Essun grows her power and asserts her will even before she leaves the Fulcrum, and increasingly afterwards. By connecting to an obelisk the first time, she attracts Stone Eater notice, triggering her eventual transformation, due to her agency, ability, and open curiosity, along with kindness toward the being therein, all in spite of oppressions she endures. A potential weak point of Jemisin's overall message in both books, from a feminist perspective, is that the women seem to need older, more powerful men to help them, even to activate them, as goddesses who can work for a better world. Still, these new goddesses appeal as neither wholly good nor evil, sufferers and agents of pain, enduring great losses, causing death and chaos at times, but also loving, serving as mothers, and proving themselves thoughtful women hopefully willing to build a better future.

Drawing Hope from Darkness

The new world that Circe, Zélie, Yeine, and Essun are willing and eager to remake "better" portends "better" fictional goddesses as well, ones more suited to our world, more complexly human and faulty, suffering in ways that resonate today, but still hopeful in a persuasive way—they know change requires difficult work but possess the will and seemingly the skill to do that work. Some critics label Jemisin's work hopepunk, a genre I argue can also be applied to work by Miller, Silko, and to some extent Walker and Adeyemi. Hopepunk perceives and portrays the world's problems but nonetheless incorporates and projects hope for change, rather than complete despair. Perhaps characters Morgaine and Ayla embrace this kind of hope as well, but not in ways as resonant with complexities or forces reflecting a contemporary world. Hold cryptic rituals, Bradley seems to suggest, and that will change the world. Build a happy family life, with men involved, and that will make everyone happy, Auel suggests. These messages and the characters conveying them seem fairly static—urging concepts and actions that have already been part of our world for some time. Silko, Walker, Adeyemi, Miller, and Jemisin leave us with characters who suffer but are still in the midst of *acting to transform their worlds*, who must continue to carve out and embrace their hard-won agency, to keep building, keep acting, keep imagining, and doing the *hard work* to enact their *will* to make their worlds into places that reflect some *hope*.

Hopepunk, found in much speculative fiction, "weaponizes optimism," and is conceived as contrasting grimdark, in which worlds and characters share similarly postapocalyptic features and themes but in which characters never fully win, ultimately "teach[ing] a different lesson [about humanity]," according to Alexandria Rowland (CBC 2019). First named and explained by Rowland in 2017, hopepunk perceives the world as troubled but also projects hope for change by offering characters who *act*, engaging their agency even in the midst of great darkness, rather than resting in despair (Romano 2017). It is neither as dark as grimdark not as bright and hopeful as noblebright, where good clearly and fully triumphs over evil (CBC 2019). Hopepunk "fits between the two ideas, where hopepunk acknowledges the world can be bad, but that people should fight to make it better," suggesting optimistically that "we can bring [goodness] back," even though it might be difficult, according to Rowland (CBC 2019). This hopeful dynamic of our time in history engages themes of resistance even during times of apocalyptic darkness, focusing on building positive social systems worth fighting for, fostering communities through cooperation, and engaging a consciousness that sees human progress as a *process* in a world where everything is dynamic and impermanent. Recent times, under a US president (Trump) who perceived the world as dark and acted troublingly, felt, especially to people of color and women, disenfranchising and threatening. Nevertheless, people, especially women of color, worked toward or imagined positive change. Such change is difficult and can be painful in real and speculative worlds, but engaging change allows for emergent possibilities. Jemisin tweeted misgivings about her work being labeled hopepunk, considering it more dystopian fiction. Hopepunk may be a passing fad, but writers imagining and creating complex characters engaged in trying to build better worlds based on conscious choice and informed experience portends positive change, fictionally and sometimes in real life, whatever its label.

Jemisin, Miller, Adeyemi, Silko, and Walker offer complex women characters who are oppressed, who suffer, and who share a fantastical mixture of human and goddess qualities (in Jemisin, Miller, and Adeyemi) or are human women inspired by goddess experiences and lore (in Silko and Walker). Essun and Circe are lovingly motherly and deadly dangerous but also women who feel their power and its consequences deeply and whom we perceive as caring, heroic, willing to put themselves at risks for changes we perceive as positive. Tashi, Indigo, and Hattie live in more realistic worlds without magical powers, but they too emerge as caring, heroic characters who endure (or in Tashi's case inspire others to endure), working against the dominant patriarchy to carve out some spaces of livable hope in their worlds. All these characters engage choices (with implications beyond the end of their novels) to focus on difficult, slow, uncertain paths toward resistance and hopeful change. These new myths offer exciting new ways of perceiving and analyzing speculative fiction and popular culture, especially works that also focus on gender and some consideration of goddesses. These works reflect intersectional feminist awareness as well, considering intersecting levels of oppression in their worlds. Nondominant genders and oppressed peoples, as much as they suffer, become wellsprings of hoped-for changes, offering some of the most realistic yet inspiring, truly *new* fiction or myths considered.

The characters in these works make mistakes, suffer, and endure in realistically imperfect (though fantastical) worlds to survive, transform, or inspire as beacons of hope to other oppressed people. Endurance, agency, and rise to goddesshood become humanistic in their complexity, with characters who perceive the faults, history, limitations, and potential of their worlds—reflecting our world. In some cases, beings enacting agency become less powerful, wounded, or die (Circe, Tashi, Hattie), but they live with some (potentially more modest) hope or leave it behind by inspiring others. In other cases (Essun, Yeine), mortal women with sparks of power (and some help) manage to shape that power to achieve goddesshood. Zélie also transforms positively via goddess power, and most of these transformations, survivals, messages, or legacies of hope require significant hard work and often much suffering. All these women's lives intersect powerlessness, moments of power, insight, great oppressions, suffering, and help from some outside forces, all of which intertwine to make them who they are.

Conclusion

Some contemporary goddesses move complexly beyond stereotyped depictions as completely good or completely bad in myths that engage issues of social justice, oppression, and sexism in thoughtful ways that resonate, reflecting recent perspectives such as intersectional gender studies. These works recognize multiple forms of oppression (like race, ethnicity, class, abilities, even species) as influencing gender dynamics. These goddesses are uniquely neither utterly destructive and chaotic nor idealized and romanticized. These emergent, more resonant, newer mythic patterns hopefully reflect our cultural moment, when we face troubling issues but want to hope and work to redress injustices and wrongs.[8] Earlier goddesses from hopeful feminists that fantasize a time when women ruled and goddesses were revered, emerged especially after second-wave feminism, when older ideas of goddess culture were most embraced as a hopeful myth that could change or save the world, though from a romanticized, essentialized perspective. Mainstream goddess myths in film and television often skew to an opposite extreme of powerful women and goddesses as chaotic forces of destruction to be feared or mocked. More intersectional feminist myths in this chapter reflect contemporary worldly concerns, modeling taking responsibility and embracing or finding agency to make and remake selves and troubled worlds—mythically or otherwise. The power of fiction, including that of goddesses, is that it can comfort, inspire, anger, cause havoc, and sometimes even reflect our world, with all its problems and complexities. Some recent goddesses and goddess cultures shimmer with potential to move beyond mere reflections of reality or affirm that we're okay in spite of our troubles.

The matrices of matriarchy that Silko imagines and the more complex relationship to and images of goddesses and related worlds analyzed in this chapter seem more thoughtfully complex and promising as new myths, reflective in a hopeful, engaged way of today's feminism, more so than many earlier goddesses. Silko's and Walker's characters suffer at the hands of the patriarchal, colonialist Western cultural norms of the twentieth century. Adeyemi, Jemisin, and Miller likewise portray oppressions and issues with twenty-first-century, real-world resonance. Goddess power emerges as more than a pseudo-utopian life, with characters who suffer and find agency to sometimes (Circe) choose living in the world as mortals among earthly friends, even if painfully. Powerful women can be conceived as more than either obnoxious and oppressive or motherly and static. Some new goddesses recognize intersectional oppressions, suffering, and hopeful but hard, gradual changes, suggesting no easy answers for the past or future.

The lack of easy answers and absolutes connects to realistic fantasies of hope, such as Silko's illuminations and comforts in small groups hiding in the shadow of patriarchy, or Walker's grassroots movement of women protecting their daughters. Circe tends her garden and family, creating spaces in which she can be independent even while powerful.[9] Yeine and Essun heal ancient rifts and take responsibility to continue correcting, healing, and forging new paths. Adeyemi's characters may break dysfunctional traditions to forge new pathways to merge factions. Even living in troubled, brutal worlds, these characters survive and find and create comfort, illumination, or joy. Such new(er) myths by women implicitly challenge and revise older assumptions of goddess culture to reimagine powerful, engaged women living amid and aware of profound challenges. Voices from the margins of our culture may be the force needed to push speculations into a more realistic, contemporary, and hopeful goddess trope. A lens of intersectional feminist theory reveals how writers less focused on past goddesses can envision new, imperfect, non-idealized, non-romanticized, and also less awful, less destructive beings who reflect contemporary human visions and lives, refashioning freshly dynamic goddess myths.

Making Mythic Sense
Living with the Goddess Myth

Let us celebrate our human ability to imagine possible pasts or futures via fiction that offers mythic visions of comfort and inspiration sometimes reflective of reality. The diversity and wonder of human expressivity allow us to mythically build past, present, and future worlds in books, on screens, and in a variety of media. Hopes that some versions of the goddess myth might work to challenge old, outdated, and harmful assumptions and cultural patterns fade as analyses of images and patterns reveal mostly reflections of the tellers and their cultures, which are usually far from utopian. Analyzing literary and popular culture versions of goddess myths through a feminist lens reveals much about our culture and the ongoing issues and dualities in our sexist, hegemonic, bureaucratic, polluted, troubled world because ultimately myths are mostly about our culture: our realities, our concerns, our anxieties, our troubles, and sometimes our hopes. Like the fake goddesses archaeologist Arthur Evans "found" on Crete, many of the newer goddesses and their myths express and create a feedback loop of a vision not only falsely projected as hope for a better world but projected onto the past as well.

Many feminists today encourage recognizing the emergent, always expanding nature of research into the past, while others urge us to ever-greater awareness of how we appropriate imagined pasts and create myths, which are often ultimately unprogressive from feminist perspectives. The goddess myth is variable but often misguided and reductionist in celebrating women as nurturing, motherly, sexual, more "natural" beings. Though many goddess myths portray gender in unsatisfying and troubling ways, some more originally conceived ones imagine goddesses and worlds that reach beyond old patterns to offer more complex characters; modest, workable moments of hope; and fresh inspiration or insight. But plenty of old patterns continue to be reproduced today. The goddess myth is often surprisingly patriarchal and un-feminist at root, rendering it largely unhelpful as a new vision for gendered and environmental futures.

Believers claim that the goddess serves "as symbol of the newfound beauty, strength, and power of women" (Christ and Plaskow 1979, 286). Contrarily, the symbolism explored herein reveals recycled images and patterns of women as domestic, nurturing, instinctive, sexual, creative, nature-based, peaceful bodies (especially in those examined in chapter 5) or otherwise as threatening, crushing forces of chaos (chapter 4). While the romanticized goddess appeals as comforting and hopeful on the surface, we can perceive old patterns and old expectations for women and our potential in these myths—a troubling, enduring "otherness" as the second sex. The hope attached to goddesses and related cultures can feel inspiring. But many myths mock or degrade women's cultures and hopes attached to them or essentialize them fantastically in distant worlds. Reflecting a truly feminist, different, or egalitarian world for women and all humans is a challenge that most goddess myths do not meet, at least not until more recent, differently patterned, hopeful myths. The newest goddesses are neither merely sexual, loving, and motherly beings nor powerfully destructive nightmares. Sometimes they carry aspects of both but also newer potential or experienced, informed perseverance. Significantly, we continue to reimagine all types of goddesses often in our world, indicating that something about such stories resonates with us today. We want or need goddesses today, though we don't always fully examine what they're communicating through a critical, feminist lens. Table 4 summarizes the myths I have examined here, the types of goddesses they imagine, the ways they present women's lives, how humans fare in their worlds, and how each world presents gender.

This comparative table of examples considered herein includes different font styles. In column 2, "Types of Goddesses," *italics* signifies romanticized views of goddesses; **bold** signifies vilified goddesses/cultures; ***bold and italics*** signifies mixed/complex views. In column 3, "Views of Women's Lives," underline highlights indicate key ways humans or women live in those worlds. Significantly, almost all works feature humans suffering in their worlds and perspectives, with women facing especially great troubles. We considered six romanticized views of goddesses and related cultures (three fully romanticized, three mixed), wherein women still mostly suffer; nine vilified views of goddesses and related cultures, where women and men suffer; and seven mixed or complex views of goddesses and related cultures, where most people

TABLE 4. CONTEMPORARY GODDESS EXAMPLES AND CHARACTERISTICS

WORK(S)	TYPE OF GODDESS (OR GODDESS CULTURE)	VIEW OF WOMEN'S LIVES (AND ALL LIFE)	PRESENTATION OF GENDER
LESLIE MARMON SILKO, *GARDENS IN THE DUNES* (2000)	Partly *romanticized*, but also **mixed, complex:** goddess culture of past romanticized (but not shown directly); no goddess characters	Small (cryptic) but strong communities of women who have all suffered greatly from patriarchy	Punished women nevertheless endure; Loving motherly women connect to nature; men are cruel, greedy, or useless
ALICE WALKER, *POSSESSING THE SECRET OF JOY* (1992)	*Romanticized* myth of idyllic previous time (no goddess characters); also **complex** in focus on women's reality	Women, especially Tashi, suffer greatly at hands of patriarchy (in recent times)	Women are sexually brutalized (FGM) and suffer, even mothers. Men are mixed—cruel or kind/caring
DAN BROWN, *THE DA VINCI CODE* (2003)	*Romanticized*—fully adopts myth of goddess prehistory as real in the past and continuing cryptically	Women, men, and culture suffer under patriarchy. Main female character knows less, grieves, and is in some danger	Men are in charge of most rituals and solving mystery (and know more), but women may help and/or be revered
THOR: RAGNAROK (2017)	Goddess Hela is **vilified** as a force of evil and chaos	Heroes must bring about terrible Ragnarok, resulting in suffering, chaos, "end of world" (at least one world)	Men excel in higher positions (including main hero), but powerful women exist and can be scarily emotional or out of control
HELLBOY II (2008)	No goddess, but giant goddess figurine **vilified** as destructive (in playful way)	Opening attack shows suffering; world in turmoil	Women have some roles of power but are secondary to men
THE 13TH WARRIOR (1999)	**Vilified**—Wendols are bloodthirsty savages; evil Mother Wendol (looks like snake goddess) poisons hero	Mother Wendol and her culture cause Norsemen to suffer and die (eating them), threatening their society	Heroic warriors are Norsemen; women are healers, nurturers, or evil savages; evil Mother Wendol somewhat sexualized
THE WICKER MAN (1973 AND 2006)	**Vilified**—goddess culture and matriarchy are real but threaten and kill the male hero	Men suffer (from hero's point of view); in matriarchal society, shown as violent and strange	Women are motherly, sexualized, tricky, deadly leaders; men are "drones," helping or victims of women
BUFFY THE VAMPIRE SLAYER (1997–2003) AND *ANGEL* (1999–2004)	**Vilified**—goddesses kill main women characters, hurt many, cause chaos; powerful women may be good (Buffy, Willow) or mixed (Jasmine, Illyria) but are also angry and destructive (Glory, Jasmine, Illyria)	Lots of suffering by all characters, but especially women who often lose their lives. Somewhat hopeful endings	Smart and clever women and men; hetero and homosexuality explored; main female characters cannot always trust sex partners (some sexual violence); absent mothers

WORK(S)	TYPE OF GODDESS (OR GODDESS CULTURE)	VIEW OF WOMEN'S LIVES (AND ALL LIFE)	PRESENTATION OF GENDER
TRUE BLOOD (2008–2014)	**Vilified**—goddesses are bloodthirsty, manipulative; Maenad causes chaos, deaths, bad feelings; Lilith is feared as original, evil goddess of death	Lots of suffering by all characters, especially main character Sookie and her friends (though series gives happy ending to some)	Goddess brings evil into world, though hero Sookie is smart, strong, and has some power; sex partners and relationships not always trustworthy; mixed mother characters
THE MAGICIANS (2015–2020)	*Mixed* to **Vilified**—some goddesses are mixed, complex (Persephone and Julia); some are fully evil (the Sister); Julia causes chaos as well as helping friends and worlds	Most main characters and the whole world are suffering often; characters must battle repeatedly to save multiple worlds; deaths, rapes, losses of souls, monsters and beasts that cause torment, etc.	Much sexuality explored for all characters (often positive), including homosexual and bisexual characters; equal experiences of power, suffering, and abuse; violent rape leads to goddesshood; absent or bad mothers (at times)
JEAN AUEL, EARTH'S CHILDREN SERIES (1980–2011)	*Romanticized*—goddesses as loving and goddess-centered matriarchy as peaceful and positive	Ayla suffers while with Neanderthals; human women are valued in matriarchal societies; Paleolithic mother goddesses are loving; less suffering than most	Women and men in conventional goddess myth roles: mostly women leaders but work evenly shared in peaceful world; much positive hetero sex and motherliness
MARION ZIMMER BRADLEY, AVALON SERIES (1983–2009)	*Romanticized*—last remnants of goddess culture (actual power) and priestesses of goddess (main character)	Women's ancient (superior) power declining due to patriarchy; suffering for women increasing	Women's power connected to magic, sexuality (somewhat troubled) and nature; men bring war
MARGARET ATWOOD, *THE PENELOPIAD* (2005)	*Romanticized*—another last glimmer of matriarchy and goddess culture), portraying its defeat by patriarchy	Women suffer abuses and are harassed and killed (hanged maidens = death of previous matriarchal goddess culture)	Women are wives or sexual slaves; "Ideal wife" Penelope used as model (lesson) and maids are used then killed by patriarchy
MADELINE MILLER, *CIRCE* (2018)	**Mixed, complex**—goddesses are real but can be good (Circe) or bad (Athena and most other goddesses); most gods (all genders) are so bad that Circe decides to be human	Circe suffers from own conscience and some mistreatment; other gods often seem unhappy, mean, or unpleasant; mortal humans' lives may be preferable to gods'	Women as mothers (some good, some bad) and wives or sexual partners; Circe and Penelope are admirable women; gender less important than inner being
TOMI ADEYEMI, *CHILDREN OF BLOOD AND BONE* (2018)	Somewhat *romanticized*—though also **mixed, complex** with multiple goddesses, some helpful/loving, some not totally so (darker, deadly)	Most characters suffer in this world—especially magi like Zélie, abused for belief in and connection to goddesses	Gender roles fairly conventional—men in positions of power and tormenting women; women trying to save society; Zélie despised/chased by love interest

WORK(S)	TYPE OF GODDESS (OR GODDESS CULTURE)	VIEW OF WOMEN'S LIVES (AND ALL LIFE)	PRESENTATION OF GENDER
N. K. JEMISIN, *THE HUNDRED THOUSAND KINGDOMS* (2010)	*Mixed, complex*—human main character has embedded goddess spark/soul and ascends to goddesshood with some identity maintained; Goddess Enefa is one of three main, ancient gods (motherly)	<u>Many humans suffer forms of oppression</u> in this world; main character Yeine (young woman) <u>is mocked and mistreated</u> but learns and adapts with positive ending	Women and men fairly evenly depicted as characters and gods, though motherhood is key to Enefa. Yeine is less knowledgeable than men; powerful women show agency; fairly positive, fluid sexuality depicted
N. K. JEMISIN, BROKEN EARTH TRILOGY (2015–2017)	*Mixed, complex*—main character. Essun, human with complex story, becomes essentially a goddess who wants to use her power to make the world better	<u>All humans suffer greatly in this broken world,</u> though the ending offers hope	Mixed gender roles—hetero, homo, and bisexual characters, and complex family dynamics

suffer. Typically, the mixed or complex views also have more complex views of gender roles and reflect some hope.

The fact that most goddess myths portray women, and often all humans, as *suffering*, living in painfully imperfect, troubled, or broken worlds, is partly the nature of story—to fictionalize all kinds of trouble and imagine ways to live with problems. Without a knotty problem for protagonists to untie, after all, stories hardly interest us. In five lengthy subsequent novels, Auel never quite recaptured the greatness of her first novel, *The Clan of the Cave Bears*, where Ayla suffers much and struggles to find a place for herself. Once Ayla is among the matriarchal, goddess-worshiping humans, the books become less exciting (critics agree). Jemisin novel *The Hundred Thousand Kingdoms* and her Broken Earth trilogy end with hope (not certainty) as Essun and Yeine work to improve their worlds, but those books mainly feature the extreme troubles the women experience. Troubled storylines with recycled-seeming heroes always reappear because there is no end to problems we experience and imagine, and dealing with trouble is fiction's point. That's why some of the newer heroes with intersectional, relevant storylines feel so hopeful. Stories help us perceive and affirm our world, where suffering is common, but those with the most poignant suffering can also imagine and hope for newer paths. We see no definitive happy endings in most works, as goddess culture imagines the distant past. But by engaging our troubled world—our puzzling existence full of tragedies, some delights, *and* potential—we can perceive human abilities and strengths to persist and resist.

Many myths that assert past and future goddess-centered, supposedly superior cultures offer minimal visions or inspirations for a brighter future for women, people of color, or people of any gender, even men. If the goddess still exists, as Morgaine perceives in Bradley's Avalon universe, her existence is cryptic and isolated, and her power minimal. Auel's Ayla perceives the future in troubling visions and urges us to be happy raising families. Such romanticized views seem happy with offering women little glimmers of potential while resting in a domestic sphere, and indeed most women do live with only glimmers of potential in a dominant patriarchy, willingly or not. Our society evinces deep concern and anger over actual women achieving power or status, as in Hillary Clinton's defeat in the 2016 election, the mistreatment and disbelief of Christine Blasey Ford's 2018 testimony of sexual harassment against a Supreme Court appointee), decline in belief of sexual misconduct allegations in the #MeToo movement by late 2018, the inability of any woman candidate to rise to the top in the 2020 election cycle, and ongoing dismay and disbelief by many about a woman of color (Kamala Harris) winning the vice presidency in 2020. There are countless real-world examples of sexism and racism today that suggest our world's progress toward potential reclaiming of goddess culture's idealized views is slow-going at best.

More than offering a means for actually changing the world and possibly bringing back women-centered cultures, many goddess myths mostly reflect our culture back to us, showing us that women who are imagined as powerful are then often punished harshly, suffering like real-world women who get too close to sources of power. Too many of the women in even the most utopian versions of the myth are left in damaged, ruined, largely hopeless worlds, with only distant promises of something different, maybe better. Or they rest in small communities with limited power to escape suffering, just surviving at best, though maybe with sincere hope. We are hopeful when Essun and Yeine wake up as new beings with powers and intentions to rebuild their broken worlds, when the women of Tashi's country promise to keep their babies whole, when Hattie and Indigo find and build communities (of mostly women) and tend their gardens, and when Circe carves out a space from her punishment as a powerful woman to embrace her humanity. These mythic women live, survive, and create, but only after suffering and battling powerful forces (that they cannot fully defeat), often in broken, troubled, difficult worlds. Nevertheless, they persist, sometimes hopefully.

In a time of real-world suffering and crises for women, including inequality, harassment, and oppression, we seek myths to help, to redress imbalance,

at least symbolically, or to offer comfort and possible hope for a better life—
though always one in a probably distant future, or possibly from an irrecover-
able past. Part of the work accomplished metaphorically by myths is to help
us accept the chaotic confusions or crises of our existence, which are often
conceived of symbolically as dualities, as well as to find a path of order (cosmos) through the confusion.[1] Myths turn chaos into cosmos, which is mythically confirmed as good.[2] Some conceive of postmodern rituals and myths of
goddess spirituality as "breathing new life into old goddess images" and helping women to "construct their ritual lives from an eclectic stew" that shows a
"dizzying variety of manifestations, both sacred and profane" because women
want an expression of the sacred in their lives (McDonald 1996, 46–52).
Believers see the myth as confirming the world that they hope they are building and their practices and beliefs as "good," an acceptable order, or new cosmos. My analysis questions the *new*ness of the cosmos that many expressions
of the myth present. They may affirm a cosmos, but what we deconstruct of
its images is hardly new; rather, it's usually a myth of patriarchy as dominant
and livable.

This mythic worldview regarding women and gender possibilities is less
new or liberated than a reinforcement of the status quo—often reducing
women to domestic, emotional beings. Motherhood is far too often a bot-
tom line or ultimate goal or reality for all these women characters. Even the
name "mother goddess" (often the kind of goddess people imagine) dictates
this reductionist, essentialized view of gender, which is limiting and problematic. Women's lives needn't be defined by motherhood, and non-mother
women can be productive, fulfilled, and happy. We resort to a reflexive base
of motherhood as essential to womanhood partly because of our culture's
gender biases, assumptions, and expectations, which are driven largely by a
patriarchal and capitalist worldview, always needing more consumers (and
thus births of consumers). We prioritize and valorize childbirth and thus
motherhood throughout all levels of our culture, at least superficially. We
rarely or minimally provide financial and other support for actual mothers,
but numerous cultural expressions, from fairy tales to songs to literature to
many other forms of popular culture, reinforce messages that being a mother
is the highest, happiest goal that women can or should strive to achieve. This
limiting and short-sighted pattern causes many problems, since motherhood is not always completely fulfilling, comfortable, or happy for all women.
Motherhood makes many women unhappy, even desperate, and can result in
other major emotional (guilt, unhappiness, and stress), financial (not having
enough money or resources to raise children), or social issues (losing jobs,

relationships, access to valued activities and education). Many autobiographies (including many by men) and much fiction, showcasing bad mothers, testify to the serious harm that bad mothers can cause. Motherhood is not a magical answer for women, nor are all mothers good mothers.

Joan Bamberger concluded back in 1974, "The myth of matriarchy is but the tool used to keep woman bound to her place. To free her, we need to destroy the myth" (280). Bamberger and many other feminist scientists perceive processes of valorizing motherhood as definitive and idealizing matriarchy as essentializing tools of the patriarchy. Those who question myths of matriarchy and goddesshood perceive how often it reinforces the status quo and hope women can access other options besides a baseline biological imperative, to which we are so often reduced, in our myths and in our lives. Motherhood can be wonderful and fulfilling but is not the only or final option for women. Surely imagining other ways of women living wonderful, fulfilled, engaged, and meaningful lives need not be threatening, sad, or horrifying. Such statements are often seen as attacks on mothers or on goddess beliefs as positive choices. Cynthia Eller (2003) clarifies, in response to attacks on her critical book *The Myth of Matriarchal Prehistory* (2000), that she doesn't intend to critique "feminist spirituality" or feminists who think this matriarchal myth is doing positive work: "I don't see myself 'criticizing feminists'; I see myself contributing to a more self-critical feminism." Calling something a myth and examining how it fulfills that genre, along with examining the messages encoded in it, are further means of critical (self-)examination. Along with Eller, Goodison and Morris, Lefkowitz, and many other feminist scholars, I believe that as feminists we can and should accept the best work of scientists, including feminist archaeologists and feminist mythologists, to examine the symbolism and deeper meanings of popular contemporary myths, allowing ourselves to question those myths' problematic and non-feminist meanings, symbols, or implications, when we find them.

Bound Up in Gender Binaries

Varied, modern, reimagined, and invented worlds that feature goddesses have become in our culture a remarkably common mythic mode that rarely breaks molds of portraying women, men, and most of our experiences and concerns in binary oppositions or dualities. The myths that vilify or romanticize goddesses are full of symbolic dualities, one of the most basic being gender—with women and men often tied to particular traits and circumstances.

Romanticized goddesses equate all that is potentially good in human culture to women, conceived in biologically determinative ways, since motherhood, and sometimes sexuality, are key to womanhood in most such versions. At the other extreme, powerful women and goddesses are bloodthirsty savages and forces of chaos, probably reflective of our culture's innate fear and rejection of the very idea of powerful women. Even those myths that do break basic cycles of vilifying or romanticizing to offer more complex characters still tend to incorporate symbolism of binary oppositions like love versus hate, body versus mind, nurturing versus destructive, nature versus culture, men versus women, and all the other qualities and aspects of tables 2 and 3. Slightly older versions of the myth in particular tend to show real and imagined women and men living in dualistic extremes, tying femininity to emotion, nurturing, and nature. Though there is no single, fully generalizable version of the myth, it often fits patterns in table 2. Perhaps such dualities are just a basic mode of human brain patterns (as Lévi-Strauss suggests), or perhaps simplifying things to binary patterns (part of lived nature) is comforting or reassuring to humans, helping make constructed, imagined worlds work. Many millennia of similar patterns in myths likely attest to perceivable dualistic patterns in nature, like night and day, hot and cold, dry and wet, life and death.

Perhaps there is a connection between nature-based stimuli (as dualistic) and the invocation of nature and ethics of place in goddess myths, where the primordial period is conceived as a time of unmatched and enviable environmentalism. Women and thus all people, since women ruled and guided society, are assumed to have been more in tune with nature, part of place in ways that later patriarchal cultures corrupted.[3] Many goddess believers contrast the healing of the planet and the oppressed gender (women), against the abusers and oppressors of both (men). If the mythic hope of saving the environment were right, and given the extent to which our culture embraces and tells the goddess myth, we might wonder why we remain in such dire and ever-worsening ecological straits. Stories help us make sense by offering answers and comforts but also sometimes by posing new questions or challenges, necessarily drawing from and reflecting our lived experiences. We experience and ponder such existential realities, including ongoing deterioration of the environment and troubled gender dynamics in our world.

Patterns of how we perceive women extend throughout our culture's representations of women, as Ortner (1974, 86–87) explained many years ago:

> We can account easily for both the subversive feminine symbols (witches,
> evil eye, menstrual pollution, castrating mother) and the feminine symbols

of transcendence (mother goddesses, merciful dispensers of salvation, female symbols of justice, and the strong presence of feminine symbolism in the realms of art, religions, ritual, and law). Feminine symbolism far more often than masculine symbolism, manifests this propensity toward polarized ambiguity—sometimes utterly exalted, sometimes utterly debased, rarely within the normal range of human possibilities.

Scholars such as Christ and Judith Plaskow (1979, 12, 7) in their *Womanspirit Rising* book decry the "problem of remaining bound to old dualisms," while calling for women to "upset the order that has been taken for granted throughout history." Yet the new "thealogy" that goddess believers describe as arising presents itself and certainly is perceived and used in popular culture in familiar dualistic patterns and symbols.[4] Six goddess myths explored herein (a sampling of what our culture creates) include "utterly exalted" symbols I'm calling romanticized and nine feature "utterly debased," vilified versions.

The reason a romanticized portrayal of goddess prehistory should be questioned as problematic and possibly harmful is that any representation that results in extreme stereotypes, whether romanticized as completely good or vilified as evil or destructive, does not represent reality. Ortner (1974, 87) refers to this reductive pattern as "a (sadly) efficient feedback system," sad because it ultimately devalues women. Either way, positively or negatively, women are cast as unrealistic "others." As existentialist philosophy explains, portraying any human as an unrealistic other is inauthentic, meaning it does not promote responsible, informed understanding or ethical, humanitarian practices rooted in reality. Inauthenticity is a worldview or philosophical perspective that might also result in art reflecting it and that hurts and limits everyone. Such art serves as a kind of fantastical escapism that can lead to harmful abuses or misunderstandings—usually of women or people of color, historically. Judgments—of the past, or of a particular sex as completely good or bad, or resting in any unrealistic extreme—and any stereotypes based on *essentialized gender*, possibly as determinative, disallow women and humans generally the space to be themselves, to be real, complex beings with shifting, emergent mixtures of good and bad, sacred and profane qualities. Nor does the "feedback system" Ortner (1974) describes allow for any of us to explore our lives and new possibilities based on our lived realities or even imagined potential. The myth can also vilify men as predominantly evil, which is equally troubling.[5] Many of these new myths rest on imagined or purported past cultures appropriated according to our current stereotypes, which tend to be sexist, patriarchal, and often discriminatory in other ways. Plus, the very way we study and discuss the myth becomes dualistic most of the time (table 3).

Harmful Mythic Clichés and Scholarship to Build Upon

At the outset, I pondered whether this myth is empowering and positive for women or whether it rests on questionable archetypes that actually reduce our options—to, for instance, motherhood, sexuality, or nature-based mysticism. Women so conceived remain in a natural or domestic sphere, as we have seen from Ayla to Essun and others. Even the powers of women in these myths, when romanticized, are often mystical and "feminine," inspired by or connected to domestic realms, for instance drawing magic from plants in gardens, saving needy humans, mothering in general, participating in cult-like religions, supporting men in their worlds, and so on. At the other extreme, the bad goddesses are often irrationally violent and chaotic, raging without reason. Although many examples of these dualistic extremes are a bit dated, from the previous century, the pattern of viewing powerful women in similar ways continues today, though not without some hopeful changes.

In both extremes of romanticized or vilified women, feminine power is connected to strong emotions. Such dualistic visions of women offer the same essential roles, always woman as other, as de Beauvoir's second sex, defined against the primary subject—man. Either mythic extreme (good or bad goddess) does not really liberate or change women's roles or possibilities, instead replaying gender stereotypes. Cliché depictions of romanticized or vilified goddesses limit gender possibilities for everyone, for instance denying men, boys, and nonbinary characters mythic space to be nurturing, emotional, caring, artistic beings. Patriarchies and most men in the myth are "aggressive, competitive, and possessive," in contrast to the more cooperative matriarchies (Eller 2000, 54). Some romanticized versions of the myth trace "a change from the peaceful, harmonious world of women to the awful, wicked world of men" (48). Patriarchy in such versions is associated with warfare, slavery, and environmental destruction, as though only men participate in atrocities or are capable of crime. In other versions, women's emotions, coupled with power, are deadly. All genders are denied a full range of human experience in such myths. Imagining or positing that there could be some human beings who are more *natural* than others is absurd. We are all human beings, all animals of nature. Science allows for no bending of this fundamental biological truth.

From a hostile, antifeminist perspective of questioning the myth, some men scholars particularly infuriated by the goddess movement cite the lack of scientific rigor to attack not only goddess culture and the myth but feminists generally, along with academic women's studies departments.[6] Feminist scholars, quoted throughout this work, also take issue with unrealistic and potentially harmful views of both genders that the myth embodies, such as the very idea of gender as an inescapable and binary system to which we are bound and by which we are determined. Neither the myth nor the scholarship thereof needs to require such definitive boundaries. Questioning the very notion of gender as binary and determinative pinpoints the unlikely, biased, and troubling nature of tying fundamental characteristics to sex. There are no predetermined, inescapable qualities of feminine or masculine, most modern gender theorists attest. Intersectional and newer writers are less absorbed with absolutes, and they offer more complexly human characters capable of good and bad actions, sometimes embracing the terms on the left side of the column, regardless of gender, other times the opposite, sometimes straddling lines. Awareness of patterns and a will to move beyond them is emerging—to smash the patterns, not just the patriarchy.

Goodison and Morris (1998) note that the pro-matriarchy movement is progressive, so they realize that many might wonder why we would scrutinize presentations or appropriations of the past. They suggest that metaphorically the concept of a matriarchal prehistory is fine; it is only literally that it is troubling. But given their concerns, and those of many others, of both literal and metaphorical messages of the myth as problematic, we should feel enabled to continue on a path of feminist inquiry and scrutiny. Many feminist scholars like me find it ironic and troubling that women have so often used archetypes created by men of essential, domestic women's roles as a "way out" of sexism.[7] Eller's (2000) subtitle, *Why an Invented Past Won't Give Women a Future*, suggests that we need not confirm or rely on unverifiable ideas to imagine a brighter feminist future. She finds "nothing inherently feminist in matriarchal myth," but she also acknowledges that many "experience the story ... as profoundly empowering," believing in "a better future for us all" (7). She affirms, "it is my feminist movement too, and when I see it going down a road which, however inviting, looks like the wrong way to me, I feel an obligation to speak up," and "the myth ignores or misinterprets" much, resting on "sexist assumptions it leaves undisturbed" (7). Goodison and Morris, Ortner, Bamberger, Lefkowitz, Meskell, and more all detail the many problems with the origins and evidence for the myth, as do I. Let us continue to question, to explore, to persist, to emerge.

The Tenacity of the Goddess Myth and Its Worldly Tethers

Since its nineteenth-century invention, the goddess myth's popularity has waxed and waned with feminist movements, finding special traction during the 1970s, probably emerging from and inspired by the second wave of feminism from that period, when more women sought spiritual roles and stories, including mythic origin stories. Lefkowitz (1993, 261) explains this "new cult": "it is not at all surprising that once modern women began to perceive themselves as a class or genre with special interests, needs, and styles of life distinctly separate . . . they would begin to develop divinities of their own." Myths particularly appeal to us and are invoked at critical times.[8] The social upheaval of women's fighting for their rights may have made the timing of Gimbutas's and Starhawk's work especially appealing to those who feel or felt their lives, roles, and history to be in crisis (the second wave of Feminism), up to now. It may have helped during the second wave to have a woman archaeologist telling the story, in the figure of Gimbutas, a sort of mother goddess herself—a mother goddess of the mother goddess concept, a role her followers seem to perceive her as filling. It is also significant that some recent and intersectional versions of the myth are offering more complex views of goddesses, perhaps reflecting third- or even fourth-wave feminism. The whole myth continues to appeal to many in our culture, though it has been questioned for years, and it is now finally evolving a little.

The Belili website devoted to her work and life describes Gimbutas as a controversial scholar who *dared* to interpret and generalize meaningfully, comparing her to other bold, groundbreaking, and underappreciated-in-their-own-day scientists, such as "Galileo and other 'heretics,'" as having "shaken the foundations of her society. . . . If her theories are correct, then peace, reverence for the earth and the honoring of life are not only human capabilities, they are the very underpinnings of European civilization itself" (Starhawk and Read 2003). Most of the women who embrace neo-paganism and the concept of goddess culture perceive such revelation as a positive new consciousness for women. But they seem to ignore recent feminist archaeologists and to minimize the concept's roots among Victorian men, instead claiming Gimbutas's work as key (Marler 2003).[9] These women are smart, well meaning, and hopeful, but they also seem to allow their hopes to obscure awareness and acceptance that patriarchal, imaginative, and often essentialized theories underpin and shape many goddess beliefs, practices, and myths.[10]

Proponents remain defiant even when confronted with strong evidence from contemporary scholars, including feminist scholars of all types. Feminist theologian Mary Daly asserts that if feminine images of the divine cannot be found (in the past), then "women should invent them" (qtd. in Goodison and Morris 1998, 11), and we have invented them, I argue—in all the examples analyzed herein and many others in our culture. We have also seen tenacious adherence to the myth by Starhawk, Christ, Marler, and others. Those who critique the myth conclude that it is valid to explore goddess ritual possibilities and other metaphors for social change but, for instance, that it is not the feminist archaeologist's task to construct "goddess" narratives but rather to demystify archaeological "facts" (Goodison and Morris 1998, 21), pointing to the truth factor so often raised in mythology. Myths are considered true and sacred by believers, even if the truth is metaphorical. But it is also the mythologist's task to demystify mythological patterns and messages, to explain what myths mean and how they function in our culture. As noted, *woman* as usually conceived and portrayed in this myth is the quintessential, fabricated other whose characteristics are remarkably unliberated in feminist terms—a mystifyingly "more natural," more emotional, motherly, more sexual being than man, one bound to be nurturing, caring, peaceful, and creative.

In some ways, the goddess movement fulfills its projected (though not always acknowledged) vision by embodying domesticity in its patterns and footprint in our world. Many iterations and experiences of goddess culture are less organized movements connected to sources of real power than grassroots series of various disunified concepts, expressions, and events (McDonald 1996).[11] Goddess culture devotees or entrepreneurs may connect via tourism, with pilgrimages to goddess shrines, as well as via sales of books, films, jewelry, bumper stickers, T-shirts, bath products, and so on. There are organized retreats, rituals, workshops, celebrations, and other gatherings, as well as artistic and publishing opportunities, including novels, histories, self-help books, coffee table books, art, films, and websites.[12] But many of these worldly aspects of the goddess myth arguably remain mostly small scale and domestic.[13] Some see the goddess-as-metaphor as important for the inner self or alternatively as a "sop" for a "radical feminist minority in the church" (McDonald 1996, 50). Daly claims that the "feminist revolution is essentially a spiritual revolution" and charged the Vatican with sexism: "As long as we believe God is male, then the male thinks he is God" (qtd. in McDonald 1996, 50–51). Such discussions confirm various inherent dualities and representations in the myth, where men and their majority institutions are cast as problematic. Bold, sweeping condemnations can feel satisfying, but they also suggest the myth's problematic limitations. Still, there is no doctrine or agreed-upon leadership council, nor any actual, generalizable, or definitive goddess culture at all. My conflation of various movements, practices, and beliefs isn't meant to ignore or deny the complexities of goddess discourse and practices. My goal remains analysis of pop culture and literary expressions of goddess myths today. Manifestations of the goddess (in all kinds of art), covens, rituals, tours, and other actions and events connected to goddess belief, though varied, lead to many broader cultural expressions that present consistent images of women in primarily domestic, natural, and emotional spheres.[14]

The Work of Myth

Gendered messages of and connections to the goddess myth may appeal or trouble us for various reasons, and many take sides on whether the myth is liberating women or keeping them in a domestic, mystical, romantic, still-not-powerful sphere. *As a myth*—whether meaning untruth or cosmogonic narrative—we rarely analyze the myth generically, but symbolically and structurally the myth communicates its messages and relevance. Lefkowitz (1993, 261) notes the self-reflexive nature of this myth, like that of most religions, quoting Xenophanes' observations on human tendencies to anthropomorphize: "humans create gods in their own image, depending upon their needs and what aspects of themselves they judge to be important at the time."[15] Most contemporary popular culture versions of this myth are neither surprising nor revolutionary; they reflect more about our culture *mythically*, as predominantly sexist and patriarchal, than they do any past cultures, however imagined.

When the goddess myth is defined as myth at all, it is typically discussed in its colloquial sense as untruth, though at times gestures (often brief) are made at defining the genre. "Truth" frames and explains this myth structurally. We have listened to scientists who question goddess-dominated interpretations of prehistory and offer compelling science-based explanations and insights. We have also examined numerous popular versions of the goddess myth to perceive how deeply they are *our* myths, not myths of any actual past. Interestingly, terms on the matriarchal side of the dualities described in table 3, like myth, utopia, and religion, reflect perceptions of untruth or intuitive, metaphoric, and symbolic knowledge, as opposed to the truth- and science-oriented terms on the patriarchal side. The fact that the myth itself invokes or reflects this framework (of truth versus untruth, with untruth-related concepts often on the matriarchal side) may explain why so many writers focus on truth or untruth when discussing the myth, as well as why they often *feel* and react strongly when the truth question is raised.

In spite of how often the term *myth* is invoked in this goddess realm, myth as a genre is rarely a prominent focus of discussions surrounding it, which may be why many have difficulty seeing what this myth reflects—our own sexist, patriarchal worldview. Eller (2000, 178, 179) mainly focuses on myth functioning as either a reflection of history (as matriarchalists perceive it) or applies a functionalist view of myth as "charter" for society (via Bronislaw Malinowski), specifically to explain men's dominance, that is, to "quell men's anxieties about their social position . . . to justify the present state of affairs." She describes women who hope such myths of an imagined past might help affect policy, including environmental policy.[16] Plus, she perceives that "messages of female specialness" continue to appeal to us, since women are still judged harshly and remain unequal (17). Mythically, such *functions* offer hope, she argues, although the truth factor bothers her.[17] Given how many symbolic "truths" of this myth reflect the status quo, she wonders whether it can achieve these lofty goals of social change, a question feminist scholars continue to pose.[18] Is this myth "simply" keeping women in the domestic sphere, albeit allowing them to feel comforted, inspired, or hopeful there?[19] Some mythologists argue that confirmation of the rightness or goodness of our cosmos *is* a large part of the work that myths and rituals accomplish, offering means of living well in the world as we know it, affirming our cosmos as it exists, and inspiring us to keep going in the world we have.[20] The order/cosmos of *our* world is neither goddess-centered nor matriarchal, except in limited spheres or via mixed-messaged media largely reflective of our cosmos.

Examining the myth as a myth, we might expect the plot to move from chaos to cosmos, since most myths show such progression. In many cosmogonic myths, the plot follows movement from a previously troubled or formless time/world (chaos) toward a superior order (cosmos), reflecting the world we know, often brought about partly by telling the myth. This is indeed how original Victorian versions of the myth of matriarchy and goddesses-as-primary were thought to progress. Goddess-centered and matriarchal cultures were considered inferior and chaotic compared to the subsequent, superior patriarchies and male gods. Neo-pagans and goddess believers reverse this view, arguing that the world began in a superior cosmos, a longed-for utopia that we should try to recapture. It is the current culture, they suggest, the evil patriarchy, that represents chaos. But this view is far from satisfying mythically, as it leaves us in chaos, which may be what many women feel we are living in, but that message isn't mythically achieving or advancing purported feminist goals (other than awareness of our suffering). The backward movement (cosmos to chaos) of this goddess myth conception contradicts the pattern of most myths structurally and is belied by many popular culture versions of it, where goddesses and related cultures *are* chaotic, evil, and destructive (film and television versions). Therein, chaos of goddess times gives way to a cosmos of our current, predominantly patriarchal society, which is where we reside, accurately enough (if also disappointingly). Only in the romanticized versions do we find a pattern of ending in the more chaotic, mythically less satisfying, men-dominated realm.

It is also typical of myths to project messages that our world and life patterns are good—that how we live, problems and all, represents the cosmos we experience.[21] Ultimately, most versions of this myth affirm *our world's* cosmos, expectedly, as we currently know it—which is neither predominantly matriarchal nor goddess centered. It's not that we can't or shouldn't imagine another, better world and not even necessarily that we approve of this world. But we must exist in this one. Utopia is nowhere; here is livable. The frequent depictions of goddess cultures or goddesses, past and present, as chaotic, deadly, or problematic, as well as the romanticized versions where patriarchal times are chaotic, both still offer dualities and patterns of our sexist, contemporary world. Beginning a myth with a lost cosmos and ending with a story of a chaotic present is not a particularly well-functioning myth—it suggests an unlivable present, contrary to messages of comfort or hope, even though believers affirm that the message is hopeful. Living in chaos, meaning void, lack of order, nothingness, is metaphorically troubling and bleak, but it does reflect reality for many. For some, the vision of past and future hope seems to be enough—comforting, even if also a bit depressing.

Powerful women throughout popular culture and literature still tend to be drawn as scary, abused, troubled, or offensive, and they often suffer greatly in their stories. Survivors in many stories analyzed herein tend to be relegated to hidden, small-scale, and personal spaces of hope (with notable exceptions of Jemisin and Adeyemi). Concomitantly, most neo-pagan or New Age communities are similarly small, relatively speaking, cryptic, or esoteric, and in our real world, politically and socially, they are mostly powerless or marginalized. Small changes and different worldviews these myths might inspire *can* evoke or provoke the profound to individuals and even small communities, but women as a whole in our society remain oppressed—de Beauvoir's other or second sex. Even the romanticized and more progressive-seeming myths present women as suffering and oppressed now, because that is our reality. One could thus argue that all such myths end by at least acknowledging our cosmos—our patriarchal order. Our world is patriarchal, our environmental, gender, class, race, ethnic, and other diversity and oppression problems globally remain largely un-advanced and sometimes feel worse now than fifty or 120 years ago—when such myths were first embraced by feminists.

Many goddess myths, like the lives of real women, remain troublingly sexist at root, though perhaps under a veneer of empowered women or promises of such. Unsurprisingly, the lives of some of the creators are also troubled or troubling, not as feminist as hoped (like their works). Remaining largely at the margins in terms of power and largely stereotyped into dualistic patterns symbolically, goddesses and their myths work as some myths can: offering comfort within the status quo, including great suffering, with some hopeful, future potential for a better world. Mixed messages of extreme goddesses (romanticized or vilified) reflect a comfort/shame dichotomy: Don't worry, there be goddesses! Go celebrate them in fantastical films or novels. They are not necessarily women you'd want to be or have any possibility of being, but at least you can enjoy fantasies, right? But at the same time, we receive another, conflicting message: Don't worry, women are unlikely to gain much real power, or if they do, many will violently oppose them. Women are, right now, used and abused without repercussion, and few women achieve significant power in any area.[22] The media, our culture, and most of these new myths communicate that powerful women, fantastical or real, goddess or human, are to be feared and avoided, postponed to or from a distant world, a fantastical future or past, or they may be hidden and only cryptically powerful. Powerful women, superheroes, even goddesses are usually not *too* powerful or too effective in terms of real change in our world. They are wish-fulfillment fantasies, but also ones that can bite or be bitten—so best be careful, of powerful women or fantasies thereof.

Given our time of cultural sexism, racial and ethnic discrimination, oppression, and environmental crises, most versions of the goddess myth fulfill the mythic role to accept as livable the world as is, with some distant, postponable hope. As I worked on a draft of this manuscript, news broke of "a brooding military veteran" with a history of harassing and assaulting women who had killed two women at a yoga studio, apparently just because they are women (Fineout 2018). Such news is all too common in our world, with a racist and misogynist president (2016–2020) who famously and without repercussion bragged that he can assault women at will.[23] For years women could not do much to respond, unless prepared to suffer. Christine Blasey Ford's testimony accusing Supreme Court nominee Brett Kavanaugh of sexual misconduct failed to block his appointment, in spite of many experts' expressing belief of her claims. Kavanaugh now sits on the Supreme Court, and Ford, who was "terrified" to testify, "has not been able to return to her home and faces a near-constant stream of threats," nor has she been able to return to teaching as of late 2018 (Visser 2018). After Stacey Abrams and Elizabeth Warren's failures as political candidates (2019–2020), many editorials and analyses question why this country can't seem to elect, support, or even listen seriously to women candidates. Though Abrams helped in the 2020 election that resulted in some change, including a woman of color in the role of vice president, we are still a patriarchal, sexist culture. As much as many women might hope, protest, and rally, as we've been hoping and rallying for a very long time, to "Smash the patriarchy!" the patriarchy is still really smashing us, backlash after backlash.[24] One woman *almost*—but did not—become a US president in 2016, and maybe another will succeed in 2024, but not without many hating her, as in our divided nation more backlashes will result. We flail, cry, grimace, protest, and *persist* in our hopes and efforts for change and in our will, but we also suffer and sometimes despair as much as we celebrate. Kamala Harris, Alexandria Ocasio-Cortez, Ilhan Omar, and others seem promisingly progressive as young women of color in office portending change. But other women also rise to power, Republicans maintain sweeping popularity, and many in our world block progressives boldly, vehemently and loudly denouncing women, especially progressive, feminist, powerful, or educated women. Advancing progressive agendas against a tide of conservatives and antifeminists in our society remains difficult.

Academically as well, women, and the study of their cultures—imagined or real—are often marginalized or given less attention.[25] The liberal arts, academically (at least historically) where women flock and where women's studies developed, are being defunded and diminished around the country, with departments, programs, and even whole colleges closing. Women and all we represent are literally under attack and belittled in ways great and small in our world, and we struggle and sometimes fail to shield ourselves, stand tall, or fight back. Real women do persist, but our imagined heroes sometimes seem better equipped to fight the forces in escapist or speculative worlds. Yet those superheroic women or goddesses are likewise often belittled, bettered by or dependent upon men counterparts, or they suffer, sometimes horrifically. We can cheer them sometimes, but rarely completely and mostly with accompanied gritting of teeth, worry, or disappointment.

Goddess myths in popular culture today appeal to us as moving, sometimes promising stories to comfort or inspire, which is also the work of myth. We still live with inequality between genders—male and female forming a basic duality that some seek to move beyond, but that is often reflected in myths and enforced in our culture. The various already-imagined, appropriated, and invented goddesses, and the myths we tell of them, often reduce women to essentialized characteristics, casting us in emotional or sexualized roles that remain discriminatory, limiting, and problematic. Belittling of and hostility toward what is often perceived as the lesser or second gender (women) continue boldly in our thriving patriarchy. Often, the stronger the woman, the greater the backlash. Seeing powerful women suffer is still too common even in the most promising goddess myths, and though real-life suffering may pale in comparison, we also have fewer powers and means of coping and fighting back in real life. Rather than opening new pathways or presenting new or realistic worldviews, many, especially older or man-dominated goddess myths, mainly reflect and reinforce our current culture, though there are emergent hopeful examples. Most goddess myths show women suffering, though some allow women and goddesses space to be more complex, more reflective of current reality, with meaningful agency, offering relatable glimmers of hope. We imagine, tentatively, possible paths toward change or means of surviving and forging new identities, roles, and relationships, though usually in limited communities, distant futures, or alternate universes. As we continue negotiating, imagining, and projecting gender roles mythically, we might consider further how inventing their shape in a distant past helps or hinders all humans and the planet.

Many women regularly feel and face deep, personal or social crises of violence, harassment, oppression, lack of opportunity, and daily pressures based on gender. Gender discrimination and concern spur plenty of mythic expression in our world of imagined pasts and projected futures. Goddess myths inspire and reflect appropriated pasts, troubled present times, and fantastical futures of all kinds, most of which incorporate cycles and centuries of suffering, reflective of our real world and women's real lives. We should hardly feel surprised over the sexist structure of most such myths, the rarity of truly new mythic moments, and the paucity of workable, inspiring goddesses today, given myth's typical function—to confirm the livability of our world, rather than to reshape a new future that challenges long-established patterns and order. Myths tell us that the cosmos in which we live *is* good, good enough anyway, livable enough (for most), and portending (sometimes, possibly) a more promising future, at least superficially or distantly. But any truly superior world requires deep changes, huge efforts, or more likely, must wait, possibly until a distant future, an afterlife, or another world. Exciting but distant, hoped-for patterns surface at times, but most of our goddess myths primarily reflect, confirm, and likely reinforce our worldview and our lived cosmos. Deeper structures and even more obvious symbols and themes show few truly new perceptions of or options for gender dynamics. The more realistic the worlds portrayed, the harder the lives of the characters therein tend to be. The closer we look, the better we perceive that the goddess myth most often fulfills its role appropriately—as a myth of our culture and our times.

Notes

Introduction

1. People use *myth* for stories that folklorists would identify as legends or folktales; it's also applied to various kind of fiction, films, television shows, and also for cultural trends, casual beliefs or rumors, etc. One example of the appeal of "myth" is the popular Australian American science entertainment television program *MythBusters* (2003–2017), which dealt largely with rumors, urban legends, adages, internet "news," film and television scenes, etc.—never any actual myths, as folklorists define them. But apparently it's understood that a more accurate moniker such as "legend busters" or "rumor busters" would not appeal as much as "myth buster."

2. "Speculative fiction" refers to literature that invents or considers past, present, future, or alternate worlds in ways that may involve advanced technology, alternate political systems, or magical or fantastical elements. It is considered fiction that asks "What if?" but in ways that make sense in and are relevant to our world. Also often known as science fiction and/or fantasy, the term *speculative fiction* is preferred by some feminist writers in the field, like Margaret Atwood, as being less about aliens and more about our world and things that could be believed to have happened in the past (Atwood 2012).

3. These are some common ways *myth* is defined, to be examined in more detail in chapter 3.

4. Founder of the academic study of popular culture in the United States, Ray B. Browne, defines the field: "Popular culture is the way of life in which and by which most people in any society live. In a democracy like the United States, it is the voice of the people—their likes and dislikes—that form the lifeblood of daily existence, of a way of life. Popular culture is the voice of democracy, democracy speaking and acting, the seedbed in which democracy grows. Popular culture democratizes society and makes democracy truly democratic. It is the every-day world around us: the mass media, entertainments, and diversions. It is our heroes, icons, rituals, everyday actions, psychology, and religion—our total life picture. It is the way of living we inherit, practice and modify as we please, and how we do it. It is the dreams we dream while asleep" (qtd. in Hoppenstand 1999, 61).

5. This famous definition was first published years earlier and is cited by many, including Hoppenstand (1999, 60).

6. Browne wrote in *Popular Culture Theory and Methodology* in 2006 that culture generally can be separated "into four main areas that are elite, popular, mass and folk. He pointed out that 'popular culture embraces all culture except elite culture'" (15). But the term remains hard to explain and define partly because of scholarship and partly because things conceived as "high culture" can at any point become "popular culture," if it's more widely distributed, appre-ciated, and understood. He considers popular culture to be "what people do when they are not working" and "the body of intellectual and imaginative work, which each generation receives as

its tradition" (21), though no definition is completely satisfactory to all (he says). Thus my use of the term specifically for film, television, and genre fiction would be more or less in line with the classic, though fuzzy, emergent scholarly definition (*X-Tomato* [blog] consulted for this summary, https://blogs.bgsu.edu/yuzheng/summary/).

7. See, for instance, Brian Boyd, *On the Origin of Stories: Evolution, Cognition, and Fiction* (Cambridge: Belknap Press of Harvard University Press, 2009); Jonathan Gottschall, *The Storytelling Animal: How Stories Make Us Human* (New York: Harcourt, 2012); Bruce Jackson, *The Story Is True: The Art and Meaning of Telling Stories* (Philadelphia: Temple University Press, 2007); Richard Kearney, *On Stories* (New York: Routledge, 2002); John D. Niles, *Homo Narrans: The Poetics and Anthropology of Oral Literature* (Philadelphia: University of Pennsylvania Press, 1999).

8. See, for instance, White (2003) and Neuendorf (2018).

9. For scholarly analyses of how violent and adult fairy tales are, see Jack Zipes, *Why Fairy Tales Stick: The Evolution and Relevance of a Genre* (New York: Routledge, 2006) and other books by Zipes, Marina Warner, Maria Tatar, Cristina Bacchilega, and others.

10. Maria Tatar (1987, 177) argues such interpretations by men "tame" the tale's sexually but maintain grisly aspects to scare women and that "reading fairy tales requires us to set aside our preconceptions about the 'lessons' imparted by specific tales." By contrast, Perrault (1697) offers this "moral" in Bluebeard: "Curiosity, in spite of its appeal, often leads to deep regret. To the displeasure of many a maiden, its enjoyment is short lived."

11. Probably the first to compare the film *Star Wars: Episode IV—A New Hope* to *The Wizard of Oz* was Roger Ebert, in his 1977 review of the first *Star Wars* film. Mark Hamill and Carrie Fisher, actors in the film, also made the comparison in a 1977 BBC interview, as documented in Gwynne Watkins, "'Star Wars' and 'The Wizard of Oz': Back in 1977, People Couldn't Stop Comparing the Two," *Yahoo*, May 2, 2017, https://www.yahoo.com/entertainment/star-wars-wizard -oz-back-1977-people-couldnt-stop-comparing-two-145943811.html. Since then, many have made similar comparisons, so that there are now memes, mash-ups, and websites devoted to such comparisons, including *Ozwars*: http://ozwars.webs.com/.

12. There are numerous articles on strong or feminist fairy tale heroes, including Larson, M.A., "10 Grimms' Girls Who Are Decidedly NOT Damsels In Distress," *Huffpost*, October 21, 2014, https://www.huffingtonpost.com/ma-larson/10-grimms-girls-who-would_b_6017816.html; Emily Jenkins, "Fairy Tale Heroine, But With Depth," *New York Times*, November 10, 2017, https:// www.nytimes.com/2017/11/10/books/review/emily-jenkins-winfield-martin-fairy-tales.html; or Nancy Ibsen, "Active Heroines in Folktales" (updated from Nancy Schimmel, *Just Enough to Make a Story: A Sourcebook for Storytellers*, Sisters' Choice, 1992), Sisters' Choice n.d., http://www .sisterschoice.com/heroines.html.

13. For arguments about why Hermione is the real hero in Harry Potter novels, see for instance: Amy Sachs, "7 Reasons Hermione Is the Best Character Ever," *Bustle*, September 4, 2015, https://www.bustle.com/articles/107868-7-times-hermione-granger-proved-she-was-the -best-female-character-of-all-time; Jo Barrow, "21 Times Tumblr Knew Hermione Was the Best Character in 'Harry Potter,'" *Buzzfeed*, March 2, 2015, https://www.buzzfeed.com/jobarrow/are -you-sure-thats-a-spell-ron; Megan Piechowicz, "Harry Potter: 15 Reasons Hermione Granger Is the Real Hero," *Screen Rant*, February 27, 2017, https://screenrant.com/harry-potter-hermione -granger-real-hero/, and many other similar arguments.

14. The Greek Hermione is daughter of King Menelaus of Sparta and Helen of Troy. Lynne Milum argues that Rowling's Hermione is goddesslike in "The Hero's Journey through Harry Potter," *MythicHero*, 2007, http://www.mythichero.com/meeting_with_the_goddess.html.

15. Jewel Queen (2018) summarizes typical criticism and argues the film isn't as progressive as some lament: "Nothing has created a greater disturbance in the Force than *Star Wars: The*

Last Jedi. While many critics and large numbers of fans have praised the film for its 'new direction,' an undeniable backlash has grown against it. Many fans of the movie have lumped all this criticism together as the same racist and misogynist fanboys who decried the inclusion of Finn from the first *Force Awakens* teaser, as well as the increase of women in Star Wars media. Those hateful detractors certainly exist, but the limited perspective that all criticism is in that bad faith has masked the flaws of *The Last Jedi* in terms of feminism and diversity. The movie diminishes the role of its own female lead, mishandles its characters of color, and gives women and POC no meaningful impact on the final story."

16. As of February 2018, Wikipedia lists *The Da Vinci Code* at no. 13 on its list of "best-selling books," with 80 million copies sold; jamesclear.com lists it at no. 10 with 85 million copies sold; ranker.com lists it at no. 9 with 80 million copies sold.

17. Cynthia Eller (2011) traces popular European versions of Amazon stories from medieval times onward, in the "Amazons Everywhere" chapter. The main message of most such stories to the ancient Greeks, Eller observes, was "to teach Athenians and other 'civilized' peoples of antiquity to conclude that the rule of women was freakish, dangerous, and certainly not to be risked in any form. . . . The Amazons were set up as the archetypal reversal of all that was good and right in patriarchal society. In fact, the Amazons were always eventually routed by the Greek heroes, no matter how bravely they fought." But this probably-fictional group "continued to exercise a powerful fascination long after the demise of classical Greek civilization" (17). Medieval Amazons existed mainly as enemies of knights, "They are not true heroines: they ultimately lose in battle" and are "not Christians" (19). They are mainly seen as "savage" cultural examples, but they did allow for the exceptional possibility of a female ruler (they were notably popular during the time of Queen Elizabeth I; 21). Many renaissance Amazons ultimately "gratefully surrender their armament and embrac[e] their true feminine nature, in subordination to men" (24).

18. Lepore (2015) notes Max Eastman's 1913 book of verse called *Child of the Amazons and Other Poems*, where an Amazonian queen falls in love with a man, though it violates their laws to marry him, as one inspiration, along with a 1914 novel by Inez Haynes Gillmore called *Angel Island*. The plot is remarkably similar to Marston's comic origin story, though here multiple men visit the Amazonian island and cut wings off the "super-humanly beautiful" women there, who try to revolt (Lepore 2015, 86). Lepore also documents a 1940 comic called "Amazona, the Might Woman," published by Planet Comics and featuring "last survivors of a super race . . . discovered by an American reporter named Blake Manners," with whom the mighty woman Amazona falls in love and with whom she returns to America (179–80).

19. There are of course nuances and variations among particular iterations of what I'm lumping together as "goddess culture." Specifics and details of such variations are profound to believers and can manifest in very different rituals, practices, beliefs, and expressions. Ethnographic studies with details of particular communities of goddess worshippers/believers are described and explained in other carefully researched books (Magliocco 2004; Pike 2001; Davies 1998). I aim not to diminish contemporary neo-pagan groups nor to deny variations and complexities within powerful contemporary religious phenomena and practices.

20. Examples of such hatred abound on the internet, including in Queen (2018). Dani Di Placido (2018), writing for *Forbes*, notes: "there's absolutely no excuse for the harassment suffered by [*Star Wars: The Last Jedi* actresses] Kelly Marie Tran and Daisy Ridley, both of whom ended up deleting their social media because of the constant abuse. Let's think about that again—both of these actresses were chased offline because of the sheer volume of raw hate, received purely for their performance in a fiction. And it wasn't some derogatory adaptation of a religious text, but a sequel to a popular cinematic franchise that received mixed audience reviews."

21. Lindsay Ellis offers a sharp analysis of The Wicked Witch character (especially in popular culture) in "The Wicked Witch of the West," *Loose Canon*, March 22, 2017, YouTube, https://www.youtube.com/watch?v=xiZB4WgjJmA&t=1s. She demonstrates how the witch's "wickedness" has varied over time, but the 1939 film *The Wizard of Oz*'s witch became the most iconic movie villain in history. Ellis also discusses how all witches symbolize to some extent a perceived danger of wise or independent women, especially mysterious, older, single women, which may represent European anxiety about women straying from their narrow cultural roles (of wife and mother). The original L. Frank Baum *Wizard* book was written during the suffrage movement, which saw many strong female characters emerge (including Wonder Woman).

22. I recorded interviews with guides on tourism of prehistory during the summers of 2003 and 2018.

23. I believe the same is true of similar sites Northern Spain, though I only visited the sites in France.

24. Sweeping, still colorful paintings in dramatic cave passages, animated by passionate guides, who manipulate lighting, suggest contexts, point out enigmatic symbols, stir imaginations.

25. Julien, a guide at Cougnac, a cave in the neighboring region of Le Lot, explained (in French): "Everywhere you go around here, there are advertisements and signs of all the prehistoric sites. There are lots of books about prehistory sold around here. I really bathed in the spirit of prehistory here." Other guides use the same language about "bathing in prehistory," suggesting a commonly heartfelt deep sense of connection.

26. In summer 2018, a guide at the museum where I first saw a reproduction of this figurine (Musee Nationale de la Prehistoire in Les Eyzies de Tayac), to whom I posed the possibility that the head was not a woman's head, responded that she and many other experts believe that the fine features of the face, including the delicate facial bones sculpted, suggest that it is likely a female face. Another guide said she thought they had never actually displayed this figure in that museum. But the museum was extensively rebuilt and reorganized since my first visit there in 2001, and the guide admitted it was possible this had been displayed earlier (as I remember).

27. Because the figurines were found so early in the history of archaeology, the science had not developed to value context very much, and thus little is known about exactly how or where the figures were found. According to the Wikipedia entry on the figurine: "Randall White observed [in 2006], 'The figurines emerged from the ground into a colonial intellectual and socio-political context nearly obsessed with matters of race.' . . . Although the style of representation is essentially realistic, the proportions of the head do not correspond exactly to any known human population of the present or past. Since the mid-twentieth century, interpretative questions have shifted from race to matters concerning womanhood and fertility." Other more identifiably female figurines (without heads, but not matching this head) were found at the site. The head is a famous image from prehistory, decorating stamps in both France and Mali.

28. What I recall seeing in the Les Eyzies museum would have been a reproduction. Later, I visited the Musée d'Archéologie Nationale at Saint-Germain-en-Laye, near Paris, to see the original. But even what was there may have been a reproduction, as the original is considered too susceptible to damage to be on permanent display (I heard).

29. For instance, I heard New York University prehistory professor Randall White speak at L'Abri Pataud (a shelter and museum in Les Eyzies). He showed a Center for the Study of Human Origins film that imagined and dramatized a few minutes of life in that exact place during the Paleolithic era. The audience of mostly guides, locals, and experts burst into enthusiastic applause for the film. White's subsequent lecture (in French) gave info on mobile art from that region housed in American museums, which evoked negative responses. White

urged everyone to be aware of how much such art is in the United States. He explained why (the transactions were legal) and suggested that it should all be studied.

30. All the articles of Goodison and Morris's (1998) *Ancient Goddesses* are written by feminist archaeologists who give careful attention to cultures whose artifacts are often called "goddesses." They offer scientific knowledge to combat the often-reflexive assumptions of the Goddess Movement, whose "treatment of the archaeological evidences ranges from the careful to the cavalier" (11). All these archaeologists find troubling, recurring ways we essentialize, stereotype, and limit female and human potential through this myth. *Ancient Goddesses* offers a wealth of actual knowledge about artifacts, contexts, and cultures. The first chapter, by Tringham and Conkey, "Rethinking Figurines: A Critical View from Archaeology of Gimbutas, the 'Goddess' and Popular Culture," particularly discusses the Paleolithic figurines like those I saw in France.

31. Goodison and Morris (1998) explain, for instance, a known ritual context from an ethnographic example in Tanzania, where adolescent boys use figurines of pregnant females in initiation rites. White (2003, 28) offers ethnographic information about Aivilik (Inuit) culture: all Aivilik community members made "art," but they had no notion of "art" in a modern sense. They believed "raw material is alive, filled the spirit of the subject that ultimately emerges . . . discovered by tempting it to present itself to the sculptor." White offers other ethnographic data from this known society living in somewhat similar conditions to Ice Age people of Europe, to show how we might "contextualize and interpret such representations" (31). He also explains how much we *do* know about prehistoric culture, urging that we should avoid "the . . . false . . . presumption that we know very little of the lives and everyday culture of prehistoric peoples," since that is used commonly as a "justification for unconstrained interpretation or the imposition of our own interpretive standards," which is problematic (31).

32. The quote first appeared in *New Directions for Women*, in May/June 1986, a feminist newsletter, and was written by Marie Shear, though it is usually misattributed to Cheris Kramarae and Paula Treichler, authors of *A Feminist Dictionary*, according to Beverly McPhail at *A Feminist Life, Etc.*, http://www.beverlymcphail.com/feminismradicalnotion.html.

33. For instance, the *Texas Heart Institute Journal* features an article from 2001 by Stephanie A. Coulter on "Gender Balance in Cardiovascular Research" at https://www.ncbi.nlm.nih .gov/pmc/articles/PMC3066814/. She notes: "Women have not shared equally in the medical revolution: up to the turn of the millennium, women experienced adverse trending rather than improvement in mortality trends."

34. Soraya Chemaly, for instance, reports on such research in a February 12, 2015, *Time* Magazine article entitled "All Teachers Should Be Trained to Overcome Their Hidden Biases," accessed September 10, 2018, at http://time.com/3705454/teachers-biases-girls-education/.

35. A whole subgenre of quilts known as "crazy quilting" began in the late 1800s, featuring irregular patterns in the patchwork textiles. Though for years African American quilting was rarely considered, the quilts by African American women in Gee's Bend, Alabama, have become famous in recent years and are now featured in numerous museum exhibits, including a touring exhibit reported on by the *Smithsonian Magazine*. Gee's Bend: The Architecture of the Quilt has been organized by The Museum of Fine Arts, Houston, and the Tinwood Alliance, according to Amei Wallach, October 2006, https://www.smithsonianmag.com/arts -culture/fabric-of-their-lives-132757004/. This one example does not mean all women's artwork is now regarded equally to men's.

36. There is no one specific case I'm thinking of nor any particular artist I'm calling out as copying quilts, but numerous art historians and artists I've known who focus on women's textile art have shared such stories and histories with me, including Ursula McCarty.

37. Google "Odalisque paintings" to see many examples.

38. The test is named for American cartoonist Alison Bechdel, who posited the test in a 1985 comic strip.

39. Charlotte Allen (2001, 1) lumps together the various iterations of "the Goddess movement, Goddess spirituality, or the Craft," including things like "Wicca and related 'neopagan' faiths," and describes them as a religion with "more than 200,000 adherents" especially in the United States, Europe, Canada, Australia, and New Zealand.

Chapter 1

1. Adler (1986), Davis (1998), Magliocco (2004), Pike (2001), etc. This study does not dispute any of that fine work and the complexity of contemporary religious communities connected to various forms of goddess worship. I do not seek to add to or be in parallel dialogue with that research; rather, this work considers the more commonly understood aspects of the myth by our culture at large, and aspects of it that influence the popular culture and literary versions analyzed herein.

2. Details of the contemporary phenomenon are documented and discussed in the works of Eller (2000 and 2011), Goodison and Morris (1998), Meskell (1995), Lefkowitz (1992 and 1993), and others. Lefkowitz (1992) specifically analyzes the ways the goddess parallels the Judeo-Christian God. These scholars also demonstrate several of the subsequent points, such as little to no evidence existing for any details of beliefs and practices associated with ancient goddesses or a unified great goddess.

3. This point is also made by all scholars referenced in the previous footnote.

4. Lefkowitz (1992, 32) and others see the "utopian notion of prehistoric religion and culture" in this myth. Goddess culture might alternatively be portrayed as backward or destructive and chaotic. I will demonstrate both the romanticized and vilified forms of goddesses in current pop culture herein.

5. Peter Steinfels (1990) demonstrates Gimbutas's connection to this tradition: "Dr. Gimbutas said in an interview that the 19th-century Swiss scholar Johann Jakob Bachofen and his followers Robert Briffault in France and James Frazer in England were among her forerunners." Davis (1998, 70, 71) affirms: "Gimbutas relied heavily on Jungian psychology [names from her bibliography offered as evidence].... Joseph Campbell ... linked Gimbutas's work to the heritage of J.J. Bachofen, the nineteenth-century pioneer of matriarchy theory whose works were partially translated into English at Bollingen.... Bachofen and Jung made vital contributions to the development of the Goddess myth in the first place."

6. Lefkowitz (1992, 31) appreciates "Gimbutas's quick eye for detail and her fine appreciation of the artifacts that she describes," also noting how she "brings to life an existence of appealing agrarian simplicity and peace, and reconstructs a religion that concentrated on essentials such as sexuality and animal life and remained remarkably stable over the millennia." But (like many others) Lefkowitz also uses her scholar's eye to question the accuracy of these theories, "Such spectacular connections between such different phenomena need to be proven. They cannot merely be assumed to have been direct or inevitable." Lefkowitz concludes that analyzing "what Gimbutas and Eisler have to say about ancient Greece, about the corner of the puzzle that I know best, does not inspire my confidence" (1992, 32). Her expertise allows her to spot errors. Many other scholars have also questioned Gimbutas's conclusive and sweeping interpretations. Davis (1998, 51–52) relates that "Gimbutas's professional colleagues essentially parted company with her when her interpretation of the recovered artifacts was pressed into the service of the Goddess movement; in professional circles, she stood virtually alone in her support for the

Goddess . . . scholars in the fields best equipped to assess the historical claims of the movement have almost unanimously discounted those claims."

7. Another scholar criticized for over-generalizing and comparing without contextual evidence, Joseph Campbell helped sing Gimbutas's praises by the late 1980s. Many other archaeologists criticized her, including (in addition to those already discussed in the text) Bernard Wailes (1992), David W. Anthony (1990), Peter Ucko (1968) and Andrew Fleming (1969), and Cathy Gere (who considers politics of archaeology; 2009).

8. Steinfels (1990) quotes four prominent contemporary archaeologists and anthropologists who seriously question her work, one of whom, Penn professor Bernard Wailes, says, "'She amasses all the data and then leaps from it to conclusions without any intervening argument. . . . Most of us tend to say, oh my God, here goes Marija again.'"

9. Steinfels (1990) explains her method: "For some time feminist writers have been seeking non-patriarchal mythologies and rituals in Jungian psychology, reconstructed notions of witchcraft, or even in pure creations of the imagination. But Dr. Gimbutas gives them something more: the seeming stamp of science and the reassurance of history . . . a dramatic story of paradise lost and now rediscovered. Originally set forth in a 1974 book, 'The Goddesses and Gods of Old Europe,' it inspired, besides feminist thinkers, a number of women artists who were captivated by the remarkable images of ancient female figurines in Dr. Gimbutas's book and later publications." Steinfels sees: "But many other investigators of prehistoric Europe have not shared the enthusiasm. Bernard Wailes, a professor of anthropology at the University of Pennsylvania, says that most of Dr. Gimbutas's peers consider her 'immensely knowledgeable but not very good in critical analysis.'" In the obituary for her by Richard D. Lyons (1994) in the *New York Times*, we see this dual reaction: "Skepticism about her thesis was widespread among scholars, but her ideas were welcomed by many feminists and by Joseph Campbell, the mythologist. Writing about 'The Language of the Goddess,' Gerda Lerner, a historian at the University of Wisconsin, said that although Dr. Gimbutas's theory could never be proved, it could 'challenge, inspire and fascinate' simply by providing an imaginative alternative to male-centered explanations."

10. Steinfels (1990) writes: "Dr. Gimbutas calls the enthusiastic reception of her work by artists and feminists 'an incredible gift' coming late in her life. But 'I was not a feminist and I had never any thought I would be helping feminists,' she said. Still, 'The Language of the Goddess' rings with a fervent belief that knowledge about a Goddess-worshiping past can guide the world toward a sexually egalitarian, nonviolent and 'earth-centered' future." Christ (2000, 173) also confirms that "Gimbutas never considered herself to be a feminist scholar." Eller and many others note this as well, though in later works, Eller says that it was only early on that Gimbutas "did not then consider herself a feminist." Eller (2005, 6) suggests she may have later welcomed such positive attention from feminists, reflected in her change of title from her 1974 publication of *Gods and Goddesses of Old Europe* to the 1982 updated edition *The Goddesses and Gods of Old Europe*. Davis (1998, 71) also discusses this change in Gimbutas, showing how feminist goddess proponents are "celebrated in the later books, and Gimbutas even adopted Eisler's neologism 'gylany.'" He references testimony of "how much Gimbutas had enjoyed participating in Goddess rituals and being fêted by 'her groupies' in the movement" (71). Most enthusiasts of her work are not archaeologists nor experts in any particular culture about which Gimbutas writes.

11. "Her work was a major scholarly source for Riane Eisler's 'The Chalice and the Blade,' a sweeping analysis of cultural evolution that has become a minor classic in the women's movement. . . . Elinor W. Gadon calls Dr. Gimbutas's research germinal and fundamentally important" (Steinfels 1990).

12. Lefkowitz (1993, 261–62) describes a few specific rituals one from 1978 at Wellesley College (where she was a student and later a professor for many years) of students praying (with a poem): "to a hamadryad, or tree nymph, of their Class Tree and seeking her protection," which she calls "an embryonic feminist ritual, in which the tree represents a young and independent Wellesley female." Lucinda Peach (2002, 350) explains that "goddess spirituality is not a single, monolithic entity but encompasses a range of different beliefs and practices that vary from group to group . . . secular and religious . . . among them [various religious practices from around the world and] a pro-environmental protections spirit. . . . If there is a commonality running through this wide variety of beliefs and practices, it might be characterized as a belief in and commitment to the cultivation and expression of women's spiritual power."

13. Goddess movement followers, like Kathryn Rountree (1997, 214, 211, 220), see the new, "good" faith as promoting positive options for women, including "a holistic world view which emphasizes connection, balance and cyclic processes," and "opening up a great range of images of the feminine." Gimbutas's editor and biographer, Joan Marler (2003, 7), also admires this movement as positive and argues against those who criticize Gimbutas' scholarship: "women's spirituality . . . is about transformation and the retrieval of inner authority which systems of domination externalize." Carol P. Christ (2003) and other supporters argue that goddess culture promotes strong ethics such as social justice and female empowerment. Other followers believe "the reclaiming of Goddess worship took on the vision of a redemption of humanity and the earth from the nadir of violence and destruction that had been unleashed by patriarchal religion and rule" (Ruether 2005, 274).

14. Goodison and Morris (1998), along with many others, demonstrate this well. Lefkowitz (1992, 31) also perceives problems: "Gimbutas must resort to speculation and imagination at almost every stage of her discussion" and shows other weaknesses of current "Goddess reconstructions."

15. There are important goddesses, including "mother goddesses," from known patriarchal cultures (such as Greece and Rome), like Gaia and Tellus, as well as an actual goddess named Venus (always depicted as a beautiful woman)—for whom many figurines from prehistory are named. But the fact that these cultures had strong goddess figures and thus worshiped women in some way does not mean that goddesses predominated or that women held power, nor that the society was focused on women as the principal force or actors. We know that these historical cultures (ancient Greece and Rome) were very patriarchal even when they had numerous goddesses (even an equal number). Lefkowitz (a classicist; 1993, 266) confirms this: "In historical Greece and Rome, there were many goddesses who coexisted alongside one another, but they considered themselves to be separate individuals," in other words not a conflated mother goddess archetype. She also affirms, "Even though they were powerful and influential, Greek goddesses always existed in a world that was controlled by male gods" (266). Most scholars believe we have no evidence for strongly goddess-centered, matriarchal cultures (in history or prehistory). Cynthia Eller (2000, 104, 105) demonstrates that many known ancient goddesses (from written records), such as Inanna or Anat, "are incredibly violent," are not necessarily mothers or motherly, and that, "goddesses are often known to support patriarchal social customs." She also argues that "goddess worship has been reported for societies rife with misogyny," and "there is simply no one-to-one relationship between goddess worship and high status for women," concluding that the type of goddess purported or assumed in the myth is "a type of goddess worship that has never been seen." Popular online references like Wikipedia and Encyclopedia Britannica agree that "The consensus among modern anthropologists and sociologists is that while many cultures bestow power preferentially on one sex or the other, matriarchal societies in this original, evolutionary sense have never existed" ("Matriarchy" entry, Encyclopedia Britannica online, accessed January 15, 2014, at http://www.britannica.com /EBchecked/topic/369468/matriarchy).

16. One story of Altamira, a famous painted cave in Spain, relates that a nineteenth-century archaeologist spent day after day there looking for artifacts. His assumptions about where and what he would find kept his eyes away from the walls and ceiling. One day, his young daughter who accompanied him pointed out the bulls on the ceiling she saw there (White 2003). In Lascaux 4 (summer 2018), I watched a film in the museum area dramatizing this scene, including the daughter pointing to the ceiling, exclaiming, "Papa, bulls!" The film emphasized the effort the archaeologist made to get others, mostly skeptics in the nineteenth century, to believe that this *is* prehistoric art from such an ancient period.

17. Most social scientists today find the word *primitive* in referring to culture to be outmoded, inaccurate, offensive.

18. Meskell (1995); Goodison and Morris (and ten other feminist archaeologists, 1998); White (2003), etc. Eller (2000) thoroughly, persuasively shows how each aspect of the myth is questionable at best, using comparative ethnography, feminist theory, human developmental theories, understanding and interpretation of prehistoric art and architecture, linguistic and genetic evidence, and more. While she admits "matriarchalists" (believers in a goddess-oriented prehistory) *might* be right in some of their assumptions and interpretations, she offers ample evidence and scholarship for why we should approach the "myth" of matriarchy skeptically. For "goddess figurines," she perceives, "the evidence of prehistoric art is simply inconclusive," and beyond confirming that prehistoric people did represent women in art, "we are given precious little information about the status of either divine or human women in prehistory" (156).

19. Tringham and Conkey (1998, 43): "the meaning of the figurines [of women from prehistory]—especially their meaningfulness—is more likely to have been varied and varying, more ambiguous than fixed, and differentially experienced, even at any one point in time."

20. Lefkowitz (2007) offers such context for Greece, White (2003) for Paleolithic art, Goodison and Morris (1998) for other ancient cultures, etc.

21. Starhawk (who has many fans) worked with filmmaker Donna Read on the documentary *Signs Out of Time* (2008) about the work of Gimbutas as it relates to the goddess. See "About Signs Out of Time," *Belili Productions*, http://www.belili.org/. Swedish artist and feminist activist Monica Sjöö also helped inspire the ecofeminist goddess movement connected to neo-paganism.

22. The trilogy of films, *Goddess Remembers*, *The Burning Times*, and *Full Circle*, known as the Goddess Trilogy is promoted on Starhawk's website, where Read is described as "Starhawk's partner in Belili Productions."

23. In her "God or Goddess" chapter of *Ancient Goddesses* (Goodison and Morris 1998), Caroline Malone, who specializes in archaeology of Ancient Malta, explains the data we have of figurines from Malta: "the traditional 'Fat Lady' or goddess figurine, that is, the classic image of prehistoric Malta, is in fact no more female than it is male. The excessive obesity (especially buttocks and thighs) has been used as the principle identifier for female gender, in spite of the missing detail of genitalia or breasts, which would normally be depicted, or the often ignored fact that Mediterranean males are frequently as obese as females." She then explains how Gimbutas interpreted the connection to temples and burials as proof of connection to "the Great Earth Mother." But "the very existence of a 'Mother Goddess' in ancient Malta is still hotly debated" (151). Of the known prehistoric figurative art from Malta, the so-called goddess figurines "probably represent only about half of the figurative art known, and few of them are actually explicitly female" (163). The idea of the "fat ladies" as female was first proposed, according to Malone, by early twentieth-century excavator Themistocles Zammit (151–52), followed by other men archaeologists, so that "the emphasis on the figurines has distorted research and popular knowledge" (157).

24. Charlene Spretnak (1992) calls "ancient images of Goddess spirituality . . . radically body-honoring and nature-oriented" and quotes Jane Ellen Harrison, Robert Graves, and

Joseph Campbell (proponents of goddess culture) to confirm the universal supremacy and importance of the great goddess to ancient people. All these older scholars based their work on earlier nineteenth-century theories that contemporary feminist archaeologists have shown to be flawed and overgeneralized.

25. As evidence, White (2003) discusses one of the earliest distasteful examples of how cultures' biases and worldview can be mapped onto the past via popular culture, reflecting our culture more than the imagined past, the case of the so-called "Hottentot Venus" in the early nineteenth century. A Khosian woman named Saartje/Sara Baartman (one of at least two Khoikhoi women from South Africa who toured), became famous as a freak show attraction because of her large buttocks and distended genitalia, when she was brought to Europe and displayed publicly, naked. Images from the time reveal that men and women ogled her with no respect. In one image, "several figures bend straining for a better look, while a male figure at the far right of the image even holds his seeing-eye glass up to better behold the woman's body. The European observers remark on the woman's body: 'Oh! God Damn what roast beef!' and 'Ah! how comical is nature'" in captions for the image (Thompson n.d.). Such blatantly disrespectful, racist, hegemonic, colonialist behavior reflects the prejudices and mindsets people carry and impose when they consider these distant past cultures or their supposed analogues in their world. Experts now believe white skin didn't appear in European populations until about eight thousand years ago, so many assumptions about the artists or original users of the material are still being revised (Gibbons 2015).

26. Racial discrimination can be seen in Baartman's exploitation and ridicule, which was considered indecent and exploitative even in her day, when her treatment was protested and debated. British abolitionists took her case to court, arguing she was "being forced to perform against her will," but her employer produced a contract and she continued to perform as a spectacle, eventually in Paris (Holmes 2008). Rachel Holmes's (2008, 187) book on Baartman explains her as "a symbol of the alienation and degradations of colonization, lost children, exile, the expropriation of female labor and the sexual and economic exploitation of black women by men, white and black." Baartman lived in poverty, died far from home in Paris, and was then dissected and displayed after death (Elkins 2007). A wax figure of Baartman along with her preserved genitalia were on display in Paris's Musée de l'homme until 2002, when apologies were made and her remains were returned for respectful burial in South Africa. Today her life symbolizes mistreatment of people considered primitive, and her story is remembered more positively in recent artwork, plays, and so on. For instance, analyzing performances of Suzan-Lori Parks's play *Venus*, a fictional depiction of Baartman's life that explores colonization and objectification, critic Cynthia Croot (2016, 76) finds, "the women playing Saartjie Baartman are able to examine their own presence as well as the audience's participation in creating a familiar, dehumanizing distance. The play demands that viewers wrestle with their historical culpability, and resonates anew in each socio-political context." Baartman's story demonstrates how our appropriative assumptions about artifacts of the past become problematic interpretations that harm real people's lives, especially the less powerful, in ways that serve the appropriators' goals, cementing gross misconceptions and discriminations. Often, even when we seem to be admiring "prehistoric women" or goddess representations, we may map very negative, demeaning, or problematic attitudes onto them, sometimes unwittingly. Our appropriative use of the art for our own cultural or personal messages often ignores, seriously misunderstands, misrepresents, or erroneously assumes how such art might have been used or understood in the distant past because it is actually more about the modern viewers and their times. Intersectional feminist insight, such as reconsidering Baartman's life, illuminates our appropriative attitude toward and (mis)use of artifacts from prehistory as deeply problematic, and such misuses continue in pop culture today.

27. I heard an exchange between a guide at Lascaux II and a tourist that shows such pre-conceptions of "primitive humans." Before they enter the reproduced portions of the cave, tourists enter museum rooms with photographs of the paintings the guides explain. One guide encouraged us to appreciate the skill of the artists in making beautiful, realistic depictions of animals, then told us that human figures in most caves (including Lascaux) are intentionally drawn more stylistically. The human figure in Lascaux has stick-like arms and legs, a small bird-like head, an erect penis, and what may be a bird staff his right hand, seemingly falling backward, next to an apparently eviscerated bull. The guide asked us to contemplate the inten-tionally stylized human, when a woman in the group asked, "Was it because they didn't know how to draw people?" The guide, frustrated by her question, gestured dramatically to several of the photographs of beautifully and skillfully drawn animals. "Look! Look! Look! How can you look at these animals and not realize that the people who could draw these animals could draw anything they wanted to? How could you question their skill or ability as artists?" Some of the crowd still seemed puzzled. Other guides told me similar stories of how some tourists just don't seem to understand or appreciate the art.

28. Impressively, most guides at the sites I visited showed integrity in their awareness of such concerns or impulses. I found few guides indulging in the kind of exaggerations, creative interpretations, and outright lies common to many guides in other tourist sites in the world. Michael Harkin (2003, 578) describes that such exaggerations or fabrications (in living pre-historic tour situations he studied) work "to heighten interest and increase tips." Most guides I knew rigorously avoided offering any answer to the most-often asked question of tourists: "What does it mean?"

29. Eller (2000, 120) wonders, "how then do feminist matriarchalists know that every ani-mal and geometrical symbol found in prehistoric art is a representation of the goddess or one of her qualities? Only by believing, before they look, that the art is religious art, and in particu-lar, an iconography of a prehistoric goddess."

30. After reviewing the most commonly argued "evidence" of the goddess—from Paleolithic Europe, Neolithic cultures, including Çatalhöyük, Malta, the Balkans, the Indus Valley civiliza-tion, and Minoan Crete, Philip G. Davis (1998, 84) similarly finds the idea of a unified goddess lacking: "In each of these cases, the story of the Goddess is a fabrication in defiance of the facts."

31. Archaeologists with more data and levels of context to consider agree that "in contrast to the essentialized prehistory of Old Europe as written by Gimbutas," which is reductionist, they instead "suggest that the interpretation of figurines should be presented in relation to, not in exclusion of, alternative interpretive narratives, . . . [which are] more complicated" than the picture that Gimbutas and others like her paint (Goodison and Morris 1998, 44–45).

32. The "we" here means our culture generally. Gimbutas discusses some variety in images and beliefs. But popular culture generally, and many specific explanations of goddess culture, seem based on a common social impulse to conflate such images and imagined beliefs.

33. "It was the discovery of Lascaux that changed ideas about the origins of art. Until the 1940s it was widely thought that the origins of art lay in ancient Greece and Rome. With Las-caux, artists and archaeologists were quick to realise that 'art' had much deeper, prehistoric origins. And what followed was a story of art that started in Lascaux and ended in the Louvre. Today we rightly challenge this Eurocentric account of the history of art, but in the 1940s it was Lascaux that challenged a very narrow definition of what was considered art" (Dowson n.d.).

34. According to a 2013 National Geographic article, "Were the First Artists Mostly Women" by Virginia Hughes, new analysis of ancient handprints finds that "three-quarters of the hand-prints in ancient cave art were left by women" (https://news.nationalgeographic.com/news /2013/10/131008-women-handprints-oldest-neolithic-cave-art/). But during fieldwork in Dor-dogne in 2018, I heard skepticism about this study from several well-versed guides.

35. There are prehistoric sites open to tourists in Dordogne, including caves, shelters, and museums. Les Eyzies de Tayac and Montignac welcome many visitors a year, and the latter features the original Lascaux (now closed) and two copies that attract many tourists (Lascaux II and Lascaux IV).

36. You can Google any named pieces to find images, and just Googling "Venus figurines" and scanning the images shown can reveal a large variation of representations.

37. E.g., Venuses of Willendorf, Lausel, Lespugue, Dolni Věstonice, Gagarino.

38. E.g., Venus Impudique, of Galgenberg, of Petřkovice, of Monruz, of Petersfels.

39. For instance, vulvas engraved in stone at places like L'Abri Blanchard or Combarelles, or the Venus of Brassempouy (a head with stylized or decorated hair).

40. E.g., some so-called Venus objects from Dolní Věstonice that are baton-like (with protrusions some read as breasts), as easily read as phallic. The most famous Laussel engraving features a woman holding horn with thirteen notches and her hand on her belly, things many observers perceive as symbolic.

41. Gimbutas, along with most scholars of prehistory (especially recently), recognize variability in an abundance of goddesses, though this apparently changed somewhat during the course of her career. Eller (2005, 8) claims that, "buoyed by the attention she received from spiritual feminists, Gimbutas grew progressively bolder in her claims, believing she had decoded the religious symbolism of Neolithic times."

Davis (1998, 70) states, "In an early book which predates the Goddess movement, *The Goddesses and Gods of Old Europe* (1974), we find that she described Old European religion as polytheistic, although the relative prominence of goddesses led her to infer 'a society dominated by the mother.' Even at this point, her fellow scholars were concerned at how glibly she assumed that humanoid figures and statuettes must be divinities, and presumed to divine the inner meaning of abstract and geometrical patterns in the decorative arts."

In a response to a critique of her faith, Starhawk (2003) refutes that most goddess traditions do not claim such homogeneity: "Allen makes a big point of asserting that ancient peoples were polytheists, and that this somehow disproves the myth that they worshiped a great goddess. She utterly misses the point that we are polytheists, now, today. No one, certainly not Gimbutas, ever postulated a monolithic, monotheistic Goddess religion of the past. But even the terms 'polytheistic' and 'monotheistic' come out of a framework that actually makes no sense to us. It's like asking 'Is water one or many?' The only possible answer is 'Huh? Hey, it's wonderful, miraculous, life giving, vital stuff that we need to honor and respect and conserve and not pollute, that's the point.'"

But as seen in *Goddess Remembered* and in many popular conceptions of the goddess (and of ancient images of women) all such images are indeed conflated as a mother goddess type from a matriarchal past. Although she does recognize multiple gods and goddesses in some of her work, Gimbutas (1982, 236–37) also makes statements like those common in popular culture: "Naturally, the goddess who was responsible for the transformation from death to life became the central figure in the pantheon of gods. . . . Significantly, almost all Neolithic goddesses are composite images with an accumulation of traits from the pre-agricultural and agricultural eras . . . [lists symbols, gods/goddesses, and myths]. The pantheon reflects a society dominated by the mother." Such statements suggest a sense of a matriarchy, "a society dominated by the mother," as well as a common image of a "central figure" of a "Great Goddess" that dominates for thousands of years in various forms (Gimbutas 1982). Even though she might have meant us to perceive variation at times, such statements and other work for more than a century have spurred many to a more monolithic conception, and it is that conception we often see in popular culture (like Read's film), and as seen also in quotes from Eller, Davis, and Lefkowitz.

42. Geometric designs including spirals were common in the Neolithic world. Issues include no evidence for homogeneity; common misunderstandings/simplifications of nuances, cultural variation, context; impulses to conflate imagery and interpret as we will. See Eller 2000; Goodison and Morris 1998.

43. "Only a "lion-headed, zoomorphic Löwenmensch figurine is older." Hohle Fels figurine information from "Venus of Hohle Fels," Wikipedia, accessed summer 2018, https://en.wikipedia.org/wiki/Venus_of_Hohle_Fels.

44. "This is about sex, reproduction," claims archaeologist Nicholas Conard (Curry 2012). Paul Mellars, an archaeologist at the University of Cambridge: "the figurine's blatant sexuality 'could be seen as bordering on the pornographic'" (Wilford 2009). This article also describes "the short, squat torso is dominated by oversize breasts and broad buttocks. The split between the two halves of the buttocks is deep and continuous without interruption to the front of the figurine. A greatly enlarged vulva emphasizes the 'deliberate exaggeration' of the figurine's sexual characteristics, Dr. Conard said" (Wilford 2009).

45. This description of the images found at the site comes from the museum that houses them: "The Laussel Venus," Musée d'Aquitaine, Bordeaux, accessed March 13, 2018, http://www.musee-aquitaine-bordeaux.fr/en/laussel-venus.

46. Many interpret the male figure, le chasseur, as "evoking a hunter by his posture." "The Laussel Venus," Musée d'Aquitaine, Bordeaux, accessed March 13, 2018, http://www.musee-aquitaine-bordeaux.fr/en/laussel-venus. See "Abri de Laussel," Hominidés, https://www.hominides.com/html/lieux/abri-laussel.php, accessed June 2018.

47. The images might portray a ritual scene (possibly with a priestess) or a fertility goddess or several (since there are at least two possibly pregnant women depicted on limestone), or, together with other figures at the site, some think it may represent a scene of hunting magic (since there seems to be a hunter depicted in a hunting scene). The images could be meant to weaken prey and strengthen the hunter's hand, or there could be multiple meanings.

48. Goodison and Morris (1998, 114) note similarly about the Neolithic "goddesses" of Crete: "Neolithic figurines from Crete and Greece, made mostly from clay, stone or marble, take very different shapes. Some are stylized, some naturalistic. Some are clothed, some naked. Some are fat, some thin. Evans linked such 'Mother idols' from Neolithic Crete back to Palaeolithic times. But what is there, really, to suggest or prove divinity for these figurines? How might one recognize a prehistoric Goddess? Certain criteria come to mind. She might be big; if she is a 'Mother Goddess,' she might be expected to have a child. If she is 'the Goddess,' there will be one of her. She might have been found in a location suitable for ritual. Better still would be evidence from a picture showing her being worshipped." But in fact we find no such evidence for most of the figurines from prehistory. "Studying the mute objects, what do we find? Certainly no mother with child," which appear only in the Late Bronze Age (rarely), and "no evidence that we should single out the female figurines as divine," nor any other such evidence (114).

49. Goodison and Morris (1998, 15) cite "Peter Ucko, one of the first critics of the 'Goddess' theory," who "pointed out that the anthropomorphic figurines were altogether a rare feature of early mainland Greek sites; indeed, from a sample he took of 300 figurines, only twenty-five were from houses and only three from a special context," such as would suggest any form of religious activity—like a shrine, temple, tomb, sanctuary, or any special place. They cite Ucko's 1968 paper no. 24 on "Anthropomorphic Figurines of Predynastic Egypt and Neolithic Crete".

50. The famous representation of a human at Lascaux is a stylized man (obvious phallus), but he has stick arms, a bird head, and probably a bird-topped staff. This might indicate his status as a shaman-type being, but no concomitantly stylized women with props are known, unless the horn of Laussel is counted.

51. Tringham and Conkey (1998, 25) quote such assumptions and interpretations about the figurines in a D. Collins and J. Onians 1978 *Art History* textbook.

52. Here Tringham and Conkey (1998, 26) quote Rainer Mack's creation of the art history interpretation of the figurine in "Reading the Female Archaeology of the Female Body" from *Qui Parle* in 1990.

53. Cook (2017) also finds it interesting that the women in figurines and ancient art are often shown pregnant or giving birth (though no sculpture is shown in the video giving birth) and believes they might reflect particular beliefs and fears regarding childbearing.

54. A *Smithsonian Magazine* article: "Some experts viewed such pieces as 'hunting magic'— representations of sought-after game animals, and therefore, survival tools," though they point out that most animals represented "don't correspond to what prehistoric people ate" (Curry 2012). White (2003, 51) also discusses Australian and African examples of animals' representations meant "to ensure success in the hunt" or sculpted pregnant women as "magical acts intended to control reproduction and fertility."

55. Curry (2012) states that some experts "perceive some prehistoric figurines—including a half-lion, half-man—not as imaginative works but literal depictions of hallucinations experienced by tribal shamans."

56. "There is little room in an evolutionary view for art as a divinely inspired struggle to create beautiful or novel forms. . . . Nothing is ever retained in evolution if it does not offer some kind of selective advantage" (White 2003, 13). In terms of interpretation, White observes that humans' ability (new in the Paleolithic Europe) to "isolate attributes and forms, and transfer them to another context, had profound organizational and adaptive implications . . . manifest[ing] gradations of social status and identity" and "that among the earliest known images are imaginary creatures, part human, part animal, that reconfigure nature in human terms" (16). He points out that "it is probably no coincidence then that the world's first representational images coincided with one of the greatest periods of technological and social innovation in all human history" (16).

57. Stanford University Professor Ian Hodder discusses some particularly plump female figurines as probably representing elderly women rather than goddesses: "Two plump women figurines unearthed at Çatalhöyük represent elderly women, not the Anatolian mother goddess Cybele as was earlier believed. . . . These figurines symbolize old women that have high status in the society instead of goddesses" (quoted in "Çatalhöyük Figurines Symbolize 'Elderly Women, Not Cybele,'" *Hurriyet Daily News*, January 15, 2017, accessed summer 2021, https://www.hurriyet dailynews.com/catalhoyuk-figurines-symbolize-elderly-women-not-cybele-108546). Hodder also discussed the figurines in Chris Kark, "Archaeologists from Stanford Find an 8,000-Year-Old 'Goddess Figurine' in Central Turkey," *Stanford News*, September 29, 2016, https://news .stanford.edu/2016/09/29/archaeologists-find-8000-year-old-goddess-figurine-central-turkey/, accessed Summer 2020.

58. Information from "James Mellaart," Wikipedia, https://en.wikipedia.org/wiki/James _Mellaart, which uses sources such as Christoph Bachhuber's chapter, "James Mellaart and the Luwians: A Culture-(Pre)History," 2013, in *Luwian Identities: Culture, Language and Religion between Anatolia and the Aegean*.

59. Google "Çatalhöyük murals" to see hunting murals and "Çatalhöyük animal figurines" to see those. Scholars such as Meskell (2018) attest that only 5 percent of thousands of figurines found are female. More about Mellaart's methods at Çatalhöyük: "Sir James Mellaart who excavated the site in the 1960s came up with all sorts of ideas about the way the site was organised and how it was lived in and so on . . . We've now started working there since the mid 1990s and come up with very different ideas about the site. One of the most obvious examples of that is that Çatalhöyük is perhaps best known for the idea of the mother goddess. But our work more

recently has tended to show that in fact there is very little evidence of a mother goddess and very little evidence of some sort of female-based matriarchy. That's just one of the many myths that the modern scientific work is undermining" (O'Brien 2009, quoting Ian Hodder from Stanford University).

60. Some details of the figurines suggest they might be goddesses, such as the material they are made from, the snakes, and more, but there is no reason to assume they are a singular goddess and attendants. It's much more plausible to consider they are multiple goddesses.

61. Mary Renault's fiction, like the novel *The King Must Die* ([1958] 1986), draws upon such beliefs and creates a fictional world of imagined goddess-based and matriarchal cultures of the time. Her fiction vilifies goddess culture and matriarchy, imagining Theseus as a great hero who helps civilize the ancient world (overcoming brutal practices of matriarchy/goddesses).

62. Visit the Brooklyn Museum of Art for images of this exhibit: Judy Chicago, *The Dinner Party*, Mixed Media, 1979, Elizabeth A. Sackler Center for Feminist Art, the Brooklyn Museum (on display since 2007), https://www.brooklynmuseum.org/exhibitions/dinner_party. See also pages on particular settings, including "Snake Goddess (Mythic)" (quoted here, including the reference that this quote comes from Chicago, *A Symbol of Our Heritage*, 1979, 60), accessed May 3, 2018, https://www.brooklynmuseum.org/eascfa/dinner_party/place_settings/snake_goddess.

63. Among the many scholars who trace this history are Lefkowitz (1992), Goodison and Morris (1998), Davis (1998), Lapatin (2002), and Eller (2011).

Chapter 2

1. Ideas of matriarchy and patriarchy as superior or inferior varied over time: "The matriarchal era, which for most Victorian anthropologists was regarded as a backward time characterized by excesses of sexual abandon, was for first-wave feminists an idyllic time for all humans, characterized by the monogamy and chastity that were considered appropriate for Victorian-era women. The patriarchal era, which most Victorian anthropologists viewed as a powerful step up the ladder of social progress, was for first-wave feminists an alarming fall from grace which could only be repaired by the reinstitution of matriarchal norms in modern-day society" (Eller 2005, 4).

2. Lefkowitz (1992, 33) agrees that the goddess myth is not feminist: "First, it reduces all representations of all women to a single representation of woman, thereby eliminating the rich differences within and between the many traditions in which women were artistically and religiously represented. And second, it reduces all of womankind to a genital identity ... [and all this] culminates in the grossest simplifications."

3. Some proponents hail the feminist aspects of "thealogy," as some term this faith, or "feminist images of God" as a force against global capitalism and environmental destruction, as well as a means for psychological female empowerment (Raphael 2000; Grey 2001). The religion can offer positive benefits of what some term "womanspirit," as Christ (and Plaskow 1979, 286) demonstrates: "The symbol of the Goddess has much to offer women who are struggling to be rid of ... devaluation of female power, denigration of the female body, distrust of female will, and denial of the women's bonds and heritage that have been engendered by patriarchal religion. As women struggle to create a new culture in which women's power, bodies, will, and bonds are celebrated, it seems natural that the Goddess would reemerge as symbol of the newfound beauty, strength, and power of women." In another book examining the history of goddess worship, including its skeptics, but concluding with its worth, Christ (1997, 177) argues that by focusing on "the beauty," "love," other messages of the Goddess: "Then we can begin again

to create communities and societies that live in greater harmony and justice with other people, all our relations, and the earth body." The book *Goddess in World Mythology* is dedicated "to all women who in the world who were unaware of their own heritage / You are descendant from a long line of sacred females / who have been respected and honored for thousands of years / Remember and make it so" (Anne and Myers Imel 1995).

4. Cynthia Eller (2000, 1) quotes feminist leader Gloria Steinem (1972): "Once upon a time, the many cultures of this world were all part of the gynocratic age. Paternity had not yet been discovered, and it was thought . . . that women bore fruit like trees—when they were ripe. . . . Women were worshipped because of it."

5. This sentiment applies even if Gimbutas is considered the "source" of the myth, since her work stems from Victorian men's theories: "Dr. Gimbutas said in an interview that the 19th century Swiss scholar Johann Jakob Bachofen and his followers . . . were among her fore-runners. In ancient laws and legends and in the beliefs of isolated tribes or communities, they found vestiges of an earlier matriarchal stage of human civilization centered on worship of a mother goddess. Dr. Gimbutas tempers her forerunners' notion of strict matriarchy, but her similarities to these predecessors divides her from many colleagues" (Steinfels 1990).

6. Lefkowitz (1992) also offers some evidence for some of the specific types of rituals enacted by practitioners of the Goddess cult, drawing from Zsuzsanna Budapest, who claims to have learned Goddess traditions through the women in her family. Lefkowitz shows that her manual, "'Z's' Holy Book of Women's Mysteries, specifies only celebrations and birth, menstruation, con-ception, hysterectomy, and menopause, as well as sexuality in all its various manifestations" (33).

7. Lefkowitz (1992, 31) also shows that "virtually all the authors of books and manuals on the Goddess and her modern cults . . . [everywhere] are confident that they are correctly recon-structing the rites and the beliefs of a lost ancient religion. They argue that the Goddess, and more generally a religion that reflected the power held by women in ancient society, preceded the male-dominated religions described in all the familiar mythologies."

8. Most critics who question the scholarship of the goddess myth (many quotes herein) suggest hope for more interpretive potential if we look beyond Victorian assumptions and conclusions. Lefkowitz, Eller, and many of the scholars in Goodison and Morris concur, for instance, "The monolithic 'Goddess' whose biology is her destiny may to a large extent be an illusion, a creation of modern need, but in acknowledging greater diversity in religious expression we allow for the possibility of finding new patterns in a rich and fascinating body of evidence" (Goodison and Morris 1998, 21). Likewise, Tringham and Conkey (1998, 45) "sug-gest that the interpretation of figurines should be presented in *relation to*, not in exclusion of, alternative interpretive narratives . . . as feminists we are sure that longer-term interpretative satisfaction is more complicated than [the 'facts' given previously]." Eller (2000, 8) laments that "the gendered stereotypes upon which matriarchal myth rests persistently work to flatten out differences among women; to exaggerate differences between women and men; and to hand women an identity that is symbolic, timeless, and archetypal, instead of giving them the free-dom to craft identities that suit their individual temperaments, skills, preferences, and moral and political commitments. . . . Innovation is possible: we are not forever condemned to find our future in our past."

9. Starhawk (1999, 4): "The truth of our experience is valid whether it has roots thousands of years old or thirty minutes old, that there is a mythic truth whose proof is shown not through references and footnotes but in the way it engages strong emotions, mobilizes deep life energies, and gives us a sense of history, purpose, and place in the world. What gives the God-dess tradition validity is how it works for us now, in the moment, not whether or not someone else worshipped this particular image in the past." Interestingly, this statement concurs with what many other feminist archaeologists and scholars who contest the reading of prehistoric

images argue, in the sense that we don't need proof of a matriarchal past to imagine a bright future for women (Goodison and Morris 1998; Eller 2000, etc.).

10. We have a better chance of offering meaningful and persuasive interpretation the more we can understand of the context of a myth, which can include the culture it came from, the individual who told it, when and for what purpose, the audience who received it, etc., as well as all of the same for the scholar doing analysis. Of course, the further back in time one goes, the harder it becomes to study context. Nonetheless, the greater the attempt to understand relevant contexts one makes, the better one's potential to interpret myths becomes.

11. Gregory Nagy (2002, 240) writes: "The meaning of myth in academic language continues to resist any definition that is uniform, universally valid." Gregory Schrempp (2012, 17) explains: "no pat definition of myth will suffice; certainly none of the pat definitions of myth proposed thus far by scholars has risen to general acceptance." G. S. Kirk (1970, 7) understands "there is no one definition of myth, no Platonic form of a myth against which all actual instances can be measured. Myths, as we shall see, differ enormously in their morphology and their social function."

12. As folklorist Richard Bauman (1991) explains of all genres of stories, they share certain characteristics of "form, function or effect, content, orientation to the world and the cosmos, truth value, tone, social distribution, manner or contexts of use, and so on."

13. Stocking (1987) explains Tylor's theory, showing how the final, most advanced stage, "civilization," was of course best represented by the men, Victorians, who were writing the theories. A good explanation of this socio-cultural evolutionary theory in Stocking's chapter 5, "The Darwinian Revolution and the Evolution of Human Culture (1858–1871)," in *Victorian Anthropology* by Georgia W. Stocking Jr. (1987). He concludes the chapter: "One studied these forms not for themselves, or in terms of the meaning they might have to the people who created them, but in order to cast light on the processes by which the ape had developed into the British gentleman" (185).

14. No culture has progressed beyond brutality, murder, war, oppression, and other grave injustices just because they may enjoy more advanced technology—in fact we could note that we use our superior technology partly to more efficiently kill other humans. Based on more than a century of ethnology (anthropological fieldwork) and research in psychology, genetics, and other disciplines, scholars now accept that humans from all eras and parts of the world have equal intellectual capacity and potential.

15. William Bascom, Alan Dundes, Schrempp, Nagy, Kirk, and others also demonstrate the range, history, and typical meanings ascribed to myth, essentially explaining aspects of its structure and function—though with an eye to those qualities needing to be considered in context as relevant to any given culture.

16. Lévi-Strauss (1971, 562) draws upon the image of one who weaves together bits and pieces of culture, helping us to live with the dualities in our world, in the image of the bricoleur, the "tinkerer" who serves as mythic hero in perceiving patterns—deeper structures like dualities—and making sense of them, and thus of the cosmos: "More rapid cross-references, together with an increase in the number of points of view and angles of approach have made it possible to consolidate into a whole what might at first have seemed to be a loose and precarious assemblage of odds and ends, all dissimilar in form, texture and color. Careful stitching and darning, systematically applied to reinforce weak spots, has finally produced a homogeneous fabric, clear in outline and harmonious in its blend of shades; fragments which at first seemed disparate, once they found their appropriate place and the correct relationship to their neighbors, come together to form a coherent picture. In this picture, the tiniest details, however gratuitous, bizarre, and even absurd they may have seemed at the beginning, acquire both meaning and function."

17. Schrempp (2012, 47) explains that "anthropologist Claude Lévi-Strauss, in his work *The Raw and the Cooked*, argues convincingly that traditional mythological stories are often structured around correlation of oppositions that in different domains contrast life in a state of nature with life in a state of culture," which we will see is part of the structure of the myth of matriarchy as this argument progresses.

18. See, for instance, Lévi-Strauss 1966. Bricolage is discussed toward the end of chapter 1.

19. "When genres are conceptualized as open-ended, flexible, and manipulable sets of discursive conventions and expectation . . . both traditional blended forms . . . as well as emergent generic syntheses become more comprehensible" (Bauman 1991, 58).

20. Folklorist Richard Bauman echoes others like Franz Boas (1898, 18), one of anthropology and folklore's founding fathers in the United States, who also recognizes the variability of generic form and content of genre when he analyzes myths of the Northwest Coast Indians: "It would seem that mythological worlds have been built up only to be shattered again, and that new worlds were built from the fragments."

21. Schrempp demonstrates that both myths and science offer explanations of the cosmos, and both often resort to narrative to relate their epistemologies. A key difference is that information about the universe presented in myths is not testable, whereas science is designed to be tested repeatedly. Science also depends on cumulative, frequently updated knowledge. Though both may be told as narratives, myth is based on fantastical characters, metaphors, and beliefs (either passed down or imagined). Myths may change over time and be modernized, and they sometimes even reflect new periods and technological developments (like space travel or other technology), but they resist testing and application of the scientific method. Myths may be enacted through rituals, told creatively in various ways, and believed in absolutely, casually, or not at all. But they usually do not have physical effects in the real world, as in leading to new technology for building cars or providing medical treatment. The effects of myth are more ephemeral, influencing beliefs or lifestyles, perhaps even changing culture, but probably not saving lives (medically). People may believe they are cured through faith, and they may find important value-laden sentiments in myths, but these "real-world results" are neither empirical nor usually repeatable (two standard criteria for science). Yet science is not completely divorced from myth. Many scientific theories are presented or understood in narrative form, which often end up sounding remarkably mythic, as Gregory Schrempp (1992, 25) demonstrates in *Magical Arrows*, where he analyzes "highly mythically tinged" literature like Greek philosopher Zeno's oblique use of a story of Achilles to illuminate his philosophy: "the invocation of myth (or at least of an 'epic' that is highly mythically tinged) ought perhaps not be regarded dismissively as a mere appeal to dramatic effect. While the invocation of Achilles, and by implication the world of heroes, may not be strictly necessary for an exposition of Zeno's technical arguments against the possibility of motion, it may be necessary for some larger intellectual purpose." Schrempp shows that Zeno and Lévi-Strauss both distinguish myth from scientific forms of discourse, yet both use myths in their own scientific discourse. In a sense, they create their own myths, even while they think they are rising above it.

22. Budapest, aka Zsuzsanna Emese Mokcsay and Z. Budapest, originally from Hungary, is a widely published American author and founder and high priestess of the first documented women-only coven. She also founded and directs a Women's Spirituality Forum. She writes on paganism for the *San Francisco Examiner* and is often cited as an important source for goddess culture practices and beliefs, which she claims comes to her from a long line of women ancestors who practiced "witchcraft" and goddess worship.

23. Another strain of "Dianic" Wiccan cults is part of a tradition of this relatively new religion. Margot Adler (1986), describing the history of various Wiccan traditions today, explains that some modern witches consider themselves worshippers of Diana. Charles G. Leland, she

explains, described "a Witch cult that worshipped Diana" in Italy at the turn of the century (46). But there is a separate "Dianic tradition that Margaret Murray made famous in a 1921 book," and that one is based on "the two-faced horned god known to the Romans as Janus or Dianus." Murray wrote that the feminine form of the name—Diana—was found throughout Western Europe as the leader of witches. Because of this, Murray called the religion the Dianic Cult, although she wrote that the god rarely appeared in female form and a male deity had apparently superseded a female one" (47). Davis (1998, 324) likewise explains that "Murray made no suggestion that witchcraft was in any way a women's religion." Eventually a later writer about paganism in Europe, Gerald Gardner, following occult order leaders like Dion Fortune and Moina Mathers (and later followers of theirs), all "emphasized goddesses," whom they considered "the Goddess herself, openly worshipped in ages before recorded history, the epitome of natural beauty, joy, and love; her immanence" (Davis 1998, 329, 330).

24. American Charles Leland claimed an Italian woman named Maddalena was a "witch informant" for his book *Aradia, or the Gospel of the Witches* (1899; Davis 1998). Gerald Gardner, an English Wiccan, follower of Aleister Crowley, and member of various occult groups like the Freemasons and the Rosicrucian Order of Crotona Fellowship, claims to have encountered the "New Forest coven" of practicing pagans in England, which he claimed initiated him in 1939 and taught him their surviving pre-Christian witch-cult ways. Davis (1998, 334) shows that "the basic framework of early Gardnerian witchcraft was taken from Margaret Murray's [1921] *The Witch-Cult in Western Europe* (1998, 333). Davis and many scholars conclude that "Gardner's own witchcraft texts were his personal creation and not something handed on to him from an ancient tradition." Scholars believe most such writers who claimed to have found still practicing survivals of ancient paganism invented their material, often based on other such writers and practitioners of their times.

25. "Goddess spirituality is neither the modern expression of an actual pre-Christian, pre-Jewish, pre-Greek, utopian, female-centered civilization, nor a creative contemporary innovation in religion; it is neither primordial nor pristine. It is, instead, one of the latest adaptations of the Western esoteric tradition as it was filtered through Romanticism—and a very effective and marketable adaptation it has proven to be" (Davis 1998, 342).

26. Gimbutas (1982, 11) mainly examines Neolithic art, but right in her introduction to *The Goddesses and Gods of Old Europe*, she also draws a likely connection to the Paleolithic era as well: "The tradition of sculpture and painting encountered in Old Europe . . . was transmitted from the Palaeolithic era. In art and mythical imagery it is not possible to draw a line between the two eras, Palaeolithic and Neolithic," though she does perceive some differences, as between "hunters and fishers" and "the first farmers." Thus the story really reaches back (at least in some inspirational and symbolic qualities), to the Paleolithic era (which in Europe dates to at least forty thousand years ago).

27. Eller (2000, 13) finds metaphorical truth key to believers: "the story is sufficiently important to some feminists that they are unwilling to discard it simply because its status as historical truth is insecure. . . . 'Truth' is thus only one consideration among others. Besides, 'metaphoric truth,' says Donna Wilshire, which 'speaks to such a deep core of our common humanity and the meaning of life' is 'more real than faculty reality.'" Schrempp (2012, 16) sees this "truth" factor in myths as complex, "Connoting in some instances a synthesis of poetic imagination and moral wisdom held as a society's unique spiritual treasure, 'myth' or 'mythology' just as readily designates ideologies perpetrated by demagogues upon gullible masses," meaning myths can either reveal powerful, "true" wisdom, or pretend to do so, harmfully.

28. Marler (2003), for instance, names eight women writers (Mary Daly, Merlin Stone, Susan Griffin, Charlene Spretnak, Starhawk, Carolyn Merchant, and Gerder Lerner), along with "numerous other scholars" whom she sees as agreeing with Gimbutas and "promoting

the second wave of feminism, the reemergence of an earth-based spirituality and the ecology movement. Collectively, their research provided an historical basis for the rejection of entrenched beliefs in the universality of male dominated religions and social structures and the reclamation of women's leadership roles as creators of culture" (*Belili* site). But such works reflect and cite each other heavily.

29. "Myth fulfills in primitive culture an indispensable function: it expresses, enhances, and codifies belief; it safeguards and enforces morality.... Myth is thus a vital ingredient of human civilization; it is not an idle tale, but a hard-worked active force; it is not an intellectual explanation or an artistic imagery, but a pragmatic charter of primitive faith and moral wisdom" (Malinowksi 1948, 101).

30. The film then shows numerous stone sculptures that depict the classical world of war—setting up another binary opposition with all the previously shown representations in stone of women from prehistory, which the film of course identifies as goddesses. Charlene Spretnak explains the relevant, goddess-centered view of history at about this time in the film: "I don't think you can understand patriarchy unless you look at the fact that fear is at the core. Fear that female sexuality will somehow become this chaotic force. That nature will become this chaotic force overtaking us. So we have to have everything tightly controlled and hierarchically ordered. In every cultural era, there have been forces that were going toward the negative, toward the destructive, and forces that were going toward the positive, toward the wisdom path" (Read 1989). Spretnak and the film connect "female sexuality" and "nature" and contrast positive, peaceful, egalitarian, female goddess culture with what comes later: the negative versus the positive, the destructive versus wisdom.

31. Again, the assumption that women are more "wild," as in more connected to nature, underpins her argument and is scientifically meaningless. Estés (1992, 7) urges readers to seek a goddesslike, fundamental version of their "woman" selves, similar in many cultures, she claims, with "no name, for she is so vast. But since this force engenders every important facet of womanliness, here on earth she is named many names, not only in order to peer into the myriad aspects of her nature but also to hold on to her." These myriad, "instinctual" aspects of womanhood are wild and natural qualities we share with wolves, she argues: "certain psychic characteristics: keen sensing, playful spirit, and a heightened capacity for devotion ... relational by nature, inquiring, possessed of great endurance and strength ... deeply intuitive, intensely concerned with their young, their mates, and their pack." These innate characteristics are in our culture, "hounded, harassed, and falsely imputed to be devouring and devious, overly aggressive, of less value than those who are their detractors" (2).

32. In *The Chalice and The Blade*, goddess culture scholar Riane Eisler (1987, 251) provides a similar chart that she titles "Comparison of Old European and Kurgan Cultures," inspired largely by the work of Gimbutas. Her book title also reflects dualities, chalice/blade (nurturing vessel vs. weapon), and history/future (goddess believers think the future could be inspired by the lost history they are recovering). The fact that she includes such a chart and bases much of her argument on such dualities supports my reading of the centrality of binary oppositions to this myth. As Eller (2000, 61–62) points out, "It is peculiar though that feminist matriarchalists like Eisler should retain this usage, as it is based on a deep dichotomy between women and men, femininity and masculinity. And arranging the world into dualisms (like feminine and masculine) is said by feminist matriarchalists to be a patriarchal practice.... In spite of this, the entire premise of feminist matriarchal myths is dualistic." Eller also shows many ways the goddess myth embodies and reflects dualities: "matriarchy and patriarchy ... are polar opposites, one good and the other evil. In feminist matriarchal thought, the goddess, who abjures dualisms, is constantly pitted in direct opposition to the patriarchal god of western cultures, whose primary failing is his penchant for separating 'us' from 'them,' 'good' from 'bad,' 'mind' from 'body,' and of course, 'women' from 'men.'

... The hope seems to be that with the one, correct, overarching dualism—whether matriarchy versus patriarchy, partnership versus dominator, goddess versus god—all the other terms will lose their polarizing grip" and she quotes Eisler as saying as much (62).

33. These terms are drawn not only from the quotes from goddess proponents already seen but also from the popular culture versions/interpretations of the myths yet to be examined.

Chapter 3

1. A significant portion of this discussion of Silko's novel was previously published in longer form as "Landscapes of Miracles and Matriarchy in Silko's Gardens in the Dunes," in *Reading Leslie Marmon Silko: Critical Perspectives through Gardens in the Dunes*, edited by Laura Coltelli, 21–36 (Pisa, Italy: Pisa University Press, 2007). It appears here with permission of the press.

2. Many find a glorious past where women ruled—a true matriarchy—unlikely. The actual stories we have of past, even mythic women show women who are no longer in power, who are subjugated, controlled, domesticated, punished, or killed: "myths of women's former dominance, whether from ancient Greece or contemporary New Guinea, are used to keep women down" (Eller 2000, 178). There are no proven cases of exclusively female rule or dominance, whether socially or in religion; male gods and heroes always exist alongside, and typically dominate, powerful women. In the long run, then, such stories support the status quo of men in power (Eller 2000). But Eller hopes nonetheless that feminists today will work toward a better future. Silko's narrative world embraces a vision of survival and potential, written for contemporary readers.

3. The recovery of Eden is also a powerful metaphor in the Judeo-Christian tradition. Eve's improper tasting of fruit leads to the fall from a perfect relationship with nature in an ideal garden. But the concept of redemption comes to fruition in the womb of another woman, Mary, the savior Christ's mother. According to Catholic theology, the Virgin Mary's womb is the enclosed garden (the new Eden) that bears fruit (Jesus) that according to Christian faith returns believers miraculously to paradise. Carolyn Merchant (2003, 53) explains: "The Virgin Mary's womb becomes a metaphor for the garden into which the Holy Ghost cast his special blessing, producing Christ as mankind's savior. The enclosed garden symbolized the womb of the virgin. Mary was a garden of sweetness, blossoming with the fullness of life. She offered hope for recovering heaven." Mary is arguably a goddess figure, still revered around the world by Catholics, who see her in visions and visitations, build shrines to her, wear and adorn their homes with images of her, and, most significantly, often put statues of her in their gardens. Dan Brown (2003) goes so far as to link her (fictionally) directly with the goddess tradition in his best-selling novel. The concept of the womb as garden inspires, according to Merchant (2003, 54), "medieval enclosed gardens" that are intricately connected in the medieval worldview to the "mysteries of womanhood." Women and gardens are both associated with the hope for the reinvention of spiritual and earthly paradise.

4. The Ghost Dance is a nineteenth-century religious movement of Native Americans who believed the circle dance (that praised Jesus) would help restore traditional Native ways and end white expansion.

5. Walker also wrote a nonfiction book called *Warrior Marks: Female Genital Mutilation and the Sexual Binding of Women* (1993), which accounts her travels to parts of Africa where FGM is practiced and her interviews with women who underwent the procedure and even a woman who performs clitoridectomies. The film, produced by Walker, is also called *Warrior Marks* and was made by Pratibha Parmar (1994).

6. There are also Sheelas in France and Spain. See any number of websites devoted to "Sheela na Gigs" (for images), including the Wikipedia entry at http://en.wikipedia.org/wiki/Sheela_na_Gig.

7. Information from John Harding, "The Sheela Na Gig Project: Researching Sheela Na Gig Sculptures in the UK," accessed summer 2021, https://sheelanagig.org/.

8. The connection between goddess culture and Jungian psychology has been demonstrated (Lefkowitz 1992).

9. "Female Genital Mutilation" fact sheet, *World Health Organization*, February 3, 2020, accessed summer 2021, https://www.who.int/news-room/fact-sheets/detail/female-genital-mutilation.

10. Lévi-Strauss and others explain that myths establish order and work to lessen chaos (see chapter 2).

11. See notes 66 and 67 for more information on Sarah Baartman, a.k.a. The Hottentot Venus, who was exploited as a sideshow attraction for her supposed resemblance to prehistoric women, particularly her large hips and genitalia.

12. See chapter 6 for hopepunk discussion.

Chapter 4

1. Others find: "It's pretty shocking that over sixteen films and nearly ten years [of the MCU], not a single woman has been the 'big bad'" (Cook 2017).

2. My Google search of "worst female movie villains" produced more than 10 million results and a rich variety of characters, including one hundred at the first hit: The Ranker Community, "The Greatest Female Villains," Ranker, December 21, 2020, accessed summer 2021, https://www.ranker.com/crowdranked-list/best-female-villains. A number of them (Cersei Baratheon, Maleficent, Bellatrix Lestrange, Annie Wilkes, and Hela) have major roles in their films or TV shows.

3. Numerous websites, blogs, and fan theories compare Thor and Jesus, including Scott Smith, "Is the Thor Myth Based on Jesus?" *The Scott Smith Blog*, November 2, 2017, accessed July 23, 2018, https://www.thescottsmithblog.com/2017/11/is-thor-myth-based-on-jesus.html.

4. Critics such as Anton K. Kozlovic see parallels between superheroes and Christ: "Superman as Christ-Figure: The American Pop Culture Movie Messiah," *Journal of Religion and Film* 6, no. 1 (2016), accessed July 31, 2018, https://digitalcommons.unomaha.edu/jrf/vol6/iss1/5/.

5. Directed by John McTiernan and Michael Crichton, starring Antonio Banderas.

6. In Crichton's novel, these prehistoric "monsters" are revealed to be Neanderthals.

7. According to the IMDB "Trivia" for the film, the original "version of the Wendol's mother was an old woman. . . . When Michael Crichton took over and did the reshoots, it was decided that brutally killing off an old lady did not reflect very well on the heroes. Crichton decided after the fact to make her younger, sleeker and tougher."

8. There is no consensus among scientists or philosophers on how old war and violence against other humans is, but some archaeologists argue that the oldest evidence of obvious intergroup violence is only ten thousand years old (the end of the Paleolithic). See for instance, Sarah Peacey, "Have Humans Always Gone to War?" *The Conversation*, April 11, 2016, accessed July 31, 2018, http://theconversation.com/have-humans-always-gone-to-war-57321.

9. Davis (1998) demonstrates that claims of found or remembered pagan life were likely invented by people who wished to find such evidence or who hoped to influence others to follow what he concludes are invented practices.

10. See also Magoulick 2006 for an argument about other such powerful women in popular culture.

11. Adam White (2017), for instance, wrote for the UK newspaper *The Telegraph*, an article titled "Five Times Joss Whedon, Self-Proclaimed 'Woke Bae,' Blew His Feminist Credentials." He specifically calls out season 4 of *Angel* as one of his worst offenses, though he also notes Whedon's infidelities, other problematic plots in his projects (such as women needing to be raped for men to learn a lesson or a bad, unused *Wonder Woman* film script). Of season 4 of *Angel*, he writes that Cordelia's "body [being] taken over by an evil higher being, and engaging in an affair with Angel's son, who she then became pregnant by. The long-running storyline was, it goes without saying, something of a disaster." More recently Charisma Carpenter, who played Cordelia (on *Buffy* and *Angel*), came forward to accuse Whedon: "[he] has created hostile and toxic work environments since his early career. . . . For nearly two decades, I have held my tongue" (Lampen 2021). She also "described being emotionally abused by Whedon on the set of Angel, alleging that he retaliated against her for being pregnant and then abruptly fired her after she gave birth" (Jeva Lange, "The Joss Whedon Problem Haunting *The Nevers*," *The Week*, April 9, 2021, accessed summer 2021, https://theweek.com/articles/976289/joss-whedon-problem-haunting-nevers). Other women *Buffy* actors also came forward expressing support for Carpenter and bad memories of working for Whedon. His wife also spoke up about years of infidelity and posing as feminist to get away with it. Actor Ray Fisher accuses him of "'gross abusive, unprofessional, and completely unacceptable' on-set behavior toward the cast and crew of *Justice League*." His work is being reconsidered by many as less feminist than some perceive (Lampen 2021).

12. Goodison and Morris (1998, 20) trace such "bad mother" conceptualizations of the Goddess back to earlier male scholars: "the 'Mother Goddess' sometimes seems to reflect our conflicting feelings about Mother. The Victorian scholars' notion of the all-powerful, all-sexual and potentially all-destructive Mother Goddess who partners the son-consort-dying god significantly mirrors the obsessive sexual love, fear and hate of the small Freudian boy in his mother's lap. Glamorizing 'matricide' as a struggle for freedom, the Jungian male hero also has to escape from the 'Terrible Mother,' the 'womb of death,' in order to achieve consciousness and identity, reflecting the dilemma of the male child who must reject the protective wing of mother, the limitations of home and traditional 'female' qualities or order to forge an acceptable identity out in a male world." Contemporary popular conceptions of the goddess as chaotic reflect long-standing Western "archetypal" fantasies of problematic women.

13. There are two descriptions of the creation of humans in Genesis, one in chapter 1, where the two beings are created at once, "Male and Female created He them," and another in chapter 2, the more familiar story of the first man being lonely, and God putting him to sleep to create a "help mate" out of his rib. For millennia, many have considered the first of these women to be Lilith, and the second to be Eve. Many consider Lilith to later become allied with demons, but she is also hailed by some as a protofeminist.

14. "The downside to the big Julia betrayal twist, unfortunately, is that the show has now suggested that the two victims of sexual assault are its villains, even if Julia hasn't gone full Dark Willow yet" (Weidenfeld 2016). That last is a reference to a plot twist in Buffy, where the character Willow, a witch in that series, becomes a dark witch threatening even her friends for a few episodes. Critics have mixed reviews about the show overall, some appreciating its creative storytelling and special effects. Many consider it a kind of grown-up version of Harry Potter. One reviewer appreciates that it doesn't shy away from "all the terrible things that could happen if magic were real. People are still fickle, amoral beings, power still corrupts, and your childhood dreams are best left in your childhood" (Weidenfeld 2016). Some find the show derivative—Fillory like Narnia; Brakebills like Hogwarts (as a university), etc., and some find troubling plot points, for instance sexual abuse (Weidenfeld 2016).

15. Murray (2016) particularly notices the weaknesses in Julia's story arc, especially compared with the more nuanced presentation of her story in the books (including false memories):

"Julia's complicated quest to reconcile her memories of trauma and become a stronger person is replaced by a plot point where god spunk gives you powers. I'm just gonna say that again—in the TV show, having the semen of a god inside your body gives you magical powers. That is why Julia has more power in the final episode. That is why Alice has more power in the final episode, too—Julia was raped and Alice drinks a mason jar of semen [of a Fillory god]."

16. When Alice asks about her magic, Julia offers her "prevailing theory": "extra sprinkles on the cupcake from when Our Lady Underground restored my Shade, but she didn't exactly leave a note, so . . . I mean, do I want to know?" Alice helps her find a way to a visionary conversation with Persephone that provides her answer, but Julia is troubled by seeing Reynard's glowing eyes connected to the seed of power. Persephone explains, "Because the seed comes from him." This makes Julia angry: "Are you kidding me? . . . You didn't think before shoving some rapist's seed inside me to ask!? You gods are real shaky on the concept of consent, you know that?" Persephone tries to reason with her: "I took it from him and gave it to you, and when you showed mercy, you *earned* this." Alice later agrees with Persephone: "This might sound horrible, but he's gone. Does it matter where it came from? It's magic" (season 3, episode 5). Julia protests that it does matter, but she retains the magic seed and learns to use her magic better as the season progresses.

17. Julia's magic grows stronger the more she uses it for good causes. She saves the Faery Skye, who is being used as a slave and tortured in this world. Faery blood and flesh is used by some, like the powerful Librarians in the series, as a source of magical power. By freeing the Faeries, Julia triggers a compromise with the Faery Queen in Fillory, who in exchange for the return to Fillory of Faery slaves on earth gives our heroes the final key they need to complete their season 3 quest. Julia's help triggers other peace accords and cooperation with the Faeries and restores Brakebills' Dean Fogg's eyesight. She restores a sentient forest on Fillory that she had previously destroyed (when without her shade). In thanks, the Fillorian people come to revere her, calling her The Lady of the Tree. She performs many good deeds as a goddess: "Julia has done us the solidest solid. After the trees, she grew food for the starving peasants. She fixed the dry wells. She even helped this one guy's bajanked case of head lice. I mean, Children of Earth are back on top!" (season 3, episode 12).

18. I witnessed this at DragonCon at a panel devoted to the show.

19. According to the Center for the Study of Women in Television and Film, "Overall, men accounted for 66% and women 34% of all directors, writers, producers, executive producers, editors, and cinematographers working on films selected and/or screened at the festivals in 2019–2020" (Martha Lauzen, "Research," Center for the Study of Women in Television and Film, 2020, accessed summer 2021, https://womenintvfilm.sdsu.edu/research/).

Chapter 5

1. Information about Auel and her books comes from her publisher's website, "Jean M. Auel," Penguin Random House, https://www.penguinrandomhouse.com/authors/1026/jean-m-auel/; and the "Jean M. Auel" Wikipedia page, https://en.wikipedia.org/wiki/Jean_M._Auel, both accessed summer 2021.

2. "The narrative is propelled by Auel's knowledge (much of it necessarily speculative) of human species interaction during the late Pleistocene epoch, roughly 35,000 to 25,000 years ago" (Hand 2011).

3. Though many contemporary humans have Neanderthal DNA, studies suggest that by 30,000 BCE in Europe (the time of the books), Neanderthals may have been extinct—by forty thousand years ago, Mateja Hajinjak et al., "Initial Upper Palaeolithic Humans in Europe Had

Recent Neanderthal Ancestry," *Nature*, July 7, 2020, accessed summer 2021, https://www.nature.com/articles/s41586-021-03335-3.pdf. Some studies suggest they might have continued until as recently as twenty-four thousand years ago, but more recent studies support the earlier date: Gunnar De Winter, "When Did the Neanderthals Go Extinct?" *Medium*, March 18, 2021, accessed summer 2021, https://medium.com/predict/when-did-the-neanderthals-go-extinct-997fea2d35f0.

4. Ayla is "an innovator who sometimes wears men's clothing and develops or adapts new technologies such as the fire-starter, spear-thrower, harness and travois. She utilizes and understands sign language (the mostly non-verbal Clan's primary means of communication); has prescient knowledge of moon phases and astronomy; possesses an excellent grasp of basic psychological counseling and legal techniques, as well as keen insight into human contraceptive and reproductive issues" (Hand 2011).

5. Ayla impresses: "Ayla's hunting prowess is just one of the many skills acquired through the years transforming her into a prehistoric MacGyver. In the course of the series, she has also become a shaman, herbalist, horse whisperer, fire starter, inventor, linguist, good cook and beautiful, loving wife" (Bradner 2011).

6. "But she never elicits the response the reader felt for the alien child among the Clan" (Elphinstone 2011); "It's striking how tedious the Earth's Children books get as they get further away from The Clan of the Cave Bear" (Oler 2014).

7. "The novel never quite apprehends the sheer difference of the deep past. The most vivid image I carry away is that of Auel marveling over the amazing cave paintings of the Dordogne, deeply appreciative of their artistry and spirituality, then returning to her hotel to shower and change for dinner. Ayla's tour reflects modern angst too accurately; there is never quite the imaginative leap that transports us to somewhere far other" (Elphinstone 2011).

8. Oler (2014) observes one key message: "Ultimately, though, Ayla's ability to learn and do both women's and men's work is key to her own survival and safety; indeed, Auel makes it clear that it's key to the evolution of humankind ... we are just as resourceful and imaginative as Ayla is. It's a truly triumphant tale not just about one girl's coming of age, but about humanity's."

9. "Le Fay" is the English pronunciation of French *la fée*, a feminine fairy, or one with magical powers. So her usual name means Morgan the Fairy. She is generally depicted in Arthurian stories as a powerful enchantress, perhaps a goddess, a fay or a sorceress (witch), or at least a healer. Earlier appearances of her do depict her as Arthur's protector (as in this version), though later depictions show her as morally ambivalent and unpredictable, and even a vindictive, predatory adversary of some knights and Arthur's wife. Malory's famed thirteenth-century *Le Morte d'Arthur* portrays her as Arthur's greatest enemy and cause of his death. There are many hundreds (possibly thousands) of modern cultural appropriations and versions of Morgan and Arthur in fiction, film, television, video games, music, art, stage productions, and so on (Wikipedia page for "Morgan le Fay," accessed summer 2021, https://en.wikipedia.org/wiki/Morgan_le_Fay).

10. "About the Fellowship," The Fellowship of the Spiral Path, n.d., accessed June 2020, https://thespiralpath.org/#:~:text=In%201981%20the%20Center%20for,for%20both%20women%20and%20men.

11. Bradley wrote (on a discontinued website): "I think the neo-pagan movement offers a very viable alternative for people, especially for women, who have been turned off by the abuses of Judeo-Christian organized religions.... [They] reach out for the gentler reign of Goddess-oriented paganism to lead them back to a true perception of the spiritual life of the Earth ... let the Mother make it clear to them—that Spirit is One and that they are, in worshipping the Goddess, worshipping the Divine by whatever name" (Bradley 1986).

12. Her brother also subsequently came forward with similar stories, that both parents committed many abusive atrocities against other children (not their own). Greyland's memories of home life are very negative, as she first expressed in an email published on a blog: "It is a lot worse than that. The first time she molested me, I was three. The last time, I was twelve, and able to walk away. I put [father] Walter in jail for molesting one boy. I had tried to intervene when I was 13 by telling Mother and Lisa, and they just moved him into his own apartment. I had been living partially on couches since I was ten years old because of the out of control drugs, orgies, and constant flow of people in and out of our family 'home.' None of this should be news. Walter was a serial rapist with many, many, many victims (I named 22 to the cops) but Marion was far, far worse. She was cruel and violent, as well as completely out of her mind sexually. I am not her only victim, nor were her only victims girls. I wish I had better news." (Moen 2014).

13. Friends I've spoken to informally who circulated in these communities years ago said the abuse was fairly well known but was largely ignored or tolerated because of Bradley's status, a claim Greyland's book supports.

14. Moira Greyland, *The Last Closet: The Dark Side of Avalon* (Kouvola, Finland: Castalia House, 2017). Unfortunately, there is also controversy over this publication, since it was published by alt-right activist Vox Day, who describes himself as a "Christian nationalist" and expresses white supremacists and sexist views (Wikipedia entry on Vox Day, accessed July 27, 2018, at https://en.wikipedia.org/wiki/Vox_Day,).

15. Guest post on a "traditional marriage" support blog. Greyland's mother lived with a woman lover for many years, while knowing her husband was a pedophile and supporting him (Greyland 2015).

16. The idea of the labrys axe being associated with goddess culture was apparently inspired by Marija Gimbutas's article "Battle Axe or Cult Axe?" published in *Man* 53 (April 1953): 51–54. Mary Renault's novel *The King Must Die* ([1958] 1986) fictionalizes this interpretation, and many other goddess culture sources accept this reading, especially in terms of the Labrys axes found on Crete being conceived as associated with goddesses, although in mainland Greece they are known to be associated with gods (like Zeus).

Chapter 6

1. Andrea Alciato, 1546; Geoffrey Whitney, 1586; James Joyce, 1922; and Margaret Atwood, 2003, among others. References at the "Circe" Wikipedia page, accessed March 1, 2019.

2. Quoting Miller: "'I learned to braid my hair back, so it would not catch on every twig, and how to tie my skirts at the knee to keep the burrs off.' It's a small detail, but it's the difference between a person of independence and skill, and some male dream of danger, foreignness, and sex, lounging with parted lips while she watches the horizon for ships" (Quinn 2018).

3. Ronald Hutton traces some of this history in *The Witch: A History of Fear* (New Haven: Yale University Press, 2017).

4. Orisha (various spellings) are human forms of god-inspired spirits in traditional Yoruba religion, from one region of Nigeria.

5. Online readers' guide from Macmillan (Adeyemi's publisher): "The Maji are citizens of Orisha who are born with the ability to summon magical powers and are easily distinguishable by their bright white hair. Each of the ten clans of Orisha and their associated Maji can harness an element of the natural world, with their magical powers based on this element." "Who Are the Maji? A Guide to the Ten Clans of Orïsha," Pan Macmillan blog, February 27, 2020, accessed summer 2021, https://www.panmacmillan.com/blogs/fiction/maji-guide-children-of-blood-bone-tomi-adeyemi.

6. For instance, during the genocide in Rwanda in the 1990s, "extremist Hutu propaganda on radio and in magazines referred to the minority Tutsis as cockroaches and a mortal threat. Similar language . . . is being used today in Myanmar, where extremists have called the Rohingya or other Muslims dogs, maggots and rapists on social media and urged that they be shot" (Finn 2019).

7. Notably, Adeyemi references the Hunger Games series in comments in her WBUR interview (Lubbock 2018), noting the backlash against the film version's casting Black actors in some roles and how openly people expressed these racist reactions.

8. This manuscript was largely revised while Donald Trump was president, the Black Lives Matter movement was under siege by white supremacists and racists, and the world dealing with the COVID-19 pandemic, including fighting harmful attacks on basic scientific understanding (summer 2020).

9. Such small, intimate changes for good reflect paths neo-pagan groups also embrace, but with the notable reversal of this goddess admitting that being human and working hard as such is all she needs, while neo-pagans suggest their comforts and workable lives depend to some extent on reigniting the goddess in themselves and the world.

Conclusion

1. Claude Lévi-Strauss (1955, 99) explains that myths and his method of analyzing them is "bringing some kind of order to what was previously chaos" and that "mythical thought always works from the awareness of oppositions toward their progressive mediation," i.e. cosmos/ order. While some people criticize this structuralist theory for being too universal and misleading (about essential human nature), even such critics often recognize that this method of interpreting myths is useful to some extent: "Attention to a myth's structure will sometimes bring palpable rewards" and "binary analysis . . . [that] myths mediate contradictions . . . is one obvious mode of thought" (Kirk 1970, 78, 83, 78).

2. Numerous myth scholars demonstrate this comforting, cosmos-affirming feature of myths, including dealing with "matters of confusion and concern" and that myth might work to "carry its own implication of a solution" (Kirk 1970, 284). If we think of Genesis, for instance (primary origin myth of Judeo-Christian culture), we note that as God creates order from chaos, he affirms at each step of the way that He *sees* that "it is good." Affirming the rightness of our cosmos offers comfort that we can live in the world as it is, compensating for potential problems that myths often reflect (like living as a disenfranchised other or second sex). Schrempp (2012, 223) shows that Ruth Benedict, among others, "hypothesized that myth, by offering fantasy, helps make up for onerous and difficult realities of life: one of the functions of myth is precisely to 'compensate' for the demands of living in society . . . [which] gives myth its power and appeal." Gregory Nagy (2002, 246) says in ancient Greek philosophy "myth" (as opposed to logic) is a powerful force for cosmos (order): "we can find a sense of nostalgia for a mythologized earlier phase of *muthos as the conveyor of a stabilized universe*" (emphasis mine); he notes a sense of myth as something that can be "saved" and "cherished" for its ability to make sense.

3. Ortner (1974) recognizes this particular binary opposition when she traces the "universal devaluation of women" related to such dualistic, simplistic oppositions as equating women to nature (versus men to culture), and we have seen that numerous goddess proponents describe their faith in such terms.

4. Wikipedia's "Thealogy" page defines the term: "Thealogy views divine matters with feminine perspectives including but not only feminism. Valerie Saiving, Isaac Bonewits (1976)

and Naomi Goldenberg (1979) introduced the concept as a neologism (new word) in feminist terms. Its use then widened to mean all feminine ideas of the sacred, which Charlotte Caron usefully explained in 1993: 'reflection on the divine in feminine or feminist terms.' By 1996, when Melissa Raphael published Thealogy and Embodiment, the term was well established." In *Introducing Thealogy*, Melissa Raphael (2000, 10) explains: "The word 'thealogy' might indicate that the Goddess is the object of a reasoned discourse; a discipline comparable to theology as reasoned discourse on God. However, that is usually far from the case. Thealogy is not founded upon a body of authoritative and sacred texts ... Most do not so much theorize the Goddess as experience her more immediately in themselves and in the natural environment." She differentiates goddess feminists as clearly distinct from "patriarchal scholarship" (11). The "practical and experiential" goddess "path" differs from the "conceptual" (11), though she discusses it academically in her book (affirming terms/concepts in table 3).

5. Numerous philosophers and feminist scholars have explained such concepts, including Jean-Paul Sartre, "Existentialism Is a Humanism," Marxists.org, 1946, accessed summer 2021, http://www.marxists.org/reference/archive/sartre/works/exist/sartre.htm; and Simone de Beauvoir, as part of her main argument in *The Second Sex* (1949). De Beauvoir sees "otherness is a fundamental category of human thought" and quotes Lévi-Strauss to support her view: "'Passage from the state of Nature to the state of Culture is marked by man's ability to view biological relations as a series of contrasts; duality, alternation, opposition, and symmetry, whether under definite or vague forms, constitute not so much phenomena to be explained as fundamental and immediately given data of social reality.'" She also writes, "Now, what peculiarly signalises the situation of woman is that she—a free and autonomous being like all human creatures—nevertheless finds herself living in a world where men compel her to assume the status of the Other." Throughout *The Second Sex*, de Beauvoir traces this otherness and shows it to be inauthentic and deeply problematic to all humanity.

6. Skeptic Robert Sheaffer's website *The Debunker's Domain* claims women embracing goddess culture "spawned a large number of uncritical, emotionally charged articles and books," which he sees as "pious" or "Noble Lies" that feminists feed our students—apparently ignoring the many feminists since at least the seventies who deny goddess claims. He also claims bad scholarship as an explanation for why women want separate women's studies departments—to evade critical scrutiny. He criticizes that the myth depicts men as cruel exploiters and women as innocent victims, which he feels causes great harm, evoking suspicion, hostility, and envy between the sexes, as well as shaping public policy. He describes this goddess myth as a variant of the "lost Garden of Eden" myth, where we are ejected from the garden for the sins of man rather than those of woman. Sheaffer is extreme in his criticism, and while well published, is not in academia. Though perhaps easy to dismiss as strident, he reveals a polarizing effect of goddess spirituality, and some of his points are demonstrable. For instance, evidence of how the Garden of Eden myth is evoked and reversed in goddess spirituality exists. Marci McDonald reports on a ritual created by Sister Elaine Weisgerber, a retired Ursuline nun in Canada, called a "false-naming" ritual that involves, "handing out apples and inviting the crowd to bite deeply 'to defy the Garden of Eden story. We don't buy into this myth that Eve caused the downfall of humanity'" (McDonald 1996, 3). A believer may embrace this ritual as empowering and healing, while a skeptic like Sheaffer will criticize it as evidence of divisiveness. Women need not make it easy for critics to object to us as scholars or artists, especially when so many women scholars do excellent work in this and many fields.

7. Eller (2000, 8) argues, "the gendered stereotypes upon which matriarchal myth rests persistently work to flatten out differences among women; to exaggerate differences between women and men; and to hand women an identity that is symbolic, timeless, and archetypal,

instead of giving them the freedom to craft identities that suit their individual temperaments, skills, preferences, and moral and political commitments."

8. David Bidney ([1955] 1974), for instance, writes that "while in times of crisis the 'noble fiction' may have its immediate, pragmatic utility in promoting social faith and solidarity" (23). "Noble fiction" means "myth."

9. Gimbutas was trained in the European, male-oriented university system (PhD at Tübingen University in 1942). The Belili site makes much of her following "the trail set in the early 19th century by female archaeologists like Jane Ellen Harrisson and historian Matilda Joslyn Gage—women who dared to challenge the findings and criteria favored by the 'establishment' of their times" (Starhawk and Read 2003). Harrison and Gage were not challenging the findings of their time, but upholding ideas about a matriarchal prehistory and goddess worship initiated and long supported by men (Goodison and Morris 1998).

10. Many scholars have also traced the roots of numerous neo-pagan practices to men progenitors, such as Englishman Gerald Gardner, himself a successor to men such as Robert Graves, Aleister Crowley, Charles Godrey Leland, who were also influenced by men-dominated groups such as the Freemasons and the Rosicrucians (at least somewhat; Davis 1998). Alex Sanders (English) and Victor Anderson (American) are credited with influencing neo-paganism as well. All these men established many common, contemporary neo-pagan practices, frameworks, and specific details (such as songs, rituals, poems, texts, and dances) before the two main women forces in the United States, Starhawk and Zsuzanna Budapest, also helped couple it with radical feminism. In analyzing this history, Philip G. Davis (1998, 341) demonstrates that in spite of some denials of the influence of men, "Gardnerian influence is still evident in the phrases 'So mote it be' and 'Blessed be,' the casting of the circle and the password 'perfect love and perfect trust,' the Murrayite esbats and sabbats, and the use of Leland's Aradia story. All of these in Gardner's books and rituals.... The fact remains that Gardnerian Wicca was the first modern Western Goddess religion." Davis lists many other earlier men from whom this tradition stems as well, including Robert Briffault, the Jungian Robert Eisler, concurring with many scholars that "Goddess spirituality is neither the modern expression of an actual pre-Christian, pre-Jewish, pre-Greek, utopian, female-centered civilization, nor a creative contemporary innovation in religion, it is neither primordial nor pristine.... There were goddesses aplenty in ancient times, but 'the Goddess' as known to twentieth-century feminist neopaganism is a different phenomenon with its own, recent pedigree" (342–43).

11. Raphael (2000) explains the more experiential nature of goddess spirituality.

12. T-shirts, bumper stickers, and other items proclaim things like "Back off, I'm a Goddess!" or "My Goddess Gave Birth to Your God." Soaps, candles, jewelry, and more are available in designs that recall the Venus of Willendorf and similar Paleolithic "goddesses." "Goddess symbols" in numerous guises and style are for sale (McDonald 1996).

13. Calling the "Goddess Market" domestic refers to the fact that most sales of goddess-themed goods and services remain largely grassroots, local, festival, or internet-based, without huge profits or visibility.

14. Eller (2000, 6) sees women as "quite narrowly" defined in goddess culture, "closely allied with the body, nature, and sex."

15. The myth reflects and serves our current culture: "Women are defined quite narrowly as those who give birth and nurture, who identify themselves in terms of their relationship, and who are closely allied with the body, nature, and sex—usually for unavoidable reasons of their biological makeup. This image of women is drastically revalued in feminist matriarchal myth, such that it is not a mark of shame or subordination, but of pride and power. But this image is nevertheless quite conventional and, at least up until now, it has done an excellent job of serving patriarchal interests" (Eller 2000, 7).

16. Mythic parallels between women and the earth are common (Eller 2000, 16–17, see also chapter 2).

17. Eller explains: "If we are not going to discover history at the end of the day, but simply create myth, then the only grounds upon which feminist political origins thinking can be justified is that it serves feminist political purposes" (2000, 185).

18. The myth's gendered assumptions are troubling: "Appraising the narrative for its functional worth, Eller applies Malinowski's thesis that 'mythic charters are said to operate especially in areas of sociological strain, such as significant differences in status or power'" (Maksel 2001, 509, qtg. Eller 2000, 176). A narrative celebrating childbirth, nurturance, and compassion uses "language virtually identical to that of contemporary right-wing antifeminists: 'the valorization of motherhood—as an ideal type separate from individual women's experiences of it—is a tactic that has served patriarchal cultures very well'" (Maksel 2001, 509, qtg. Eller 2000, 65).

19. Eller helps Maksel (2001, 509) realize: "The matriarchal myth seeks to explain male dominance, but its rhetoric binds women to a past and future based solely on anatomy, certainly a permanent condition."

20. Schrempp (2012, 70) shows Lévi-Strauss's perceiving myth operating "to justify the shortcomings of reality, since the extreme positions are only *imagined* in order to show that they are *untenable*" (qtg. Lévi-Strauss). Schrempp (2012, 70) agrees that "mythic thought is thus stacked in favor of the status quo." Our myths reflect our reality and confirm it as cosmos, even when it is confusing and lacking (non-ideal).

21. As noted, numerous myth scholars demonstrate this comforting, cosmos-affirming feature of myths, including dealing with "matters of confusion and concern" and that myth might work to "carry its own implication of a solution" (Kirk 1970, 284). If we think of Genesis, for instance, we note that as God creates order from chaos, he affirms at each step of the way that He sees that "it is good."

22. Women's lack of power in our world extends to women in film and television, where women hold many fewer jobs, especially as writers, producers or directors, and most characters, especially significant or admirable ones, are men, according to the *Center for the Study of Women in Television and Film* (statistics listed), Martha Lauzen, "Research," 2018, Center for the Study of Women and Film, accessed summer 2020, https://womenintvfilm.sdsu.edu /research/.

23. Trump famously said on tape: "When you're a star, they let you do it. You can do anything. . . . Grab 'em by the pussy. You can do anything" (Makela 2016).

24. Like the one Susan Faludi wrote about in 1991.

25. Emily Toth (1997), a.k.a. Ms. Mentor, advises women academics in tenure-track jobs to stop playing the role of nurturers in academia, say no to committee work, and focus more on writing and publishing, as do their male counterparts, who earn jobs and tenure at research institutions at a higher rate.

References

Adeyemi, Tomi. 2018. *Children of Blood and Bone*. New York: Macmillan.

Adler, Margot. 1986. *Drawing Down the Moon: Witches, Druids, Goddess-Worshippers, and Other Pagans in America Today*. Revised and expanded edition. New York: Penguin/Arkana.

Aldama, Frederick Luis. 2000. "Leslie Marmon Silko: *Gardens in the Dunes*." *World Literature Today* 74, no. 2 (Spring): 457–58.

Allen, Charlotte. "The Scholars and the Goddess." *The Atlantic*, January 2001, 1–12. Accessed October 2, 2008. http://www.theatlantic.com/issues/2001/01/allen.htm.

Alvarez, Ana Cecilia. 2015. "Why It's Time We Drop Gender from Our Goddess Worship." *Broadly*, December 11, 2015. Accessed September 2018. https://broadly.vice.com/en_us/article/d7ab5q/why-its-time-we-drop-gender-from-our-goddess-worship.

Angel. 1999–2004. Created by Joss Whedon. Transcriptions by author, sometimes amended from fan sites.

Anne, Martha, and Dorothy Myers Imel. 1995. *Goddesses in World Mythology: A Biographical Dictionary*. London: Oxford University Press.

Asbjørnsen, Christen Peter, and Jørgen Moe. 1859. *Popular Tales from the Norse*. Translated by George Webbe Dasent. New York: D. Appleton. https://www.pitt.edu/~dash/norway034.html.

Atwood, Margaret. 1985. *The Handmaid's Tale*. Toronto: McClelland & Stewart.

Atwood, Margaret. 2005. *The Penelopiad*. India: Penguin Random House.

Atwood, Margaret. 2012. *In Other Worlds: SF and the Human Imagination*. New York: Anchor.

Auel, Jean. 1980. *The Clan of the Cave Bear*. New York: Bantam.

Auel, Jean. 2002. *Shelters of Stone*. New York: Crown.

Auel, Jean. 2011. *The Land of Painted Caves*. New York: Crown.

Bamberger, Joan. 1974. "The Myth of Matriarchy: Why Men Rule in Primitive Society." In *Woman, Culture, and Society*, edited by M. Z. Rosaldo and L. Lamphere, 263–80, Stanford: Stanford University Press.

Baring, Anne, and Jules Cashford. 1993. *The Myth of the Goddess: Evolution of an Image*. London: Arkana.

Bascom, William. 1965. "The Forms of Folklore: Prose Narratives." *Journal of American Folklore* 78: 3–20.

Bauman, Richard. 1991. "Genre." In *Folklore, Cultural Performance, and Popular Entertainments: A Communications-Centered Handbook*. Oxford: Oxford University Press.

Bell, Robert E. 1991. *Women of Classical Mythology: A Biographical Dictionary*. New York: Oxford University Press.

Bidney, David. (1955) 1974. "Myth, Symbolism, and Truth." In *Myth: A Symposium*, edited by Thomas A. Sebeok, 3–23. Bloomington: Indiana University Press.

Boas, Franz. 1898. "Introduction to James Teit." In *Traditions of the Thompson River Indians of British Columbia: Memoirs of the American Folklore Society*, vol. 6.

Bradley, Marion. 1983. *The Mists of Avalon*. New York: Alfred A. Knopf.

Bradley, Marion. n.d. "Thoughts on Avalon." *Marion Zimmer Bradley Literary Works Trust*. Accessed June 7, 2010. http://en.academic.ru/dic.nsf/enwiki/33928.

Bradner, Liesl. 2011. Review: "'The Land of Painted Caves' by Jean M. Auel." *Los Angeles Times*, March 27, 2011. Accessed August 8, 2018. http://www.latimes.com/entertainment/la-ca-jean -auel-20110327-story.html.

Britt, Ryan. 2017. "Lev Grossman Is Surprised by What Happens on 'The Magicians.'" *Inverse*, January 25, 2017. Accessed March 21, 2019. https://www.inverse.com/article/26772-lev -grossman-magicians-season-two-books-syfy.

Brown, Dan. 2003. *The Da Vinci Code: A Novel*. New York: Anchor Books.

Browne, Ray B. 2006. "Popular Culture: Notes toward a Definition." In *Popular Culture Theory and Methodology*, edited by Harold E. Hinds Jr., Marilyn F. Motz, and Angela M. S. Nelson, 15–29. Madison: University of Wisconsin Press.

Budapest, Zsuzsanna. 1989. *The Holy Book of Women's Mysteries (Complete in One Volume): Feminist, Witchcraft, Goddess Rituals, Spellcasting, and Other Womanly Arts*. Oakland: Wingbow Press.

Buffy the Vampire Slayer. 1997–2003. Created by Joss Whedon. Transcriptions by author, sometimes amended from fan sites.

Caputi, Jane. 2004. *Goddesses and Monsters: Women, Myth, Power, and Popular Culture*. Madison: University of Wisconsin Press.

Cartwright, Mark. 2013. "Kali." In *Ancient History Encyclopedia*, June 21, 2013. Accessed March 2019. https://www.ancient.eu/Kali/.

CBC Radio. 2019. "A Guide to Hopepunk: What to Read, Watch and Listen To When All Seems Lost." *Tapestry*, March 8, 2019. Accessed January 10, 2020. https://www.cbc.ca/radio/tapestry /when-hope-is-punk-and-grudges-are-forgiveness-1.5046927/a-guide-to-hopepunk-what -to-read-watch-and-listen-to-when-all-seems-lost-1.5046937.

Charles, Ron. 2018. "The Original Nasty Woman Is a Goddess for Our Times." Review of *Circe*. *Washington Post*, April 9, 2018. Accessed March 15, 2019. https://www.washingtonpost.com /entertainment/books/the-original-nasty-woman-is-a-goddess-for-our-times/2018/04/09 /742c54d0-3b88-11e8-974f-aacd97698cef_story.html.

Chicago, Judy. 1974–79. *The Dinner Party*. Elizabeth A. Sackler Center for Feminist Art at Brooklyn Museum. Accessed July 2018. https://www.brooklynmuseum.org/eascfa/dinner_party /home. See also https://www.brooklynmuseum.org/eascfa/dinner_party/place_settings.

Christ, Carol P. 1997. *Rebirth of the Goddess: Finding Meaning in Feminist Spirituality*. Reading, MA: Addison-Wesley.

Christ, Carol P. 2000. "Reading Marija Gimbutas." *National Women's Studies Association Journal* 12, no. 1 (Spring): 169.

Christ, Carol P. 2003. "Musings on the Goddess and Her Cultured Despisers—Provoked by Naomi Goldenberg." *Belili Productions*. Accessed November 22, 2013. http://www.belili.org /marija/carol_christ.html.

Christ, Carol P., and Judith Plaskow, eds. 1979. *Womanspirit Rising: A Feminist Reader in Religion*. San Francisco: Harper & Row.

Cook, Jill. 2017. "The Female Gaze." Video of the British Museum exhibit of *Ice Age Art*. Accessed June 2018. http://www.britishmuseum.org/whats_on/exhibitions/ice_age_art.aspx.

Cook, Tommy. 2017. "Cate Blanchett on Playing Marvel's First Female Villain in 'Thor: Ragnarok.'" *Collider*, October 5, 2017. Accessed July 20, 2018. http://collider.com/cate-blanchett -thor-ragnarok-interview/.

Croft, Janet Brennan. 2015. "Giving Evil a Name: Buffy's Glory, Angel's Jasmine, Blood Magic, and Name Magic." *Slayage: The Journal of the Whedon Studies Association* 12, no. 2. Accessed June 2019. https://www.whedonstudies.tv/uploads/2/6/2/8/26288593/croft_slayage_12.2-13.1.pdf.

Croot, Cynthia. 2016. "Venus Embodied Performing the role of Sartjie Baartman in Suzan-Lori Parks' Venus." *Theatre Forum* 49: 69–76.

Crossley-Holland, Kevin. 1980. *The Norse Myths*. New York: Pantheon.

Curry, Andrew. 2012. "The Cave Art Debate." *Smithsonian Magazine*. March 2012. Accessed March 13, 2018. https://www.smithsonianmag.com/history/the-cave-art-debate-100617099/.

Daley, Mary. 1973. *Beyond God the Father: Toward a Philosophy of Women's Liberation*. Boston: Beacon Press.

Davis, Philip. G. 1998. *Goddess Unmasked: The Rise of Neopagan Feminist Spirituality*. Dallas: Spence.

de Beauvoir, Simone. 1949. "Introduction: Woman as Other." In *The Second Sex*. Accessed July 18, 2013. http://www.marxists.org/reference/subject/ethics/de-beauvoir/2nd-sex/introduction.htm.

Dekker, Nusi. 1999. "Depictions of Goddesses in Xena: Warrior Princess." *Whoosh!*, IZXS project 231, no. 31. Accessed August 2, 2018. http://www.whoosh.org/issue31/dekker3.html.

Demarest, Donald, and Coley Taylor, eds. 2004. *The Dark Virgin: The Book of Our Lady of Guadalupe*. In *The Heath Anthology of American Literature: Concise Edition*, edited by Paul Lauter, 72–80. New York: Houghton Mifflin.

Dickson, Katie. 2007. Review: "Earth's Children (Series) by Jean M. Auel." *Smart Bitches, Trashy Books*, October 4, 2007. Accessed August 7, 2018. http://smartbitchestrashybooks.com/reviews/earths_children_series_by_jean_m_auel/.

Di Placido, Dani. 2018. "Why Is There Still Controversy Surrounding 'Star Wars: The Last Jedi?'" *Forbes*, June 28, 2018. Accessed July 30, 2018. https://www.forbes.com/sites/danidiplacido/2018/06/28/why-is-there-still-controversy-surrounding-star-wars-the-last-jedi/.

Doty, William G. 1986. *Mythography: The Study of Myths and Rituals*. Tuscaloosa: University of Alabama Press.

Dowson, Thomas. n.d. "Why Lascaux 4 Is Not Just a Bigger & Better Lascaux 2." *Archaeology Travel*. Accessed June 20, 2018. https://archaeology-travel.com/reviews/is-lascaux-4-better-than-lascaux-2/.

Dundes, Alan. 1984. *Sacred Narrative: Readings in the Theory of Myth*. Berkeley: University of California Press.

Eisler, Riane. 1987. *The Chalice and the Blade: Our History, Our Future*. San Francisco: Harper & Row.

Elkins, Caroline. 2007. "A Life Exposed." *New York Times*, January 14, 2007. Accessed June 2018. https://www.nytimes.com/2007/01/14/books/review/Elkins.t.html.

Eller, Cynthia. 2000. *The Myth of Matriarchal Prehistory: Why an Invented Past Won't Give Women a Future*. Boston: Beacon Press.

Eller, Cynthia. 2003. "A Response from Cynthia Eller." *Belili Productions*. Accessed March 26, 2008. http://www.belili.org/marija/c_eller_response.html.

Eller, Cynthia. 2005. "The Feminist Appropriation of Matriarchal Myth in the 19th and 20th Centuries." *History Compass* 3, no. 179 (January 1, 2005): 1–10.

Eller, Cynthia. 2011. *Gentlemen and Amazons: The Myth of Matriarchal Prehistory, 1861–1900*. Los Angeles: University of California Press.

Elphinstone, Margaret. 2011. Review: "The Land of Painted Caves, by Jean Auel." *Globe and Mail*, May 1, 2011. Accessed August 8, 2018. https://www.theglobeandmail.com/arts/books-and-media/the-land-of-painted-caves-by-jean-auel/article576541/.

Estés, Clarissa Pinkola. 1992. *Women Who Run with the Wolves: Myths and Stories of the Wild Woman Archetype*. New York: Ballantine.

Fineout, Gary. 2018. "Yoga Shooter Appeared to Have Made Misogynistic Videos." *US News*, November 3, 2018. Accessed November 6, 2018. https://www.usnews.com/news/us/articles /2018-11-03/police-search-for-motive-in-florida-yoga-studio-slayings.

Finn, Tom. 2019. "'It Shames Us All': Rwandan Genocide Survivor Says Myanmar Persecution a Repeat of History." *Reuters*, July 11, 2019. Accessed May 24, 2020. https://www.reuters.com /article/us-rwanda-genocide-myanmar/it-shames-us-all-rwandan-genocide-survivor-says -myanmar-persecution-a-repeat-of-history-idUSKCN1U61U9.

Fleenor, S. E. 2019. "Book vs. TV: The Magicians," *SyfyWire*, January 8, 2019. Accessed March 21, 2019. https://www.syfy.com/syfywire/book-vs-tv-the-magicians.

Flood, Alison. 2014. "SFF Community Reeling after Marion Zimmer Bradley's Daughter Accuses Her of Abuse." *The Guardian*, June 27, 2014. Accessed July 27, 2018. https://www.the guardian.com/books/2014/jun/27/sff-community-marion-zimmer-bradley-daughter -accuses-abuse.

Fry, Carrol L. 1993. "The Goddess Ascending: Feminist Neo-Pagan Witchcraft in Marian Zim- mer Bradley's Novels." *Journal of Popular Culture* 27, no. 1 (Summer): 67–80.

Gibbons, Ann. 2015. "How Europeans Evolved White Skin." *Science Magazine*, April 2, 2015. Accessed July 27, 2018. http://www.sciencemag.org/news/2015/04/how-europeans-evolved -white-skin.

Gibson, Clare. 1998. *Goddess Symbols: Universal Signs of the Divine Female*. New York: Barnes & Noble.

Gimbutas, Marija. 1982. *The Goddesses and Gods of Old Europe 6500–3500 BC: Myths and Cult Images*. New and updated edition. Berkeley: University of California Press.

Gimbutas, Marija. 1989. *The Language of the Goddess*. San Francisco: Harper & Row.

Gimbutas, Marija. 2001. *The Living Goddesses*. Los Angeles: University of California Press.

Goodison, Lucy and Christine Morris, eds. 1998. *Ancient Goddesses: The Myths and the Evi- dence*. Madison: University of Wisconsin Press.

Grey, Mary. 2001. *Introducing Feminist Images of God*. Sheffield, England: Sheffield Academic Press.

Greyland, Moira. 2015. "The Story of Moira Greyland (Guest Post)." *Ask the "Bigot"* (blog), July 23, 2015. Accessed July 27, 2018. https://askthebigot.com/2015/07/23/the-story-of-moira -greyland-guest-post/.

Greyland, Moira. 2017. *The Last Closet: The Dark Side of Avalon*. Excerpts at Goodreads. Accessed summer 2019. https://www.goodreads.com/notes/37494480-the-last-closet /65456598-gene.

Grimm, Jacob. 1882. *Teutonic Mythology: Translated from the Fourth Edition with Notes and Appendix*, Vol. I. Trans by James Steven Stallybrass. London: George Bell and Sons. Via "Hel (being)," *Wikipedia*, accessed July 20, 2018. https://en.wikipedia.org/wiki/Hel_(being).

Grossman, Lev. 2009. *The Magicians*. New York: Viking Penguin.

Hand, Elizabeth. 2011. Review: "'The Land of Painted Caves' by Jean M. Auel." *Washington Post*, May 2, 2011. accessed August 7, 2018. https://www.washingtonpost.com/entertainment /books/book-world-elizabeth-hand-reviews-the-land-of-painted-caves-by-jean-m-auel /2011/03/07/AF5Ue7cF_story.html.

Hansen, William. 2002. "Meanings and Boundaries: Reflections on Thompson's 'Myth and Folk- tales.'" *Myth: A New Symposium*, edited by Gregory Schrempp and William Hansen, 19–28. Bloomington: Indiana University Press.

Hansen, William. 2004. *Classical Mythology: A Guide to the Mythical World of the Greeks and Romans*. Oxford: Oxford University Press.

Harkin, Michael. 2003. "Staged Encounters: Postmodern Tourism and Aboriginal People." *Eth- nohistory* 50, no. 3: 575–85.

Harris, Hunter. 2017. "I Didn't Give a Sh*t about Marvel Movies till I Saw Tessa Thompson in *Thor: Ragnarok.*" *Vulture*, November 9, 2017. Accessed July 23, 2018. http://www.vulture.com /2017/11/in-praise-of-tessa-thompson-in-thor-ragnarok.html.

Hellboy II: The Golden Army. 2008. Written and directed by Guillermo del Toro. Transcription by author.

Hoffman, Curtiss. 2002. *The Seven Story Tower: A Mythic Journey through Space and Time.* New York: Basic Books.

Holmes, Rachel. 2008. *The Hottentot Venus.* London: Bloomsbury.

Homer. 1632–33. *The Odyssey.* Translated by Theodoor van Thulden. Accessed March 2019. https://www.poetryintranslation.com/PITBR/Greek/Odhome.php.

Homer. 1897. *The Odyssey.* Translated by Samuel Butler. Accessed March 2019. https://www .gutenberg.org/files/1727/1727-h/1727-h.htm.

Hoppenstand, Gary. 1999. "Ray and Pat Browne: Scholars of Everyday Culture." In *Pioneers in Popular Culture Studies,* edited by Michael T. Marsden, 33–66. Madison: University of Wisconsin Press.

Jemisin, N. K. 2010. *The Hundred Thousand Kingdoms: Book One of the Inheritance Trilogy.* New York: Hatchette.

Jemisin, N. K. 2015. *The Fifth Season.* New York: Hatchette.

Jemisin, N. K. 2017. *The Stone Sky.* New York: Hatchette.

Jernigan, Jessica. 2017. "The Book That Made Me a Feminist Was Written by an Abuser." *Electric Literature,* December 14, 2017. Accessed July 27, 2018. https://electricliterature.com/the -book-that-made-me-a-feminist-was-written-by-an-abuser-4c6891f548cf.

Jesch, Judith. 1991. *Women in the Viking Age.* Woodbridge, UK: Boydell.

Jorgensen, Jeana. "#FolkloreThursday: Exploring Tale Type 510B." *Foxy Folklorist* (blog), September 14, 2017. https://www.patheos.com/blogs/foxyfolklorist/folklorethursday-exploring -tale-type-510b/.

Keats, John. 1818. "Endymion." *Poems by John Keats.* Accessed June 10, 2020. http://keats-poems .com/poems/endymion/.

Kemp, Ella. 2017. "In Praise of Tessa Thompson's Valkyrie, Marvel's Long-Awaited Saviour." *Little White Lies,* October 24, 2017. Accessed July 23, 2018. http://lwlies.com/articles/tessa -thompson-valkyrie-marvel-female-characters/.

Kirk, G. S. 1970. *Myth: Its Meaning and Functions in Ancient and Other Cultures.* Berkeley: University of California Press.

Kit, Borys. 2015. "Cate Blanchett Joining 'Thor 3.'" *Hollywood Reporter,* December 10, 2015. Accessed July 20, 2018. https://www.hollywoodreporter.com/heat-vision/cate-blanchett -joining-thor-3-847912.

Knox, Bernard M. W. 1997. "Ancient Greece and the Formations of the Western Mind." In *The Norton Anthology of World Masterpieces,* edited by Maynard Mack, 87–95. New York: W. W. Norton.

Lampen, Claire. "A Brief Tour of Joss Whedon's Many Controversies." *The Cut,* April 6, 2021. Accessed summer 2021. https://www.thecut.com/2021/04/joss-whedons-controversies-and -alleged-bad-behavior-a-guide.html.

Lapatin, Kenneth. 2003. *Mysteries of the Snake Goddess: Art, Desire, and the Forging of History.* Cambridge, MA: Da Capo Press.

Lefkowitz, Mary R. 1992. "The Twilight of the Goddess." *New Republic* 207, no. 6: 29–33.

Lefkowitz, Mary R. 1993. "The New Cults of the Goddess." *American Scholar,* no. 2 (Spring): 261–69.

Lefkowitz, Mary R. 2007. *Women in Greek Myth.* 2nd ed. Baltimore: Johns Hopkins University Press.

Lepore, Jill. 2015. *The Secret History of Wonder Woman*. New York: Vintage Books.

Lévi-Strauss, Claude. (1955) 1974. "The Structural Study of Myth." *Myth: A Symposium*, edited by Thomas A. Sebeok, 81–106. Bloomington: Indiana University Press.

Lévi-Strauss, Claude. 1966. *The Savage Mind*. Chicago: University of Chicago Press.

Lévi-Strauss, Claude. 1971. *The Naked Man: An Introduction to a Science of Meaning*. Vol. 4. New York: Harper and Row.

Lubbock, Robin. "YA Author Tomi Adeyemi Wants to Show Black People 'They Can Be the Heroes.'" *Here and Now*, WBUR, July 31, 2018. https://www.wbur.org/hereandnow/2018/07/31/children-of-blood-and-bone-tomi-adeyemi.

Lyons, Richard D. 1994. "Dr. Marija Gimbutas Dies at 73; Archaeologist with Feminist View." *New York Times*, February 4, 1994. Accessed July 19, 2013. http://www.nytimes.com/1994/02/04/obituaries/dr-marija-gimbutas-dies-at-73-archaeologist-with-feminist-view.html.

The Magicians. 2015–2020. Produced by Syfy network. Transcriptions by author, amended from fan sites.

Magliocco, Sabina. 2004. *Witching Culture: Folklore and Neo-Paganism in America*, Philadelphia: University of Pennsylvania Press.

Magoulick, Mary. 2006. "Frustrating Female Heroism: Mixed Messages in *Xena*, *Nikita*, and *Buffy*." *Journal of Popular Culture* 39, no. 5 (Fall): 729–55.

Magoulick, Mary. 2007. "Landscapes of Miracles and Matriarchy in Silko's *Garden's in the Dunes*." *Reading Leslie Marmon Silko: Critical Perspectives through* Gardens in the Dunes, edited by Laura Coltelli, 21–36. Pisa, Italy: University of Pisa Press.

Makela, Mark. 2016. "Transcript: Donald Trump's Taped Comments about Women." *New York Times*, October 8, 2016. Accessed November 5, 2018. https://www.nytimes.com/2016/10/08/us/donald-trump-tape-transcript.html.

Maksel, Rebecca. 2001. "Review of *The Myth of Matriarchal Prehistory: Why an Invented Past Won't Give Women a Future*." *Journal of American Folklore* 114, no. 454 (Fall): 508–9.

Malinowski, Bronislaw. (1948) 1992. *Magic, Science and Religion and Other Essays*. Reprint, Prospect Heights, IL: Waveland Press.

Malone, Caroline. 1998. "God or Goddess: The Temple Art of Ancient Malta." *Ancient Goddesses: The Myths and the Evidence*, Edited by Lucy Goodison and Christine Morris, 148–63. Madison: University of Wisconsin Press.

Marler, Joan. 2003. "The Myth of University Patriarchy: A Critical Response to Cynthia Eller's *Myth of Matriarchal Prehistory*." *Belili Productions*, Accessed March 26, 2008. http://www.belili.org/marija/eller_response.html.

May, Herbert G., and Bruce M. Metzger, eds. 1977. *The New Oxford Annotated Bible with the Apocrypha, Revised Standard Version*. New York: Oxford University Press.

McCoy, Daniel. n.d. "Hel (Goddess)." *Norse Mythology for Smart People*. Accessed July 20, 2018. https://norse-mythology.org/gods-and-creatures/giants/hel/.

McDonald, Marci. 1996. "Is God a Woman?" *Maclean's* 109, no. 15: 46–52.

McDowell, John, Walter Strauss, Gregory Schrempp, Camille Bacon-Smith, Wendy Doniger, Lee Haring, Stephanie Kane, Donald Williams, Bruce Lincoln, and Donald Cosentino. 1998. "Perspectives: What Is Myth?" *Folklore Forum* 29, no. 2: 75–89.

Mendelson, Scott. 2017. "Review: Tessa Thompson and Cate Blanchett Steal 'Thor: Ragnarok.'" *Forbes*, October 19, 2017. Accessed July 20, 2017. https://www.forbes.com/sites/scottmendelson/2017/10/19/thor-ragnarok-review-tessa-thompson-rocks-cate-blanchett-slays-in-witty-mcu-sequel/.

Merchant, Carolyn. 2003. *Reinventing Eden: The Fate of Nature in Western Culture*. New York: Routledge.

Meskell, Lynn. 1995. "Goddesses, Gimbutas and 'New Age' Archaeology." *Antiquity* 69, no. 262 (March): 74–85.

Meskell, Lynn. 1998. "Twin Peaks: The Archaeologies of Çatalhöyük." In *Ancient Goddesses: The Myths and the Evidence*, edited by Lucy Goodison and Christine Morris, 42–62. Madison: University of Wisconsin Press.

Meskell, Lynn. 2017. "On Archaeology and Prehistoric Materialities at Çatalhöyük." Transcribed by author. YouTube, August 30, 2017. Accessed April 25, 2018. https://www.youtube.com /watch?v=Kt7j7OoBAG0.

Messud, Claire. 2018. Review: "Turning Circe into a Good Witch." *New York Times*, May 28, 2018. Accessed June 15, 2018. https://www.nytimes.com/2018/05/28/books/review/circe -madeline-miller.html.

Michelle, Heron. 2017. "Shopkeeper Sagas: From the Ashes a Fire Shall be Woken" *Witch Fire* (blog), March 29, 2017. Accessed July 26, 2018. http://www.patheos.com/blogs/witchonfire /2017/03/shopkeeper-sagas-ashes-fire-shall-be-woken/.

Miller, Madeline. 2018. *Circe: A Novel*. New York: Little, Brown.

Moen, Deirdre Saoirse. 2014. "Marion Zimmer Bradley: It's Worse than I Knew." *"Sounds Like Weird"* (blog), June 10, 2014. Accessed June 10, 2018. https://deirdre.net/marion-zimmer -bradley-its-worse-than-i-knew/.

Murphey, Kathleen. 2018. "Science Fiction/Fantasy Takes on Slavery: N.K. Jemisin and Tomi Adeyemi." *Pennsylvania Literary Journal* 10, no. 3 (Fall): 106–15.

Murray, Katherine. 2016. "Everything That's Wrong (and a Few Things That Are Right) with 'The Magicians.'" *Bitch Flicks*, April 18, 2016. Accessed July 24, 2018. http://www.btchflcks.com /2016/04/everything-thats-wrong-and-a-few-things-that-are-right-with-the-magicians.html.

Nagy, Gregory. 2002. "Can Myth Be Saved?" In *Myth: A New Symposium*, edited by Gregory Schrempp and William Hansen, 240–48. Bloomington: Indiana University Press.

Neuendorf, Henri. 2018. "What Gave Humans the Edge Over Neanderthals? It Was Art, a New Study Claims." *Artnet News*, February 14, 2018. Accessed July 30, 2018. https://news.artnet .com/art-world/prehistoric-art-helped-hunters-1224005.

Newkirk, Vann R., II. 2018. "Where Fantasy Meets Black Lives Matter." *The Atlantic*, April 2018. Accessed August 9, 2018. https://www.theatlantic.com/magazine/archive/2018/04/children -of-blood-and-bone-tomi-adeyemi/554060/.

Norman, Jeremy. n.d. "The Venus Impudique: The First Discovery of a Venus Figurine." *History of Information*. Accessed March 13, 2018. http://www.historyofinformation.com/expanded .php?id=4457.

Novik, Naomi. 2015. "Review of 'The Fifth Season,' by N.K. Jemisin." *New York Times*, August 6, 2015. Accessed August 22, 2018. https://www.nytimes.com/2015/08/09/books/review/the -fifth-season-by-nk-jemisin.html.

O'Brien, Jeremy. 2009. "New Techniques Undermine 'Mother Goddess' Role in Ancient Community." *Irish Times*, September 10, 2009. Accessed June 10, 2019. https://www.irishtimes .com/news/new-techniques-undermine-mother-goddess-role-in-ancient-community -1.734909.

O'Hehir, Andrew. 2017. "Book Review of THE STONE SKY: The Broken Earth: Book Three." *New York Times*, September 26, 2017. Accessed September 15, 2018. https://www.nytimes .com/2017/09/26/books/review/nk-jemisin-stone-sky-broken-earth-trilogy.html.

Oler, Tammy. 2014. "Out of the Cave: The Extraordinary Image of Girlhood at the Center of *Clan of the Cave Bear*." *Slate*, May 6, 2014. Accessed August 8, 2018. http://www.slate.com /articles/arts/books/2014/05/clan_of_the_cave_bear_and_feminism_dystopian_precedent _to_the_hunger_games.html.

Oliver, Myrna. 1999. "Marion Bradley; Writer of Fantasy Novels." Obituary. *Los Angeles Times*, September 30, 1999. Accessed July 27, 2018. http://articles.latimes.com/1999/sep/30/news /mn-16625.

Ortner, Sherry B. 1974. "Is Female to Male as Nature Is to Culture?" *Woman, Culture, and Society*, edited by M. Z. Rosaldo and L. Lamphere, 68–87. Stanford: Stanford University Press.

Paxson, Diana L. 2007. *Marion Zimmer Bradley's Ravens of Avalon: A Novel*. New York: Viking.

Paxson, Diana L. n.d. "Marion Zimmer Bradley." *Diana L. Paxson: Welcome to My Worlds.* Accessed July 27, 2018. https://diana-paxson.com/writing/avalon/marion-zimmer-bradley/.

Peach, Lucinda Joy. 2002. *Women and World Religions*. Upper Saddle River, NJ: Prentice Hall.

Pearse, Emma. 2015. "Why Can't Romance Novels Get Any Love?" *Smithsonian Magazine*, March 12, 2015. Accessed June 2019. https://www.smithsonianmag.com/arts-culture/why -cant-romance-novels-get-any-love-180954548/.

Peel, Ellen (Susan). 1990. "Utopian Feminism, Skeptical Feminism and Narrative Energy." In *Feminism, Utopia and Narrative*, edited by Libby Falk Jones and Sarah Webster Goodwin, 34–49. Knoxville: University of Tennessee Press.

Pike, Sarah M. 2001. *Earthly Bodies, Magical Selves: Contemporary Pagans and the Search for Community*. Berkeley: University of California Press.

Queen, Jewel. 2018. "The Inclusive Illusion of *Star Wars: The Last Jedi.*" *The Mary Sue*, March 20, 2018. Accessed March 10, 2019. https://www.themarysue.com/the-inclusive-illusion-of-star -wars-the-last-jedi/.

Quinn, Annalisa. 2018. Review: "'Circe' Gives the Witch of the Odyssey a New Life." *NPR*, April 11, 2018. Accessed March 15, 2019. https://www.npr.org/2018/04/11/599831473/circe-gives-the -witch-of-the-odyssey-a-new-life.

Radin, Paul. 1950. "The Basic Myth of the North American Indians." In *Eranos-Jahrbuch: Der Mensch und die Mythische Welt*, 359–419. Winterthur, Switzerland: Rhein-Verlag Zurich.

Raphael, Melissa. 2000. *Introducing Thealogy: Discourse on the Goddess*. Cleveland: Pilgrim Press.

Read, Donna, dir. 1989. *Goddess Remembered*. Transcription by author.

Renault, Mary. (1958) 1986. *The King Must Die*. Reprint, New York: Vintage.

Romano, Aja. 2018. "Hopepunk, The Latest Storytelling Trend, Is All about Weaponized Optimism." *Vox*, December 27, 2018. Accessed September 10, 2019. https://www.vox.com/2018 /12/27/18137571/what-is-hopepunk-noblebright-grimdark.

Rosenberg, Alyssa. 2014. "Re-reading Feminist Author Marion Zimmer Bradley in the Wake of Sexual Assault Allegations." *Washington Post*, June 27, 2014. Accessed July 27, 2018. https:// www.washingtonpost.com/news/act-four/wp/2014/06/27/re-reading-feminist-author- marion-zimmer-bradley-in-the-wake-of-sexual-assault-allegations/.

Ross, Jacquelyn. 2001. "Review of *Gardens in the Dunes.*" *News from Native California* 15 (Winter): 34–35.

Rountree, Kathryn. 1997. "The New Witch of the West: Feminists Reclaim the Crone." *Journal of Popular Culture* 30, no. 4: 211–29.

Ruether, Rosemary Radford. 2005. *Goddesses and the Divine Feminine: A Western Religious History*. Berkeley: University of California Press.

Schrempp, Gregory. 1992. *Magical Arrows: The Maori, the Greeks, and the Folklore of the Universe*. Madison: University of Wisconsin Press.

Schrempp, Gregory. 2012. *The Ancient Mythology of Modern Science: A Mythologist Looks (Seriously) at Popular Science Writing*. Montreal: McGill-Queen's University Press.

Schrempp, Gregory, and William Hansen, eds. 2002. *Myth: A New Symposium*. Bloomington: Indiana University Press.

Sheaffer, Robert. 1995. "Feminism, the Noble Lie." *Free Inquiry* 15, no. 2 (Spring): 13.

Sheaffer, Robert. 1999. Review: "The Goddess Has No Clothes." *Skeptical Inquirer* 23, no. 3 (May/June): 51–53.

Silko, Leslie Marmon. 1999. *Gardens in the Dunes*. New York: Scribner.

Sjöö, Monica, and Barbara Mor. 1987. *The Great Cosmic Mother: Rediscovering the Religion of the Earth*. San Francisco: HarperOne.

Smith, Scott. 2017. "The Hidden Christian Meaning of the Myth of Thor." *Church Pop*, November 14, 2017. Accessed July 31, 2018. https://churchpop.com/2017/11/14/the-hidden-christian-meaning-of-the-myth-of-thor-at-ragnarok/.

Spretnak, Charlene. 1992. *Lost Goddesses of Early Greece: A Collection of Pre-Hellenic Myths*. With new preface. Boston: Beacon.

Starhawk. 1999. *The Spiral Dance: A Rebirth of the Ancient Religion of the Great Goddess*. Special 20th Anniversary Edition. San Francisco: HarperCollins.

Starhawk. 2002. "Power-Over and Power-from-Within." In *Sacred Voice: Essential Women's Wisdom through the Ages*, edited by Mary Ford-Grabowsky, 273–74. San Francisco: Harper.

Starhawk. 2003. "Starhawk's Response to Charlotte Allen's article." *Belili Productions*. Accessed July 22, 2013. http://www.belili.org/marija/allen_response.html.

Starhawk and Donna Read. 2003. "About Marija Gimbutas." *Belili Productions*. Accessed June 7, 2010. http://www.gimbutas.org/marija/aboutmarija.html.

Steinfels, Peter. 1990. "Idyllic Theory of Goddesses Creates Storm." *New York Times*, February 13, 1990. Accessed July 19, 2013. http://www.nytimes.com/1990/02/13/science/idyllic-theory-of-goddesses-creates-storm.html.

Stone, Merlin. 1984. *Ancient Mirrors of Womanhood: A Treasury of Goddess and Heroine Lore from around the World*. 1979. Reprint, Boston: Beacon Press.

Tatar, Maria. 1987. *The Hard Facts of the Grimms' Fairy Tales*. Princeton: Princeton University Press.

The 13th Warrior. 1999. Film produced and directed by John McTiernan (with Michael Crichton and Ned Dowd). Script amended from https://subslikescript.com/movie/The_13th_Warrior-120657, accessed summer 2018.

Thompson, Krista A. n.d. "Exhibiting 'Others' in the West." *Postcolonial Studies at Emory*. Accessed June 7, 2010. http://english.emory.edu/Bahri/Exhibition.html.

Thor: Ragnarok. 2017. Directed by Taika Waititi. Script from Walt Disney Studios. Accessed July 23, 2018. https://waltdisneystudiosawards.com/media/scripts/thor_ragnarok.pdf.

Toth, Emily. 1997. *Ms. Mentor's Impeccable Advice for Women in Academia*. Philadelphia: University of Pennsylvania Press.

Tringham, Ruth, and Margaret Conkey. 1998. "Rethinking Figurines: A Critical View from Archaeology of Gimbutas, the 'Goddess' and Popular Culture." In *Ancient Goddesses: The Myths and the Evidence*, edited by Lucy Goodison and Christine Morris, 22–45. Madison: University of Wisconsin Press.

True Blood. 2008–2014. Produced by HBO. Transcriptions by author amended from various fan sites.

Ucko, Peter. 1996. "Mother, Are You There?" *Cambridge Archaeological Journal* 6: 300–304.

Van Gelder, Lindsay. 1986. "Speculative Fiction." *Ms.* 14, no. 9 (March): 64, 70.

Visser, Nick. 2018. "Christine Blasey Ford Can't Return Home due to 'Unending' Threats, Lawyers Say." *Huffington Post*, October 8, 2018. Accessed October 25, 2018. https://www.huffingtonpost.com/entry/christine-blasey-ford-home-unending-threats_us_5bbaa112e4b0876eda9f3317.

Walker, Alice. 1992. *Possessing the Secret of Joy*. New York: The New Press.

Wardlow, Ciara. 2017. "Movies Need More Female Villains like This One." *Hollywood Reporter*, November 4, 2017. Accessed July 20, 2018. https://www.hollywoodreporter.com/heat-vision/thor-ragnarok-cate-blanchetts-hela-is-a-remarkable-female-villain-1054937.

Weatherford, Jack. 1989. *Indian Givers: How the Indians of the Americas Transformed the World.* New York: Ballantine Books.

Weidenfeld, Lisa. 2016. "The Magicians Leaves Itself a Whole Mess of Problems to Fix in Season 2." *AV Club*, April 11, 2016. Accessed July 24, 2018. https://tv.avclub.com/the-magicians-leaves-itself-a-whole-mess-of-problems-to-1798187341.

Weigle, Marta. 1989. *Creation and Procreation: Feminist Reflections on Mythologies of Cosmogony and Parturition.* Philadelphia: University of Pennsylvania Press.

Wessel, Thomas R. 1976. "Agriculture, Indians, and American History." *Agricultural History* 50 (January): 9–20.

White, Adam. 2017. "Five Times Joss Whedon, Self-Proclaimed 'Woke Bae,' Blew His Feminist Credentials." *The Telegraph*, August 21, 2017. Accessed August 1, 2018. https://www.telegraph.co.uk/tv/0/joss-whedon-5-times-blew-feminist-credentials/.

White, Lynn, Jr. 1996. "The Historical Roots of Our Ecological Crisis." *The Ecocriticism Reader*, edited by Cheryll Glotfelty and Harold Fromm, 3–14. Athens: University of Georgia Press.

White, Randall. 2003. *Prehistoric Art: the Symbolic Journey of Humankind.* New York: Harry N. Abrams.

The Wicker Man. 1973. Directed by Robin Hardy. Transcription based on Script-o-rama. Accessed summer 2018. http://www.script-o-rama.com/movie_scripts/w/wicker-man-script-transcript.html.

The Wicker Man. 2006. Directed by Neil LaBute. Transcription based on Scripts.com. Accessed summer 2018. https://www.scripts.com/script/the_wicker_man_23451.

Wilcox, Clyde. 1994. "The Not-so-Failed Feminism of Jean Auel." *Journal of Popular Culture* 28, no. 33: 63–70.

Wilford, John Noble. 2009. "Full-Figured Statuette, 35,000 Years Old, Provides New Clues to How Art Evolved." *New York Times*, May 13, 2009. Accessed March 13, 2018. http://www.nytimes.com/2009/05/14science/14venus.html.

Yarnall, Judith. 1994. *Transformations of Circe: The History of an Enchantress.* Urbana: University of Illinois Press.

Zinski, Dan. 2017. "The 3 Reasons Cate Blanchett Wanted to Be in Thor: Ragnarok." *Screen Rant*, September 2, 2017. Accessed July 20, 2018. https://screenrant.com/thor-3-ragnarok-cate-blanchett-villain-casting-reasons/.

Index

Page numbers in **bold** indicate tables or illustrations.

About the Author

Credit: Melissa D. Gerrior

Mary J. Magoulick is professor of English at Georgia College. She writes and teaches on folklore, women's studies, mythology, and popular culture. She did fieldwork with Native Americans for her dissertation and loves traveling and learning about cultures.

CPSIA information can be obtained
at www.ICGtesting.com
Printed in the USA
BVHW091449060122
625024BV00005BA/14